HESPERIA: SUPPLEMENT XIII

MARCUS AURELIUS

ASPECTS OF CIVIC AND CULTURAL POLICY IN THE EAST

BY

JAMES H. OLIVER

AMERICAN SCHOOL OF CLASSICAL STUDIES AT ATHENS

PRINCETON, NEW JERSEY

1970

PRINTED IN THE UNITED STATES OF AMERICA
BY J. H. FURST COMPANY, BALTIMORE, MARYLAND

TO

THE

PANHELLENION

PREFACE

This work grew out of the author's long interest in the edicts and epistles of Roman emperors and in the history of Roman Athens. It took its present form after the discovery of a lengthy and difficult inscription which was found in 1966 in the Roman Market Place at Athens and is now in the Epigraphical Museum with the number EM 13366. For permission to study the stone under convenient conditions the writer is indebted to the good offices of successive Ephors of the First District, N. Platon, the late N. Verdeles and B. Kallipolites, and of the Directrix of the Epigraphical Museum, Mme. D. Peppas-Delmouzou. For the authorization to make the first extensive publication he is deeply grateful to J. Kondes, former Director General of Antiquities and Conservation; he is deeply grateful also to Mme. D. Peppas-Delmouzou, George Dontas and John A. Papapostolou. Eugene Vanderpool and Homer A. Thompson kindly facilitated arrangements; he particularly thanks them and also Henry S. Robinson for various courtesies. An admirable early report of the contents came from Daniel J. Geagan, to whom we are greatly and continuously indebted for help and clarification. The writer took up the inscription in a seminar at the Johns Hopkins University in 1968/9. The following participated, contributed and aided him in compiling the Greek index: Robert Boughner, James Joseph Bowes, Ellen Everson, Gretchen Kromer, Ellen Slotoroff, Gretchen Southard and Wesley Walton. Finally the writer would express to the editor Lucy Shoe Meritt his appreciation of her ubiquitous care and good sense, and he thanks his wife for compiling laboriously the General Index.

JAMES H. OLIVER

BALTIMORE, MARYLAND
OCTOBER 28, 1969

TABLE OF CONTENTS

BIBLIOGRAPHY

Amelotti, Mario, *Il testamento romano attraverso la prassi documentale*, I, *Le forme classiche di testamento* (Studi e testi di papirologia editi dall'Istituto papirologico " G. Vitelli " di Firenze diretti da Vittorio Bartoletti, I), Florence, 1966.

Barns, T. D., " Hadrian and Lucius Verus," *Journal of Roman Studies*, LVII, 1967, pp. 65-79.

Bengtson, Hermann, *Grundriss der römischen Geschichte mit Quellenkunde*, I, Munich, 1967.

————, " Das Imperium Romanum in griechischer Sicht," *Gymnasium*, LXXI, 1964, pp. 150-166.

Benjamin, Anna S., " Two Dedications in Athens to Archons of the Panhellenion," *Hesperia*, XXXVII, 1968, pp. 338-344.

Béranger, Jean, *Recherches sur l'aspect idéologique du Principat*, Basel, 1953.

Birley, Anthony, *Marcus Aurelius*, Boston and Toronto, 1966.

Bleicken, Jochen, *Senatsgericht und Kaisergericht: Eine Studie zur Entwicklung des Prozessrechtes im frühen Prinzipat* (Abhandlungen der Akademie der Wissenschaften in Göttingen, Phil.-hist. Kl., Dritte Folge, Nr. 53, 1962).

Bowersock, Glen Warren, *Greek Sophists in the Roman Empire*, Oxford, 1969.

Carrata Thomes, Franco, *Il Regno di Marco Aurelio*, Turin, 1953.

Day, John, *An Economic History of Athens under Roman Domination*, New York, 1942.

Delz, Josef, *Lukians Kenntnis der athenischen Antiquitäten*, Inaug.-Diss. Basel, 1950, reviewed in *A.J.P.*, LXXII, 1951, pp. 216-219.

De Martino, Francesco, *Storia della Costituzione Romana*, IV, 1-2, Naples, 1962, 1965.

De Visscher, Fernand, *Les Édits d'Auguste découverts à Cyrène*, Louvain and Paris, 1940.

Dobiáš, Josef, " La seconda spedizione germanica degli imperatori Marco e Commodo alla luce delle iscrizioni," *Atti del III Congresso Internazionale di Epigrafia Greca e Latina*, Rome, 1959, pp. 1-14.

Duff, A. M., *Freedmen in the Early Roman Empire*, Oxford, 1928.

Farquharson, A. S. L., *The Meditations of Marcus Aurelius*, I-II, Oxford, 1944.

Gagé, Jean, *Les classes sociales dans l'empire Romain*, Paris, 1964.

Garzetti, A., *L'impero da Tiberio agli Antonini*, Bologna, 1960.

Geagan, Daniel J., *The Athenian Constitution after Sulla* (*Hesperia*, Supplement XII), 1967.

Gilliam, J. F., " The Plague under Marcus Aurelius," *American Journal of Philology*, LXXXII, 1961, pp. 225-251.

Gordon, Mary L., " The Freedman's Son in Municipal Life," *Journal of Roman Studies,* XXI, 1931, pp. 65-77.

Graindor, Paul, *Athènes sous Auguste*, Cairo, 1927.

————, *Athènes de Tibère à Trajan*, Cairo, 1931.

————, *Athènes sous Hadrien*, Cairo, 1934.

————, *Un milliardaire antique: Hérode Atticus et sa famille*, Cairo, 1930.

Groag, Edmund, *Die römischen Reichsbeamten von Achaia bis auf Diokletian* (Akademie der Wissenschaften in Wien, Schriften der Balkankommission, Antiquarische Abteilung, IX, 1939), reviewed in *A.J.P.*, LXIX, 1948, pp. 434-441.

Hammond, Mason, *The Antonine Monarchy* (Papers and Monographs of the American Academy in Rome, XIX), 1959.

Hampl, Franz, " Kaiser Marc Aurel und die Völker jenseits der mittleren Donau," *Festschrift zu Ehren Richard Heubergers*, Innsbruck, 1960, pp. 33-40.

Hertzberg, Gustav Friedrich, *Die Geschichte Griechenlands unter der Herrschaft der Römer*, I-III, Halle, 1866, 1868, 1875.

Hopkins, Keith, " Élite Mobility in the Roman Empire," *Past and Present*, XXXII, 1965, pp. 12-26.

Jones, A. H. M., *The Cities of the Eastern Roman Provinces*, Oxford, 1937.

————, *The Greek City from Alexander to Justinian*, Oxford, 1940.

————, *Studies in Roman Government and Law*, Oxford, 1960.

Kaser, Max, *Das römische Zivilprocessrecht*, Munich, 1966.

Keil, Bruno, *Beiträge zur Geschichte des Areopags* (Berichte über die Verhandlungen der Sächsischen Akademie der Wissenschaften zu Leipzig, Phil.-hist. Kl., LXXI, 1919, 8. Heft).

Keil, Josef, " The Greek Provinces," *Cambridge Ancient History*, XI (1936, reprinted 1954), Ch. XIV.

Kelly, John Maurice, *Princeps Iudex: Eine Untersuchung zur Entwicklung und zu den Grundlagen der kaiserlichen Gerichtsbarkeit* (Forschungen zum römischen Recht, 9. Abh.), Weimar, 1957.

Kunkel, Wolfgang, " Der Prozess der Gohariener vor Caracalla, " *Festschrift Hans Lewald*, Basel, 1953, pp. 81-91.

————, " Die Funktion des Konsiliums in der magistratischen Strafjustiz und im Kaisergericht," *Zeitschrift der Savigny-Stiftung für Rechtsgeschichte*, Roman. Abt., LXXXIV, 1967, pp. 218-244 and LXXXV, 1968, pp. 253-329.

Lambrechts, P., " L'empereur Lucius Verus: Essai de réhabilitation," *L'Antiquité classique*, III, 1934, pp. 173-201.

Larsen, J. A. O., " Roman Greece " in Tenney Frank's *An Economic Survey of Ancient Rome*, Baltimore, 1938, pp. 259-498.

————, " Cyrene and the Panhellenion," *Classical Philology*, XLVII, 1952, pp. 7-16.

————, " A Thessalian Family under the Principate," *Classical Philology*, XLVIII, 1953, pp. 86-95.

Litewski, W., " Die römische Appellation in Zivilsachen," *Revue internationale des droits de l'antiquité*, 3ᵉ série, XII, 1965, pp. 347-436, XIII, 1966, pp. 231-323, XIV, 1967, pp. 301-403, XV. 1968, pp. 143-351.

Magdelain, André, *Auctoritas Principis*, Paris, 1947.

Mazzarino, Santo, *Trattato di Storia Romana*, Rome, 1956.

Mommsen, Theodor, *Römisches Staatsrecht*, I-II, 3. Auflage, Leipzig, 1887.

————, *The Provinces of the Roman Empire* (English translation by W. P. Dickson in 1886, edited with an introduction by T. Robert S. Broughton), *The European Provinces*, Chicago, 1968.

Nörr, Dieter, *Imperium und Polis in der hohen Principatszeit* (Münchener Beiträge zur Papyrusforschung und antiken Rechtsgeschichte, L, 1966).

Oliver, James H., *The Civilizing Power: A Study of the Panathenaic Discourse of Aelius Aristides Against the Background of Literature and Cultural Conflict* (Transactions of the American Philosophical Society, N. S., LVIII, 1), 1968.

————, *The Ruling Power: A Study of the Roman Empire in the Second Century after Christ through the Roman Oration of Aelius Aristides* (Transactions of the American Philosophical Society, N. S., XLIII, 4), 1953, supplemented by " Aristides, In Romam 65," *La Parola del Passato*, CXVIII, 1968, pp. 50-52.

————, *The Sacred Gerusia* (*Hesperia*, Supplement VI), 1941.

Orestano, Riccardo, *L'appello civile in diritto romano*, 2nd ed., Turin, 1953.

————, *Il potere normativo degli imperatori e le costituzioni imperiali*, Rome, 1937.

d'Ors, Alvaro, " Epigrafía jurídica griega y romana," well documented report appearing every three years in *Studia et Documenta Historiae et Iuris*.

Palm, Jonas, *Rom, Römertum und Imperium in der griechischen Literatur der Kaiserzeit* (Skrifter utgivna av Kungl. Humanistiska Vetenskapssamfundet i Lund, LVII, 1959).

Pekáry, Thomas, " Studien zur römischen Währungs- und Finanzgeschichte von 161 bis 235 n. Chr.," *Historia*, VIII, 1959, pp. 443-489.

Robert, Jeanne and Louis, " Bulletin épigraphique," indispensable survey published annually in the *Revue des études grecques*.

Rostovtzeff, Michael, *Social and Economic History of the Roman Empire,* Oxford, 1926; revised edition edited by Peter Fraser, 1957.

Schiller, A. Arthur: *See* Westermann, Youtie.

Stanton, C. R., " The Cosmopolitan Ideas of Epictetus and Marcus Aurelius," *Phronesis,* XIII, 1968, pp. 183-195.

Taubenschlag, Raphael, " The Imperial Constitutions in the Papyri," *Journal of Juristic Papyrology,* VI, 1952, pp. 121-142.

Tod, Marcus Niebuhr, " Epigraphical Notes on Freedmen's Professions," *Epigraphica,* XII, 1950, pp. 3-26.

————, " Greek Inscriptions from Macedonia," *Journal of Hellenic Studies,* XLII, 1922, pp. 167-183.

Vitucci, G., " Libertus," *Dizionario epigrafico di antichità romane,* IV, fasc. 29-30, 1958, pp. 905-946.

Weaver, P. R. C., " Freedmen Procurators in the Imperial Administration," *Historia,* XIV, 1965, pp. 460-469.

————, " Social Mobility in the Early Roman Empire: The Evidence of the Imperial Freedmen and Slaves," *Past and Present,* XXXVII, 1967, pp. 3-20.

Weber, Wilhelm, *Untersuchungen zur Geschichte des Kaisers Hadrianus,* Leipzig, 1907.

Westermann, W. L., and Schiller, A. Arthur, *Apokrimata: Decisions of Septimius Severus on Legal Matters,* New York, 1954.

Woodward, A. M., " *I.G.,* V, 1: Some Afterthoughts," *Annual of the British School at Athens,* XLIII, 1948, pp. 209-259.

Youtie, Herbert C., and Schiller, A. Arthur, " Second Thoughts on the Columbia *Apokrimata* (P. Col. 123)," *Chronique d'Égypte,* XXX, 1955, pp. 327-345.

Ziegler, K. H., *Die Beziehungen zwischen Rom und dem Partherreich,* Wiesbaden, 1964.

Zwikker, W., *Studien zur Markussäule,* I (Allard Pierson Stichting, Archaeologisch-historische Bijdragen, VIII), Amsterdam, 1941.

LIST OF ILLUSTRATIONS

LIST OF NUMBERED INSCRIPTIONS CONCERNING REFORMS OR PANHELLENION

INTRODUCTION

One who surveyed the world from the standpoint of Greeks and Romans on the day that Marcus Aurelius ascended the throne would find that a great civilization had been created in the classical canons of literature and art, in the philosophy of Plato and of the Hellenistic schools, in the establishment of peaceful intercourse throughout the oecumene and of an international or supranational administration which provided unprecedented security and offered few grounds of reasonable complaint. A series of military crises and a plague were soon to shake confidence in that security, but apart from these new and intermittent distractions various administrators, jurists and others tried to perfect the rules under which men of a world empire could live together most fairly, justly and happily. Of Roman Law, surely one of the greatest constructions of ancient man, the classical period runs from Augustus to Diocletian, and its culmination from the accession of Trajan to the death of Alexander Severus.[1]

Toward the middle of this period came the reign of Marcus Aurelius, when well known military emergencies and the will of influential groups produced important innovations that are not well known and which were followed by reaction and compromise. The battles of Marcus Aurelius were both military and social; his deep concern for justice and the ancient culture led to much legal activity and to many interesting decisions of policy. In some he tried to maintain the distinction and balance between the aristocratic and the democratic elements of cities and federal states.

Many would not hesitate to call him the noblest of the Roman emperors. The *Meditations* of Marcus Aurelius have inspired sympathy and admiration, which have induced Renan to exaggerate the emperor's political wisdom. Undoubtedly more recent studies give a truer picture. The conscientious emperor's wisdom may not everywhere have equalled his courage, but his decisions can be defended; the writer finds no evidence of hypocrisy or base opportunism or sterile indecision in Marcus Aurelius. He gave thought to the solution of the problems presented, and in his reign the principles of what Mazzarino calls the humanistic empire still guided policy. Pius, Hadrian and Augustus showed him the way.

---

[1] F. Schulz, *History of Roman Legal Science*, Oxford, 1946, p. 99: " The culminating point in the course of this development lies unquestionably in the age of Trajan and Hadrian . . . Julian's *Digesta* are the greatest product of Roman jurisprudence; they dominate legal science till the end of the Principate. After Julian a slight decline is sometimes observable, but on the whole the science of law remained on the same high level till the middle of the third century."

CHAPTER I

MARCUS AURELIUS ON APPEALS FROM ATHENS

The new inscription here published illustrates the interest of Marcus Aurelius, which both Dio and the Vita mention, in judicial questions, and it shows him answering his critics, as the Vita says he did. Secondly it brings a document of the first importance on questions related to the quarrel of the Athenians with Herodes Atticus and so clarifies the life of Herodes in Philostratus, *Vitae sophistarum*, II, 1. Thirdly—and this is perhaps the chief contribution of the inscription—it shows specific attempts of the emperor to reform the cities by reviving old laws and then his merely temporary compromise in standards demanded. Fourthly it brings prosopographical information in which the implied position of the Quintilii has an importance not only for students of Roman Achaia but for those of the Second Germanic Expedition of Marcus Aurelius. In fifth place the record of appeals and their disposition contains much to interest students of Athenian and Roman institutions and throws a new light on the role of the Attic Panhellenion.

GREEK TEXT

Three fragments of an inscription of white " Pentelic " marble were found in the American Excavations of the Ancient Athenian Agora during the seasons 1936, 1937 and 1939. The writer copied them in 1939 and then soon recognized seven more fragments stored by the Greek archaeologists in the Old Mosque at the so-called Roman Market Place. The smooth back and elegant lettering made recognition possible although the thickness varied from 0.028 m. in the case of two pieces in the American Excavations to 0.033 m. in the case of pieces in the Old Mosque.

Of the pieces in the American Excavations two join as one; the three will be shown below as fragments A (= I 4457 + 4083) and B (I 5754). Of the seven pieces in the Old Mosque six join as one; they will be shown below as fragments C and D. Having waited for more than twenty-six years for the publication of the latter, the writer made a search for them in September 1966 but failed to discover either fragment D or any of the six pieces of fragment C. In 1969, however, S. N. Koumanoudes found, in the Tower of the Winds, fragment D, most of C plus a new piece which joins above, and a new fragment F, all of which he and Mr. Dontas kindly placed at my disposal.

In the regular spring weeding of the Roman Market Place in 1966, the discovery of some small inscribed fragments led to the raising of a paving slab. Afterwards with the approval of the Ephor, the fragments were carried to the Stoa of Attalus where they were put together by the technician, Spyro Spyropoulos.

1

John Travlos and Homer A. Thompson say that the inscribed slab from the Market Place was surely one of several thin slices into which a substantial block had been sawn to provide flooring; that several of the uninscribed slices from the interior of the block could be recognized near by; that these slabs formed part of a huge cross which had been worked out in the middle of the floor of the Market Place, light marble contrasting with dark; and that a similar design was followed in the latest floor of the Tholos, probably in the same period (*Hesperia,* Supplement IV, p. 63).

From Daniel J. Geagan's report of the new text the writer noted the similarity with the content of fragments A, B, C and D. In September 1966, when he himself went to Athens, he saw the inscription while it was in the Stoa of Attalus; he ascertained that the new slab was a second plaque of the inscription from the American Excavation with the same variance in thickness. From B. D. Meritt in 1966 the writer asked and obtained permission to publish the Agora fragments (A and B). The two hundred fragments and slivers of the new plaque were transported in the summer of 1967 to the Epigraphical Museum, where Mme. Peppas-Delmouzou has had it splendidly reconstructed as EM 13366, skillfully cleaned and augmented by the placing of five more slivers.

Plaque I, fragment A, from the American excavations, consists of a piece which was found April 28, 1936 in a Late Roman context in the NW corner of the Market Square beyond the railway (F2), Agora Inventory No. I 4083, and of a piece which was found January 28, 1937 in late fill in front of the S. end of the Stoa of Attalus (P 12), Agora Inventory No. I 4457. I 4083 and 4457 join as one piece, 0.13 m. high and 0.21 m. wide, broken above, below and at the sides.

Plaque I, fragment B, from the American excavation, broken above, below and at the sides, was found May 28, 1939 in a Mycenean well on the north slope of the Acropolis (V 24). It is 0.165 m. high and 0.17 m. wide. Agora Inventory No. I 5754.

Plaque I, fragment C, now in the Tower of the Winds, consisted of six pieces including two small pieces from the right side which have disappeared. With the new piece added by S. N. Koumanoudes we now have five fragments which join as one, 0.30 m. high and 0.48 m. wide, broken above, below and at the left. There is a right edge which dates in my opinion from the recutting of Plaque I, because there is no margin as on the left side of Plaque II. If on Plaque I, as on Plaque II, not more than two to five letters are missing along the new right edge, my restoration at the end of line 18 overruns the available space and belongs partly at the beginning of line 19.

Plaque I, fragment D, now stored in the Tower of the Winds, is 0.13 m. high and 0.22 m. wide, broken above, below and at the sides.

Plaque I, fragment F, identified by S. N. Koumanoudes and now stored in the Tower of the Winds, is 0.12 m. high and 0.12 m. wide, broken above, below and at the sides.

Plaque II, the paving block from the so-called Roman Agora, with its inscribed face partly illegible because of wear, fracture or adhering concrete, consists of many fragments which join as one piece, fragment E, 2.31 m. high and 0.88 m. wide. It preserves top, bottom and left side, but the right edge is not original.

Height of letters, 0.01 m.

PLAQUE I

A

$$]ον\ υἱὸ[ν$$
$$]αχθήσεται\ ^{vv}\ [$$
$$ὁ\ κράτι]στος\ ἀνὴρ\ εἰσ[$$
$$]ας\ ὑποτρέφειν\ [$$
5
$$]ο[\ .\ ]\ Ἡρώιδου\ μετ[$$
$$]\ ἀπευθύνεται\ προσυ'[$$
$$]\ πέρχωνται\ διαδοχη\ [$$
$$]ονο[\ .\ .\ .\ ]ασου[$$

B

$$]ω\ ἐφθη[$$
$$]τηνουκε[$$
$$]ησ[\ .\ .\ ]σ[\ .\ .\ .\ .\ ]ν[$$
$$]οναγαραλι[$$
5
$$]νοίας\ εἰς\ τὴν\ ἀσφ[άλειαν$$
$$]\ ὁρῶμαι\ γὰρ\ μηι[$$
$$]\ δεσπότου\ τῶ[ν$$
$$]ημα\ τοῦ\ [$$

C

$$]νεντ[$$
$$]\ καὶ\ προσ[$$
$$ἐ]ξοικισθῆναι\ δ[$$
$$]λιοις\ Ἀθηναίοις\ ἀλγεῖ\ ολμ[$$
5
$$]\ ὑπέμεινα\ εἰς\ νῆσον\ ἔδοξεν\ κατα[$$
$$]ον\ καὶ\ πολύπλοκον\ ὡς\ βαρὺ\ τοῖς\ ε[$$
$$]ς\ ἐτεχνάζετο\ ἀρι[\ \ \ ]ντοι\ προσγ[$$
$$]ται\ ^{vv}\ Εὔοδος\ Ὀνησίμ[ο]ν\ οσανεν[$$
$$]ικῆς\ ἐπιτεχνησάμενος\ ἐφ[$$
10
$$]ιε[\ .\ .\ .\ ]λιω,\ ἐπεὶ\ μηδὲ\ ταῖς\ προτέραι[ς$$
$$τῆς\ πατρί]δος\ καὶ\ [τ]ῶν\ νήσων\ αὐτῆς\ ἀπε[χ]έσθω\ ^{v}\ [$$
$$τοῦ]\ κρατίστου\ ἀνδρὸς\ ἔτι\ καὶ\ δοῦλον\ λύσιν\ οὐκ\ [$$
$$τοῖ]ς\ πραχθεῖσιν\ οὐδὲν\ ὁρίσαι\ ἔδοξεν,\ βουλοίμην\ [$$
$$πε]ριέμειναν\ μέχρι\ τοῦ\ ταῦτα\ ἀποφήνασθαί\ με\ συνεχῶς\ [$$
15
$$]ν\ ἐνκλημάτων\ ἄνωι\ καὶ\ κ[άτ]ωι\ στρεφομένων\ ^{vv}\ Ἐπεὶ\ δὲ\ τα[$$
$$]σας\ ἐπὶ\ τῆς\ παρ᾽\ ἐμοὶ\ [λεχθείσης]\ καὶ\ τὰ\ μάλιστα\ εἰς\ αὐτὴν\ ἐνδ[$$
$$]ο\ τὰς\ ἀποδεο[μένας\ -------\ ]ι\ ὁ\ κράτιστος\ ἀνὴρ\ ἴδιον\ δ[$$
$$]λας\ ὑπ[\ ----------\ κριτὴν]\ δίδωμι\ Ὀφίλλιον\ Ἰνγ[ένουον$$
$$]που[\ --------------\ ]μοι\ πραχθέντω[ν$$

D

$$]ορω\ διαφερον[$$
$$]μὴ\ περαιτέρωι\ καὶ\ το[$$
$$]ν\ τετυχήκασιν\ παρὰ\ τῆς\ [$$
$$]ν\ οὔτε\ ἀπελευθέρους\ α[$$
5
$$]τους\ μετ᾽\ αὐτὰ\ οἵτιν[ες$$
$$]\ ἐπὶ\ τῆς\ ἀγορᾶς\ συνηθ[$$
$$]ι\ Ἀθηναίων\ δίκαιοι\ σ[$$
$$]\ Ἡρώιδου\ καὶ\ [$$
$$]αι\ προσο[$$

F

$$]λα[$$
$$]\ παραγρα[$$
$$]ολλιου\ προ[$$
$$τ]ὴν\ ἐξέτασιν\ [$$
5
$$]πως\ δὴ\ σχ]$$
$$]\ καὶ\ μον[$$

E   PLAQUE II

[Ἔκκλητοι ἃς] ἐποιήσαντο Αἴλ Πραξαγόρας, Κ̅λ̅ Δημόστρατος, Αἴλ Θεμίσων
    πρὸς Α̅ἴ̅λ̅ Διονύσιον δίκαιοι εἶναι ο[− − ±12 − −]
[− − ±10 − −] ἐφέσ[ε]ων ἐδέησεν ἀκροάσασθαι ἐξαρκεῖν ἔδοξεν τὸ τὰς
    ἀρχαιρεσίας ἐνθεσμῶς ἀχθείσας ξ[− − ±12 − −]
[− − ±10 − −] ὧν τῶν ἀνδρῶν οὐχ ἡγησάμην ἀνανκαῖον εἶναι ὑποστῆναι
    τῶι μηδὲ Ἀθήνησιν αὐτὴν γ[− − ±11 − −]
γεμην τὸν ἐξῆς χρόνο[ν] ἵνα μή τι ἀμφίβολον καταλειφθῆι· τοὺς μὲν
    δαιδουχίαν ἤ τινα ἑτέραν ἐθελου[σίαν διέ]
5 τοντας ἱερ[ε]ωσύνην μέμ[ον]α, ἧς φθάνουσιν ἔχειν, προκατατίθεσθαι ἀεὶ
    τὸ τρόφιον ἐννόμως· εἰ δέ τις [ὑπὸ]
τοῦ δήμου καλοῖτο, οὐκ ἔσται πρὸς τοῦτον ἀμφισβήτησις ἐὰν μὴ
    προκαταθῆται τὰ πρότερα σύμ[β]ολα πρὶν ἀ[πο]
δειχθῆναι, χειροτονηθεὶς μέντοι καὶ οὗτος τὸ προϋπάρχον αὐτῶι
    καταθήσεται ⟨ Ἔκκλητοι ἃς ἐποιήσαντο Σ[έν]
[τ]ιος Ἄτταλος καὶ Κλήμης Κλήμεντος καὶ Κλ Χρύσιππος ἀπὸ τοῦ
    δικαστηρίου καὶ ἀπὸ τοῦ βασιλέως Κλ Εὐπραξίδο[υ]
πρὸς Οὐαλέριον Μαμερτεῖνον περιγεγράψο[ν]ται· Μαμερτεῖνος μὲν
    οὖ[ν], ἐπεὶ Εὐμολπίδης ὢν οὐδέτερον τ[ῶν]
10 γονέων ἔσχεν ἐκ τοῦ τῶν Κηρύκων γένους, ἐπιδεῖται καθ᾽ ὅνπερ
    μόνον ἐφεῖται τρόπον τοῖς ἐξ ⟨ἑ⟩κατέρου τῶν [δύ]
[ο] τούτων γενῶν πρὸς θάτερον μεθίστασθαι, ἀφέξεται τοῦ τῆς
    ἱεροκηρυκείας ἐφείεσθαι ⟨ αἱ δὲ ἀρχαιρεσία[ι με]
ταξὺ τῶν ἄλλων τῶν τε ἤδη ἐπιδικασαμένων καὶ τῶν νῦν ἐθελησόντων
    παραν⟨γ⟩έλλειν κατὰ [τοὺ]ς νόμους το[ὺς]
Ἀθηναίων ἐπαναλημφθήσονται ⟨ Μαμερτεῖνος οὔτε τοῦ ἀριθμο[ῦ] τῶν
    Εὐμολπιδῶν ἐξαιρεθ[ή]σεται καὶ τὴν [ἱερε]
ωσύνην ἀνακομιεῖται ⟨ τὸ δὲ ἐπὶ τούτου μοι παραστὰν λαβόντι τὴν
    γνώμην ἐκ τῆς παρούση[ς δ]ίκης οὐκ ἂν[ήσει]
15 τὸ μέλλον συνχέαι τὰ παραφυλαττόμενα ⟨ Λάδικος Πολυαίνου ὁ
    ἐκκεκλημένος πρὸς Σωφάνην Σω[φά]
[ν]ους ἀπὸ Ἰουλ Δαμοστράτου τοῦ ἄρχοντος τῶν Πανελλήνων φαίνεται
    κατὰ τὸν ὡρισμένον χρόνο[ν ἀπεῖ]
ναι τόσου ἔξεστιν δικάζεσθαι πρὸς τοὺς κεχειροτονημένους Πανέλληνας·
    κληθεὶς ἐπὶ τὴν κρίσιν, ἀπ[ενε]
χθεὶς δέ, καίτοι μετὰ τὴν νενομισμένην προθεσμίαν τῆς χειροτονίας
    γεγενημένης, ὑπὸ τὴν ἔννο[μον]

10 ⟨ἑ⟩κατέρου, ΑΚΑΤΕΡΟΥ lapis.
12 παραν⟨γ⟩έλλειν, ΠΑΡΑΝΤΕΛΛΕΙΝ lapis.

ἡλικίαν γεγονὼς οὐδὲ τότε, καὶ οὐδεμίαν ἀρχὴν πρότερον ἄρξας ὡς
  ὁ θεὸς πάππος μου ὥρισεν, ἀδίκως [ἐφει]
20 κένα[ι δ]οκεῖ ᵛ Ἐπίγονος Ἐπικτήτου ἐκκαλεσάμενος ἀπὸ Ἰουλ
  Δαμοστράτου πρὸς Εὔδημον Ἀφροδεισί[ου πα]
  ρὰ τοῖς [ἐ]μοῖς Κυιντιλίοις ἀγωνιεῖται περὶ τῆς τοῦ Πανελληνίου
  κοινωνίας· καὶ γὰρ αὐτὸς ἠξίωσεν ἐπὶ τὴν π[αρ᾽ ἐ]
  [κ]είνο[ι]ς πεμφθῆναι κρίσιν, καὶ πολλὰ τῶν εἰς ἐμὲ καθηκόντων
  μερῶν ἐν τοῖς πράγμασιν τοῖς ἐπὶ τῆς ἔδ[ρας]
  ὑπ᾽ ἐκείν⟨ω⟩ν ἐκτελεῖσθαι δῆλόν ἐστιν ᵛ Ἀθηνόδωρος Ἀγρίππου
  ἀπὸ Παπίου Ῥούφου τοῦ τῶν [Π]ανελλήν[ων ἄρ]
  ξαν[τος] ἐπὶ τῆς προτέρας πεντετηρίδος ἐφεικὼς πρὸς τοὺς διοικητὰς
  τῶν τοῦ κρ Κλ Ἡρώιδου, ἐπεὶ μήτ[ε τὰ ὑ]
25 πομνήματα τῶν Πανελλήνων μήτε τὴν γνῶσιν τὴν ἐξενεχθεῖσαν παρέσχετο,
  ἐπὶ τῶν ἐμῶν Κυιντιλ[ίων ἀ]
  γωνιεῖται, ἵνα μὴ μετὰ τοσοῦτον τοὺς καιροὺς ἐν οἷς ἐξέσται μοι
  καὶ παρὰ τὰς στρατιωτικὰς πράξεις τὰ κρίσ[εως δε]
  όμενα ἐκδικάζειν ἀναγκασθῇ περιμένειν ᵛ Νόστιμος Διονυσίου γεγενῆσθαι
  κ[α]τὰ τοὺς νόμους Ἀ[ρεοπα]
  γείτης οὐκ ἔδειξεν, ἀλλ᾽ εἰ ἔστιν ἐν τούτωι, ὡς τῆι ἐξ Ἀρείου πάγου
  βουλῆι, προσγραφῆναι δύνασθαι, δ[ιαγνώ]
  σουσιν οἱ Κυιντίλιοι· διότι δ᾽ ἂν ἀπεωσθείη τῆς κοινωνίας τοῦ
  συνεδρίου τῶν Πανελλήνων [.........]
30 [....]ν δικάζοντί μοι περὶ τῆς ἐκκλήτου τῆς πρὸς Εὐφρᾶν Νίκωνος
  γενομένης ᵛ Ποπιλί[ωι Πείωι]
  [τ]ῶι δικαίωι τῆς πολειτείας τῆς Ἀθηναίων μενεῖ καθ᾽ ἃ ἐπέγνωσαν
  οἱ Ἀρεοπαγεῖται· χρ[ὴ γὰρ τῆς στά]
  σε[ως αὐτῶι] τὴν βεβαιότητα ὑπάρχειν καὶ τοῖς ἄλλοις, ὅσοι, τῆι
  δοθείσηι ἐξουσίαι ὑπὸ φόβ[ου ἐκ τοῦ ἀν]
  τιπάλου ἐπακολουθοῦντες, τοῖς Ἀρεοπαγείταις τὰ ἑαυτῶν δίκαια
  παρέσχοντο· εἰς [δὲ] τὸ μέλλο[ν κατὰ]
  τοὺς νόμους καὶ κατὰ τὰ πάτρια ἔθη παραφυλαχθήσεται καὶ δοκιμασθήσεται
  εἴ τις ἐκ γένους [δίκαι]
35 ός ἐστιν ᵛ Ἔκκλητος ἣν Αἴλ Πραξαγόρας ἀπὸ Γαουινίου Σατορνείνου
  ἐποιήσατο· ἐπὶ τῆς δίκης [τῶν]
  καλουμένων κωδικίλλων ἐπ᾽ ὀνόματι Πρατολάου προκομισθέντων ἡ ζήτησις
  ἐγένετο· δικα[ιωθῆ]
  ναι φαίνεται ᵛ Εἰ μέντοι βούλοιτό τις ἐντὸς δύο μηνῶν ἢ δημοσίαι
  ἢ ἰδίαι μετὰ τὸ ἀναγνωσθ[ῆναι]

23 ἐκείν⟨ω⟩ν, EKEINON lapis.

τὴν ἐπιστολὴν ταύτην Ἀθήνησιν περὶ τῆς δωρεᾶς ἣν προὔθεσαν ὀφείλεσθαι
    τῆι πόλει [ἄγειν, προ]
σ[ι]έναι ἐφείσθω ταύτωι δύο ἄλλων μηνῶν προθεσμίας παραφυλαττομένης
    πρὸς τὸ ἐπί[δικον]
40 τοῖς ἐμοῖς Κυιντιλίοις· εἰ δὲ ἐν τῶι μεταξὺ τούτωι διαστήματι
    ἐνδεήσειεν, οὐκ ἂν ἐν[ί]στ[ασθαι ἢ]
ἀγῶνα ἐπαναλαμβάνειν ἐπιχειροίη{ι}· εἰς δὲ τὴν τῶν χωρίων νομὴν
    Πραξαγόρας ἐπανελεύ[σεται καὶ]
λή[μψ]εται παρὰ τῶν κρ Κυιντιλίων διαιτητὴν περὶ τῶν καρπῶν ⌄
    ἐπί γε μὴν τὰ χωρία ἃ τῶι κρ Ἡρώ[ιδηι]
κατα[λελ]εῖφθαι ἐλέγετο, ἤδη ἐπανήξει ⌄ περὶ τῶν καρπῶν Ἰνγένουος
    δικάσει ⌄ ἐὰν δὲ τὴν βραδυ[τῆτα]
παραδόσεως μέμψηται Πραξαγόρας, ὑπὸ τῶν ἡγεμόνων τοῦ ἔθνους
    εἰσαχθήσεται ⌄ τῆι δεήσει τῆι [Ἀθη]
45 ναίων — ἦν γὰρ τῆι ἡλικίαι τοῦ πατρὸς καὶ τῶι μόνον αὐτὸν τῶι
    οἴκωι ὑπολελεῖφθαι — ἔνειμ' ἂν δύναιμι· [ἴσως]
εἴ⟨η⟩ ἂν [ὠ]φείλιμον ἀνακληθῆναι μὲν ἐκ τῆς νήσου εἰς ἣν
    εἰσεφυγαδεύετο κατὰ τὴν ἐξέτασιν τοῦ πράγ[ματος],
τῶν δὲ ὅρων τῆς Ἀττικῆς πρὸς τὸ λοιπὸν ἀπέχεσθαι ⌄ Ἀγαθοκλεῖ
    Ἀγαθοκλέους ἡ διὰ τὰς πρεσβε[ί]ας ἀξίωσ[ις ἃς πα]
ρ' ἐμο[ὶ] συντελεῖ ⌄ ἀποδοθήσεται δή· καὶ τῆι πατρίδι καὶ τῶι
    τῶν Ἀρεοπαγειτῶν συνεδρίῳ καὶ ἐγγύαι τῶν [ἐκκλή]
των δικῶν ἃς ἐποιήσαντο οἱ διοικηταὶ τῶν τοῦ κρ Ἡρώιδου πρὸς
    Αἴ[λ] Ἀμεινίαν ⌄ ὁμοίως καὶ ἐγγύαι ἐκ[κλ]ήτω[ν ἃς]
50 ἐπὶ ταῖς δίκαις ταῖς παρ' ἐμοὶ λεχθείσαις ἐποιήσαντο Αἴλ Πραξαγόρας,
    Κλ Δημόστρατος, Αἴλ Θεμίσων, Σέγ[τιος]
Ἄτταλος, Κλήμης Κλήμεντος, Οὐαλέριος Μαμερτεῖνος, Λάδικος
    Πολυαίνου, Εὔοδος Ὀνησίμου, Νόστιμο[ς Διο]
ν[υ]σίου, Ποπίλιος Πεῖος, ἀποδοθήσονται. Ἐπιγόνου δὲ καὶ
    Ἀθηνοδώρου τὰς ἐκκλήτους περιγεγράφθ[αι οὐ]
δέπ[ω] φθάνω προειπών ⌄ εἴ τινες ἄλλαι ἐφέσεις ἀπηρτημέναι
    ταύτης τῆς διαγνώσεως, περὶ ὧν οὐδὲν ἐδ[ήλω]
σα πρὸ ἀποφάσεως, εἶεν γεγενημέναι, περιγεγράψονται, ὥστε
    ἐξετασθῆναι παρὰ τῶι δικαστῆι κατὰ τὰ αὐ[τὰ]
55 καθάπερ καὶ ἔμελλον ἐξετασθήσεσθαι καὶ μηδεμίας οὔσης ἐκκλήτου
    δίκης, τίνων δ' ἂν εἶεν ἐπιστε[λεῖ]
πρὸς ἐμὲ Ἰνγένουος· εἰ δέ τινες μετὰ τὴν γνῶσιν ἀπηνέχθησαν,
    τούτων κατὰ τὴν προσήκουσαν τά[ξιν]

46 εἴ⟨η⟩, ΕΙꞱ lapis.

αὐτὸς ἀ[π]οκ[ρινεῖ] ᵛ Ὅσην εἰσφέρομαι σπουδὴν ὑπὲρ τῆς δόξης
 τῶν Ἀθηνῶν, ὡς τῆς παλαιᾶς αὐτῆ[ς ἐ]
πικρατεῖν σεμνότητος, ἱκανῶς δεδηλωκέναι νομίζω, καὶ ἡνίκα
 τὸ παρ' αὐτοῖς ἔκκριτον συνέδρι[ον]
ἐπαναγαγεῖν ἐπειράθην πρὸς τὸ παλαιὸν ἔθος, καθ' ὃ τούτους
 μόνους εἰς Ἄρειον πάγον εἰσεδέχον[το]
60 τοὺς ἀπὸ τῆς τριγονίας ἐξετασθέντας· καὶ εἴθε ἦν περιουσία
 τῶν ἐνδόξων γενῶν, ἵν' ἐξῆι μοι κα[ὶ νῦν]
ἔτι τὴν γνώμην τὴν ἡμετέραν φυλάξαι, ἀλλ' ἐπειδὴ τὰ συμβάντα
 διὰ τὴν τύχην ὑπολογιζομένο[υς, ἐ]
φ' οἷς πολλὰς καὶ ἄλλας πόλεις οἶδα θεραπείας εἰς τὰ μάλιστα
 ἐπιδικασαμένας, τὰ μὲν ἐπανειένα[ι] δε[ῖ τῆι]
πρὸς τὸ παρεληλυθὸς φιλανθρωπίαι, τὰ δὲ τῆι πρὸς τὸ μέλλον
 αὐτάρκως ἱδρῦσαι, μέχρι τοσούτου συν[τιθέ]
μενος Ἀθηναίοις ἐνδώσω, ὡς ἐπὶ μὲν τοῦ παρεληλυθότος χρόνου
 πρὸς τοῦτο μόνον ἀφορᾶν, εἴ τ[ινι πα]
65 τὴρ εὐγενής, κἄν τις τῶν ἐξ Ἀρείου πάγου διὰ τὸν κανόνα τῆς
 τριγονίας ἐξεῶσθαι φαίνηται, τὸ ἀξίωμα ἀ[να]
κομιεῖται, μετὰ ταῦτα δὲ τὸ ἐξ ἀμφοῖν τῶν γονέων εἶναί τινα
 εὖ γεγονότων· ἀρκέσει τοῖς μετὰ τὴν ἐπ[ιστο]
λὴν ἐ‹μ›ὴν ἑτέραν ἀπελευθέρου πατρὸς οὖσιν καὶ εἰς Ἄρειον πάγον
 ἑαυτοὺς ἐνβεβληκόσιν τῆς ἀγν[οίας ἐν]
ὥρᾳ τεθεᾶσθαι ᵛ Εἰ μέντοι τις πρὸ τῆς ἐπιστολῆς ἀπελευθέρου πατρὸς
 γεγονὼς ὑπ' οὐδενὸς δικαστηρ[ίου]
τῶν ἐπὶ τούτο[ι]ς ἀποδοθῆναι δυναμένων ἐξεώσθη, μενεῖ ᵛ Ὅσοι μετὰ
 τὰ ἡμέτερα γράμματα διὰ τὸ τὸν [πάπ]
70 πον ἀπηλευθερῶσθαι ἢ ὑπεξήχθησαν τῆς ἐν Ἀρείωι πάγωι βουλῆς ἢ
 ἑκόντες ὑπεξῆλθον, τὴν τιμὴν ἔ[χειν]
ἀπ[είργ]ονται· τούς γε μὴν ὑπεξστησομένους διὰ τὰ προειρημένα ἐκ
 τοῦ συνεδρίου χρὴ μηδὲν ἐκ τοῦ τοι[ού]
του π[α]ραλυπεῖσθαι πρὸς τὸ τὰς ἄλλας τιμὰς καὶ τάξεις μετιέναι ᵛ
 Εἴ τινες εἶεν ὑπεναντίον τοῖς ὑφ' ἡμῶν ἐ[πε]
σταλμένοις κατειλεγμένοι, οἷς οὐδὲ μετὰ τὴν νῦν ἐξενεχθεῖσαν
 γνῶσιν οἷόν τέ ἐστιν ἐν Ἀρείωι π[άγωι]
καθῆσθαι, ἀπαλλαττέσθωσαν ἐντὸς ἐνιαυτοῦ ᵛ Ὃς δ' ἂν καὶ μετὰ τὰ
 ἀπηγορευμένα διατελέσηι μένω[ν ἢ καὶ]
75 παρὰ τὰ προγεγραμμένα εἰσδύηται, ἐν ἴσωι ταχθήσεται τοῖς ὑπεξαχθεῖσιν
 διὰ τοῦ δικαστηρίου ἐλάττοσ[ίν τε]

67 ἐ‹μ›ὴν, ΕΙΝΗΝ lapis.

ἐκ τούτου καὶ ἐν τῶι μετιέναι τὰς καταδεεστέρας τάξεις κ[α]ὶ
    τιμάς ᵛ Ἐάν τινες ἐξ Ἀρεοπαγειτῶν ἐν τοῖς [Πανέλ]
λησιν ὄντες τήμερον καταλημφθῶσιν τὴν τριγονίαν παρασχεῖν μὴ
    δυνάμενοι, οὐ διὰ τοῦτο ἀπ[οδιω]
χθήσονται τοῦ συνεδρίου, πρὸς δὲ τὸ μέλλον οὐδεὶς ἄλλος ἐξ
    Ἀρεοπαγειτῶν τοῖς Πανέλλησιν ἐνγρ[αφή]
σεται ἢ ὅσοι πρὸς τὰς χειροτονίας ἀφικνεῖσθαι δύνανται τὴν τριγονίαν
    ἔχοντες· τὸ πρὸς τὴν βου[λὴν]
80 τῶν Πεντακοσίων φέρον [ἀ]ποχρώντως ἔχει ταύτηι τετάχθαι ὥστε
    αὐτοὺς τοὺς καταλεγομένους ε[ὖ γε]
γονέναι ᵛ Ἰνγένουος ταῖς ἐ[ξ ἑκ]ατέρου τῶν μερῶν ἀμφισβητήσεσιν
    αὐτὸς ἔσται δικαστής, δικάσε[ι δὲ]
[κ]αὶ πρὸς ἐκείνους τοῖς προνοουμένοις τῶν τοῦ κρ ἀνδρός, οἵπερ
    ἂν μηδὲν ἀντε[ι]σπράτ[τ]ωσιν [εὔλο]
γοι ᵛ Οἱ διοικήσαντες τὰ δημόσια τῆς πόλεως χρήματα καὶ λογισμοὺς
    ὀφείλοντες ἔχουσιν δικασ[τὰς]
τοὺς ἐμοὺς Κυιντιλίους, παρ' οἷς οἱ τῶν Ἀθηναίων σύνδικοι
    προνοήσονται τὰ αὐτῶν ἐκπλῆσαι π[λήθη]·
85 Ἰνγένουος Ἀθηναίων μὲν τοῖς κρίσεως δεομένοις ἐν Ἐλευσεῖνι
    δικάσει καὶ ἐν Πειραεῖ, καθ' ὃ[ν ἂν ἑ]
τερῶθι βούληται χρόνον ᵛ τοῖς δὲ ἐκ Λακεδαίμονος ὁριεῖ τόπον ἐν
    ταῖς πλησίον πόλεσιν κατὰ τὸ ἐ[πιτη]
[δει]ότατον αὐτὸς δοκιμάσας ᵛ Ἡγοῦμαι δεδηλῶσθαι, δι' ὧν
    ἀπεφηνάμην, ὅτι ἕκαστα π[ρ]οϊδόμην ο[ὐ διὰ]
π[αρ]ουσίας μᾶλλον ἢ φροντίδος, ἵνα πρὸς τὸ μέλλον Ἡρώιδηι τε
    ὑπάρχοι παρὰ Ἀθηναίοις συνευφ[ροσύ]
νια περί τε τὰ θεῖα καὶ τὰ ἀνθρώπινα ἔχειν σὺν τῆι εὐκλεεῖ περὶ
    παιδείαν σπουδῆι, καὶ Ἀθηναῖοι τῆς πρό[τερον]
90 γν[ωτ]ῆς εἰς αὐτοὺς εὐποιίας τοῦ κρ Ἡρώιδου μεμνημένοι τὸ
    θάρσος τῆς πρότερον περὶ ἀλλ[ήλ]ους [οἴκει]
ότητο[s] ἀνανεώσαιντο, δι' ἣν οὐδὲ ἐμοῦ διαλλακτοῦ δέονται.
    τί γὰρ ἂν ἔτι ὑποκαθέζοιτο ἐν γνώμ.[ηι τι]
νὸς μετὰ τὸ ἀπαλειφθῆναι τὴν ἐπὶ [τ]αῖς αἰτίαις μνήμην; τῆς
    θεραπείας ἐπὶ πᾶσιν ἐκπεπο[ν]ημένης [ἆρ' οὐκ]
Ἀθην[α]ίοις ἐξ[ῆν] τὸν ἐμὸν καὶ τὸν ἴδ[ι]ον αὐτῶν Ἡρώιδην
    στέργειν οὐδενὸς ἔτι ἑτέρου τῆι εὐνοίαι με[γάλου]
ἀντικρούοντος; Ὅ γε μὴν ἐπὶ πᾶσι τούτοις κατὰ τὴν Ἑλλήνων
    φωνὴν περὶ τῶν δικασθέντων συντετ[αγμέ]

91 οὐδὲ aut οὐδὲ⟨ν⟩

95 νοις προσενεθυμήθην ὡς, ἐν οἷς ἀπεφηνάμην, παρειμένον, ἀπὸ
　　μὲν τῆς γνώμης τῆς ἐμῆς, εἰ καὶ [ἀπῆν]
　　τῶν τῆς ἀποφάσεως ῥημάτων, νοεῖσθαι δυνάμενον, ἐξηγήσεως
　　δέ τινος προσδεόμενον. Ἵνα μή τι [νέαν]
　　ἀμφισβήτησιν παράσχοι, προσήκειν ἔδοξεν σαφῶς καὶ τοῦτο
　　διορίσασθαι· εἴ τινες ἐκ πατέρων ἀπε[λευ]
　　θέρων γεγονότες τῆς βουλῆς τῶν Πεντακοσίων ἐξανέστησαν, τούτοις
　　ἐπανιέναι πάλιν εἰς τὴν [ἐξέ]
　　τασιν κατὰ [τ]ὰ αὐτὰ συνκε[χω]ρήσθω καθὰ καὶ τοῖς ἐξ Ἀρείου
　　πάγου· ἀποδεικνύτωσαν δὲ οἱ ἐκ τ[ῆς τῶν]
100 Πεντακοσίων βουλῆς σφᾶς αὐτοὺς ἐν ἐλευθερίᾳ γεγενῆσθαι· χρὴ
　　γὰρ οὐ τοὺς ἐκ πατέρων ἀπ[ελευ]
　　θέρων ἀλλὰ τοὺς αὐτοὺς ἀπελευθερωθέν[τα]ς εἴργεσθαι μόνους,
　　ὅπερ καὶ πρὸς τὸ μέλ[λ]ον [περὶ αὐ]
　　τῶν διηκρίβωται　　　　　vacat

PUNCTUATION: A letter of unusual size, epsilon on C, lines 8 and 15, and on E pi in line 43, omicron in line 57, epsilon in line 68, iota in line 81, seems to mark the beginning of a new sentence, but irregularly. The only other punctuation is an occasional blank and in one case (E, line 94) a sign > at the end of a paragraph.

ORTHOGRAPHY: The forms Ἀρεοπαγεῖται (E, line 31, 33, 76 and 78) and Ἐλευσεῖνι (E, line 85) are normal for this period, likewise the spellings Μαμερτεῖνος (E, lines 9, 13 and 51) and Σατορνείνου (E, line 35), while Πειραεῖ (line 85) might occur in any period. Nor are ἐφείεσθαι (E, line 12), πολειτείας (E, line 31), Πεῖος (E, line 52), ἐπανειένα[ι] (E, line 62) and ὑπεξστησομένους (E, line 71) very surprising. Nu ephelkystikon occurs four times on the fragments of Plaque I and twenty-two times on Plaque II. Where possible, it is missing in only one case (line 94). The iota adscript is usually added where it belongs, but it is incorrectly added on C, line 15 ἄνωι καὶ κ[άτ]ωι, on D, line 2 περαιτέρωι, and on E, line 41 ἐπιχειροίηι. The following more serious errors on E can probably be attributed to the stonecutter: ΑΚΑΤΕΡΟΥ for ⟨ἑ⟩κατέρου in line 10, ΠΑΡΑΝΤΕΛΛΕΙΝ for παραν⟨γ⟩έλλειν in line 12, ΕΚΕΙΝΟΝ for ἐκείν⟨ω⟩ν in line 23, ΕΙΙΑΝ for εἴ⟨η⟩ ἂν in line 46, ΕΙΗΗΝ for ἐ⟨μ⟩ὴν in line 67. On the other hand, ἐφείσθω (E, line 39) is a variant rather than an error, likewise [ὠ]φείλιμον (E, line 46).

WORDS:

New words: ἀντεισπράττω (E 82), εἰσφυγαδεύω (E 46), ἐννόμως (E 5), ἱεροκηρυκεία (E 11), συνευφ[ροσύ]νια (E 88). Old word with new meaning: τρόφιον (E 5). Verbs with double prefix: ἀντεισπράττω (E 82), ἐξανίσταμαι (E 98), ἐπαναλαμβάνω (E 13 and 41), ἐπανάγω (E 59), ἐπανέρχομαι (E 41), ἐπανήκω (E 43), ἐπανίημι (E 62), προκατατίθημι (E 5 and 6), προσενθυμέομαι (E 95), ὑπεξάγω (E 70 and 75), ὑπεξέρχομαι (E 70), ὑπεξίσταμαι (E 71), ὑποκαθέζομαι (E 91). Atticisms: παραφυλαττόμενα (E 38), παραφυλαττομένης (E 39), ἀπαλλαττέσθωσαν (E 74), ἐλάττοσ[ιν] (E 75), τήμερον (E 77), ἀντε[ι]σπράτ[τ]ωσιν (E 82), and a predilection for optatives, which are found in C 13, E 6, 29, 37, 40, 41, 45, 46, 54, 55, 60, 72, 88, 91 twice, and 97. Latinism: [τῶν] καλουμένων κωδικίλλων (E 36).

COMMENTARY

Plaque I

Fragment A: The phrase ὁ κράτιστος ἀνήρ, which occurs in line 3, occurs again on C, lines 12 and 17, and on Plaque II, line 82, τοῦ κρ ἀνδρός. It refers to Herodes Atticus, whose name appears in line 5 and on D and frequently on Plaque II. See footnote 9 of this chapter.

Fragment B: The first person singular in line 6 constitutes one more link with C (line 16) and Plaque II.

Fragment C, line 5: " It seemed best that he be relegated to an island." See the case discussed in lines 35-47 of Plaque II.

C, line 8: Euodus son of Onesimus, who reappears on Plaque II, line 51 as if exonerated, cannot be the man relegated to an island.

C, line 11: τῆς πατρί]δος καὶ [τ]ῶν νήσων αὐτῆς ἀπε[χ]έσθω. The verb has been restored from the parallel in line 47 on Plaque II. The restoration γῆς Ἀτθί]δος seemed too poetical, but the restoration here adopted attributes to the emperor a complete dactylic hexameter! Attica and the subject isles make a formulaic phrase for Athenian territory as in the Ulpius Eubiotus inscription (Oliver, *The Sacred Gerusia*, No. 31), lines 19-20, καὶ τὰ χρήματα αὐτῶν τελῶ[ν | ἀπολύεσθαι ἔν τε τῇ ἀ]πάσῃ Ἀττικῇ καὶ ταῖς ὑπηκόοις νήσοις. Hexameters are occasionally found in prose, e. g. Demosthenes, V, 41.

C, line 13: τοῖ]ς πραχθεῖσιν and εἰ]σπραχθεῖσιν are equally possible. See line 16.

C, line 15: ἐνκλημάτων and ἔνκλημα τῶν are equally possible readings in themselves, but the former goes better with the participle.

C, line 16: ἐπὶ τῆς παρ᾽ ἐμοὶ [λεχθείσης] has been restored on the basis of the parallel in line 50 of Plaque II.

C, line 18: Ὀφίλλιον Ἰνγ[ένουον. The third letter of the cognomen could be read as either a dotted gamma or a dotted pi, but not as an epsilon. The man is mentioned again in lines 43, 81 and 85 on Plaque II as a *iudex datus*, but by his cognomen alone. Ofillius Ingenuus is otherwise unknown, but the nomen occurs earlier at Ephesus (*AE* 1950, No. 100 and 1958, No. 52), at Caenepolis (*I.G.*, V, 1, 1246), and at Gythium (*S.E.G.*, XIII, 258), later at Athens (Ofillius Ariston, *I.G.*, II², 2111/12). Though there is no indication of equestrian rank, he surely had membership in the *decuriae*, because he appears as a *iudex* in line 43. For the relation of equestrian rank and *iudex* status see R. Duncan-Jones, " Equestrian Rank in the Cities of the African Provinces under the Principate," *Papers of the British School at Rome,* XXXV, 1967, pp. 147-188.

Fragment D: The name Herodes constitutes another link with A and Plaque II. Line 9 probably reads αἱ πρόσο[δοι.

Fragment F: Compare Plaque II, lines 98-99 and 46.

PLAQUE II = EM 13366

Line 1: The name of Aelius Praxagoras, known from *I.G.*, II², 2067, 2342, 3693, 3710, 3713, 4088 and from Philostratus, *V. S.*, II, 1 (p. 67 Kayser, p. 168 Wright), belonged to a man (or two men) who served as *dadouchos* and, in A.D. 154/5, archon at Athens. He reappears in lines 35, 41, 44 and 50. Claudius Demostratus (son of Sospis, of Melite), a relative by marriage, is known from *I.G.*, II², 2342 (line 10), 3609, 3613, 4077, 4088 and *Hesperia*, XI, 1942, p. 43, No. 12, XVI, 1947, p. 175, No. 77, XXIX, 1960, p. 62, No. 105, and Philostratus, *V.S.*, II, 1, pp. 63, 67 and 71 Kayser. Since he is often confused with his homonymous grandfather, the interested reader would do well to consult the section on " The Claudii of Melite " in J. H. Oliver's *The Athenian Expounders*, Baltimore, 1950, pp. 76-81. See also E. A. Kapetanopoulos, 'Αρχ. 'Εφ., 1964, pp. 120-123, and *B.C.H.*, XCII, 1968, pp. 493-518, and especially Michael Woloch's still unpublished dissertation, *Roman Citizenship and the Athenian Elite . . . A.D. 96-161* (Johns Hopkins University, 1966), pp. 179-183. The name of the third man, Aelius Themison, is new, and so is that of their opponent Aelius Dionysius—at least with the Roman nomen. For Praxagoras, Demostratus (and Mamertinus, *infra*) see also G. W. Bowersock, *Greek Sophists in the Roman Empire*, Oxford, 1969, pp. 92-100.

Line 4: δαιδουχίαν. This word in the sense " priesthood of the *dadouchos* " occurs in the decree in honor of the *dadouchos* Themistocles published by J. Chr. Threpsiades in K. Kourouniotes, 'Ελευσινιακά, I, 1932, pp. 223-236 and republished by P. Roussel, *Mélanges Bidez*, II, 1934, pp. 819-834, in lines 34, 49, 51 and 65.

Lines 4-5: ἐθελου[σίαν διέ]|ποντας ἱερ[ε]ωσύνην. The opposite of the adjective " voluntary " would seem to be " elected." For the candidates themselves A. H. M. Jones, *The Greek City from Alexander to Justinian*, pp. 182 and 342, cites the adjectives ἑκούσιος (*Die Inschriften von Milet*, No. 176) and αὐθαίρετος. For the participle compare Herodian, *Ab excessu divi Marci*, IV, 1, 3, οἱ τὴν ὕπατον ἀρχὴν τότε διέποντες.

Line 5: φθάνουσιν ἔχειν. For the verb φθάνω with infinitive see the edict of Tib. Julius Alexander, lines 35-36, ὁσάκις ἔπαρχος ἐπ' αὐτὸν ἀχθέντα ἔφθα|σεν κρίνας ἀπολῦσαι.

Line 5: προκατατίθεσθαι τὸ τρόφιον ἐννόμως, to make their prior payments (of grain) as the law requires. The adverb ἐννόμως occurs here for the first time. The word τρόφιον (rather than τροφῖον = τροφεῖον) is connected with the verb τρέφω and with the noun τροφεύς, which were commonly used in reference to donations of free grain. The evidence on the latter was brought together by L. Robert, *Hellenica*, VII, 1949, pp. 74-81 (see also *Bull. ép.*, 1960, p. 438). At Apamea inscriptions honor a man θρέψαντα τὴν πόλιν . . . σείτου ἐπιδόσει, and at Synnada there were coins with the legend ἐπὶ 'Αρτέμωνος ἀρχιερέως or ἐπὶ 'Αρτέμωνος τροφέως (cited by Robert).

We are more familiar with cash requirements in the sale of priesthoods. The *diagraphe* of Dionysus Phleos, *Inschr. von Priene* 174 = Sokolowski, *Lois sacrées de l'Asie Mineure* 37, reads: καταβαλεῖ δὲ ὁ πριάμενος τῶι νεωπόῃ τὸ μὲν ἐπιδέκατον παραχρῆμα, τῆς δὲ λοιπῆς τιμῆς τὸ μὲν ἥμισυ μηνὸς Μεταγειτνιῶνος ἔτους τοῦ αὐτοῦ, τὸ δὲ ἥμισυ μηνὸς Ἀνθεστηριῶνος ἐπὶ στεφανοφόρου Κλεομένου. The minimum price was fixed, but the exemptions depended on the extra amount he paid. The Milesian inscription, Sokolowski, *Lois sacrées de l'Asie Mineure* 48, reads: τὴν δὲ τιμὴν καταβάλλειν ἐν ἔτεσιν [δέ]κα, δέκατον μέρος ἔτους ἑκάστου. And there are other examples, but apparently the word τρόφιον had not previously appeared in this sense. The τρύβλιον at Cyrene was something else (L. Robert, *Hellenica*, I, 1940, pp. 14 f.). Compare Claude Moussy, *Recherches sur* ΤΡΕΦΩ *et les verbes grecs signifiant " nourrir "* (Études et commentaires, LXX, 1969), pp. 85-89. The noun προκαταβολή (*Hesperia*, X, 1941, p. 16, line 36) has similarity.

Line 6: " called by the Demos." Compare *I.G.*, IV, 609 (Argos, second century after Christ), κληθέντα ἐπὶ πᾶσαν ἀρχὴν καὶ ἐπὶ τῇ τελευτῇ [τ]ειμ[ηθ]έντα ταῖς μεγίσταις τιμαῖς.

Lines 7-8: Sentius Attalus (of Gargettos), who reappears in lines 51-52, ephebe around 166/7 (*I.G.*, II², 2094) and hoplite general in 181/2 (*I.G.*, II², 1791), served in the Council during A.D. 182/3 (prytany catalogue published in *Hesperia*, IV, 1935, p. 48, No. 11 and XXXVI, 1947, pp. 47 f.). Claudius Chrysippus (of Phlya) may have been son of the homonymous cosmete of 142/3 (*I.G.*, II², 3740) and grandson of the homonymous archon known from *Hesperia*, XI, 1942, p. 37, No. 7. He appears in the inscription published by B. D. Meritt, *Hesperia*, XXIX, 1960, pp. 29-32, No. 37, which J. H. Oliver, " The Athens of Hadrian," *Colloque International à Madrid sur les empereurs romains d'Espagne*, Paris, 1965, pp. 126-129 interpreted as a list of property on which the fiscus had some claim. His son appears as an ephebe gymnasiarch in *I.G.*, II², 2113.

Line 8: ἀπὸ τοῦ δικαστηρίου καὶ ἀπὸ τοῦ βασιλέως Κλ Εὐπραξίδο[υ]. There is no indication that dicasteries of the type described by Aristotle, *Ath. Pol.*, 63-69 any longer existed. The word, however, may have continued in use for a court of a different type. At Cyrene, as we know from the first edict of Augustus, there were jury courts empaneled from a roll of those with a certain census; Augustus referred to the jurors as the κριταί. At Athens as we know from Hadrian's Oil Law, *S. E. G.*, XV, 108, certain criminal cases were tried before the Council of the Five Hundred and other criminal cases with larger sums involved were tried before the Ecclesia of the Demos; no mention of a dicastery occurred in the extant section of the Oil Law. Two other references to a dicastery will be found in lines 68 and 75. Line 68 speaks of a plurality of courts; whether or not they were old, how they were empaneled and with how many jurors we cannot say. Here in line 8 repetition of the preposition ἀπό indicates that these appeals are from two courts, one of which is probably a jury court, the other is the archon basileus. The legality of the adoption here mentioned had to be tried in the dicastery. Since Aristotle, *Ath. Pol.*, 57, 2 says that the basileus decided disputes concerning hereditary priesthoods, we presume that the case concerning the recovery of a Eumolpid priesthood came to the emperor on appeal from the decision of the basileus. Claudius Eupraxides is otherwise unknown.

Line 9: Valerius Mamertinus, who reappears in line 51, is known from Philostratus, *V.S.*, II, 1, p. 67 Kayser, p. 168 Wright, as one of the main enemies of Herodes Atticus along with Praxagoras and Demostratus of line 1. He was archon in 166/7 (*I.G.*, II², 1773) and hoplite general in 168/9 (text published by D. J. Geagan, *The Athenian Constitution after Sulla* [*Hesperia*, Suppl. XII], 1967, p. 195).

Lines 9-11: Mamertinus, a Eumolpid who desired an office reserved for the Ceryces, could have claimed a precedent in the family of T. Flavius Straton of Paeania and his homonymous son. An inscription at Eleusis, *I.G.*, II², 3984, shows that whereas Straton senior served as hierophant, hence belonged to the Eumolpidae, Straton junior served as altar priest, hence belonged to the Ceryces. Straton junior, who transferred from the genos of the Eumolpidae to that of the Ceryces, probably based his right to transfer on his mother's and maternal grandfather's membership in the Ceryces.

Line 12: παραν⟨γ⟩έλλειν. *Posse et alios profiteri, si gratiae aut meritis confiderent*, as Tacitus, *Ann.*, I, 81, 3 quoted Tiberius.

Lines 13-14: τὴν [ἱερε]|ωσύνην ἀνακομιεῖται. The parallel passage on one who will recover his status as a member of the Areopagus occurs in lines 65-66: τὸ ἀξίωμα [ἀνα]|κομιεῖται. The restoration [ἱερε]|ωσύνην seems imposed, but its interpretation is not certain. Presumably he relinquished a lesser priesthood when he transferred himself hopefully out of the Eumolpidae. The catalogue of those entitled to a distribution at the festival at Eleusis contains a list of priesthoods: see J. H. Oliver, " The Eleusinian Endowment," *Hesperia*, XXI, 1952, pp. 381-399, especially p. 394. But we do not know what lesser priesthoods were reserved for Eumolpidae, apart from expounding priesthoods.

Line 14: τὸ δὲ ἐπὶ τούτου μοι παραστὰν λαβόντι τὴν γνώμην ἐκ τῆς παρούση[ς δ]ίκης, " the decision which ripened in me in this case after I had formed my opinion from the present trial ": In the edict remitting the *aurum coronarium, P. Fay.* 20, line 2 Severus Alexander says ὅθεν μοι παρέστη τὸ βούλευμα τοῦτο (a plan in imitation of Trajan and Marcus). The metaphor is that of grain ripening on the stalk cf. Ptolemy III in *O.G.I.S.*, 56, line 68, ὅταν ὁ πρώιμος σπόρος παραστῆι). The decision was supposed to remedy the situation, but the emperor first had to form his opinion on the merits of the case.

Lines 14-15: " will not let that which is likely to confuse the traditional, carefully guarded procedures slip by." With the phrase τὸ μέλλον συνχέαι τὰ παραφυλαττόμενα compare Herodotus, VII, 136, κείνους μὲν γὰρ συγχέαι τὰ πάντων ἀνθρώπων νόμιμα ἀποκτείναντας κήρυκας, and S.I.G.³, 45, τὸν νόμον τοῦτον εἴ τις θέληι συγχέαι. The decision will not establish a dangerous precedent. Compare also Trajan to Pliny (X, 115), *in futurum autem lex Pompeia observaretur; cuius vim si retro quoque velimus custodire, multa necesse est perturbari.* Τὰ παραφυλαττόμενα are *quae velimus custodire.* Συνχέαι means *perturbare.*

Lines 15-16: Ladicus son of Polyaenus (mentioned again in line 51) and Julius Damostratus (mentioned again in line 20) were previously unknown. Sophanes seems to appear in *I.G.*, II², 12731.

Lines 16-20: That Hadrian himself established the rules for eligibility to membership in the Panhellenion might have been inferred but is first explicitly stated here. The sense requires a verb like ἀπεῖναι or ἀπελθεῖν in the lacuna of lines 16-17. The crucial restoration ἀπ[ενε]|χθείς in lines 17-18 is suggested by Demosthenes, *Against Meidias* 86, where a ruling is reported with the words ἀνώμοτος ἀπηνέχθη, " he was disqualified as unsworn."

Line 19: " and had previously exercised rule in no office." Compare the maxim in the Vatican parchments *De eligendis magistratibus*, lines 210-215: χρὴ δ' ὅλως οὐδένα ἄναρχον [ἄ]ρχειν ἕως τὸν ἀβούλευτον. In this treatise from the end of the fourth century B.C. published by W. Aly, *Studi e testi* 104 (Vatican City, 1943) and by Fr. Sbordone, *La Parola del Passato*, IX, 1948, pp. 269-290, the advantage of training a man in the lower offices before admitting him to higher offices appears long before the Romans established for themselves a *cursus honorum* by law. Hadrian's ruling, however, did not demand a series of offices before a man became eligible for the Panhellenion.

Lines 19-20: " appeal without justification." Scaevola *libro secundo digestorum* (Digest, IV, 4, 39 pr.): *finita appellationis apud imperatorem cognitione et iniusta appellatione pronuntiata.*

Line 20: Eudemus son of Aphrodisius was an ephebe in 142/3 and is already known from *I.G.*, II², 2049, 3630 and 3740, but Epigonus cannot be identified elsewhere.

Line 21: For " my Quintilii " see pp. 66-70.

Lines 22-23: ἐπὶ τῆς ἕδ[ρας]|ὑπ' ἐκείν⟨ω⟩ν (lapis EKEINON) ἐκτελεῖσθαι. If, as in line 21, only three letters are missing at the end of line 22, or four at the most, we are almost obliged to assume ἕδ[ρας] as the mutilated word. It refers to the sitting of a magistrate's court. In the Spartan inscription cited *infra* as No. **2** the praetorian prefect who handled much of the court business for Antoninus Pius is called τὸν ἐπὶ τῇ καθέδρα τοῦ Αὐτοκράτορος Καί(σαρος).

Line 23: Athenodorus son of Agrippa (of Eitea) is known from the prytany catalogue *I.G.*, II², 1793, in which he appears just after his relative Agrippa son of

Asmenus, who presumably outranked him. Around A.D. 180 (see *Harvard Theological Review*, XLIII, 1950, p. 234 on the uncertainty of the year) another catalogue, *I.G.*, II², 1794, is dated ἐπ' ἄρχοντος Ἀθηνοδώρου τοῦ Ἀσμένο[υ] | τοῦ καὶ Ἀγρίππου Ἰταίου. The phrase " called Agrippa " has since Dittenberger's edition, *I.G.*, III, 1040, been applied to Athenodorus, but to the writer it now seems that the archon Athenodorus of Eitea was the son of Asmenus called Agrippa. Our Athenodorus, accordingly, was the attested archon, his father was Asmenus called Agrippa, and his grandfather was Asmenus of Eitea. The father, having the same name as the grandfather, came to be distinguished by a second name.

Lines 23-24: Papius Rufus is otherwise unknown. That the archon's term was four years constitutes new information.

Line 24: The administrators of the estates of the vir clarissimus Claudius Herodes (= Herodes Atticus) are mentioned again in lines 49 and 82. They are the freedmen against whom Marcus had turned his anger after the trial at Sirmium (Philostratus, *V.S.*, II, 1, p. 69 Kayser, p. 172 Wright).

Line 25: It is significant that the *acta* of the Senate too were called ὑπομνήματα in Greek: Cassius Dio, LXXVIII, 22, 2, τὰ τῆς βουλῆς ὑπομνήματα διὰ χειρὸς ἔχων.

Line 27: Nostimus son of Dionysius (mentioned again in line 51) was ephebe in 145/6 as we see from *I.G.*, II², 2052, where his name appears first in the panel of the tribe Acamantis, ἀγορανόμος Νόστιμος Διονυσίου Χολαρ.

Lines 27-29: The first difficulty is the meaning of the phrase ἐν τούτωι. The three previous cases concerned appeals of men from the court of the archon of the Panhellenes. The court, if any, from which Nostimus was appealing is not mentioned, but it should therefore be a similar case to the preceding which concerned membership in the Panhellenion, so that the phrase ἐν τούτωι is better interpreted to mean " in the Panhellenion." The second difficulty concerns the phrase κατὰ τοὺς νόμους. If he had become Areopagite in the face of some legal impediment, the emperor would hardly have considered his enrollment permissible. Therefore, Nostimus probably received an honorary appointment for a service other than that prescribed by the laws. He was not ineligible because of a taint upon his ancestry, but he had not earned the appointment by the usual service foreseen in the laws, the perfect performance of an archonship. Some post he must have held, if we are right in thinking that this case too concerned membership in the Panhellenion. An *agonothesia* comes to mind. Or an *epimeleteia*? For we see from line 19 that a man who had never held any previous post could not be a Panhellene.

Lines 30-35: The name of Popilius Pius appears again in line 52. The complete cognomen, being short, came at the end of line 30, and the two first visible letters of line 31 are not part of the name. If this case too concerned the Panhellenion, Popilius Pius would have to be a man of importance, perhaps a kinsman of Popillius Theotimus of Sunium, archon in 155/6 (*I.G.*, II², 2068), and of the naturalized (?)

director of the Epicurean School at Athens, Popillius Theotimus, to whom Hadrian wrote at Plotina's request (*I.G.*, II², 1099). It is possible that while content to see foreigners with honorary Athenian citizenship assuming the expense of the archonship, rivals begrudged Pius the distinction of being a Panhellene from Athens. The last visible letters of line 31 are a chi and a letter with a vertical hasta; the restoration is suggested by the parallel in line 100. With the phrase τὴν βεβαιότητα ὑπάρχειν in line 32, compare the passage on Alexandrians, *C.P.J.*, 153, lines 53-59, especially βέβαιον διαφυλάσσω τὴν Ἀλεξανδρέων πολιτείαν and εἶναι βούλομαι βέβαια and [ὁ] θεὸς Σεβαστὸς ἐβεβαίωσε. The phrase τῆι δοθείσηι ἐξουσίαι in line 32 recalls the phrase in which a choice of jurors was granted in the first edict of Augustus at Cyrene, δοθείσης ἐξουσίας αὐτῷ πότερον, κτλ. So here the interpretation, " following because of fear of the adversary the option granted to them," is recommended rather than an interpretation which takes the preposition ὑπό as expressing agency. The option was, I think, trial before the Areopagus, trial before the Panhellenes under presidency of the archon of the Panhellenes, trial in a Roman court, which was usually that of the proconsul of Achaia. The plaintiff brought against Popilius [Pius] a charge of ineligibility to a seat in the Panhellenion on the ground that he was not legally an Athenian. Since the court of the Panhellenes judged the eligibility of its own members, the plaintiff expected the case to be tried in the Panhellenion, but the defendant, who considered the Panhellenion under the influence of the plaintiff, demanded trial in the Areopagus. The emperor upholds the right of the plaintiff in any such situation to choose the court of his own city. A question of citizenship would naturally go to whatever court the defendant chose. The evidence which leads to this impression will be found in the rescript of Diocletian and Maximian to a certain Alexander, Cod. Iust., III, 13, 2: *Iuris ordinem converti postulas, ut non actor rei forum, sed reus actoris sequatur: nam ubi domicilium habet reus vel tempore contractus habuit, licet hoc postea transtulerit, ibi tantum eum conveniri oportet.* On the *reiectio* of a whole *iudicium* see Peter Garnsey, *J.R.S.*, LVI, 1966, pp. 182-185. For τὰ δίκαια see L. Robert, *Revue de philologie*, 3ᵉ série, XXXII, 1958, pp. 30 f. The order in line 34 to preserve the ancestral customs may be compared with the phrase *salvo iure gentis* in the Tabula Banasitana.

Line 35, Gavinius Saturninus: One could divide Γα Οὐινίου as praenomen plus nomen or read Γαουινίου as nomen alone. The nomen Vinius (see W. Schulze, *Zur Geschichte lateinischer Eigennamen*, p. 425) is rare and praenomina are apparently not used in this inscription. Therefore, we might better read the nomen as Gavinius (Schulze, p. 76).

Lines 35-37: Mario Amelotti, *Il testamento romano attraverso la prassi documentale*, I, pp. 209-215 shows what the codicils were in theory and practice, and on pp. 22 f. he discusses codicil cases from the time of Marcus Aurelius. The Latin word κωδικίλλων is found in another Athenian inscription, *Hesperia*, XXX, 1961,

p. 236, No. 32 (reinterpreted *ibidem*, p. 403) and in *Inscr. Cret.*, IV, 300. Minor, or theoretically minor, dispositions could be made in codicils, but *codicillis hereditas neque dari neque adimi potest.* See particularly Institutes, II, 25 *de codicillis*, Digest, II, 29, 7 *de iure codicillorum*, and XXX-XXXII *de legatis et fideicommissis.* Since the case concerns an inheritance and the appeal is brought by a Roman citizen from the court of Gavinius Saturninus, the unidentified Gavinius Saturninus, who has neither the title of an office in the polis or Panhellenion nor the predicate of rank becoming to a Roman senator, appears to be the *procurator hereditatum.* Compare P. A. Brunt, " Procuratorial Jurisdiction," *Latomus*, XXV, 1966, pp. 461-489; W. Litewski, *R.I.D.A.*, XIII, 1966, p. 290.

Line 38: The subject of the verb προὔθεσαν has to be inferred from the plural noun in line 36 (the codicils).

Line 39: δύο ἄλλων μηνῶν προθεσμίας παραφυλαττομένης. Compare *I.G.*, II², 1104, reedited by J. H. Oliver, *Colloque . . . Madrid sur les empereurs romains d'Espagne,* Paris, 1965, p. 129: μέχρι μηνῶν ἄλλων δύο, and the three references to the original term of sixty days.

Line 42: For the restoration λή[μψ]εται compare ἐπαναλημφθήσονται and καταλημφθῶσιν in lines 13 and 77.

Lines 42-43: References to Herodes Atticus and to Ingenuus show that we are still dealing with the case mentioned on Plaque I, fragment C, lines 16-17. Ingenuus is Ofillius Ingenuus, otherwise unknown, whom the emperor, without giving him the predicate of high rank, named as the man he was appointing as *iudex.* On this expert, perhaps from Laconia, compare commentary on fragment C, line 18.

Line 44: What does the phrase τῶν ἡγεμόνων τοῦ ἔθνους mean? Practically the same phrase was used by Hadrian in his letter to the Ephesians (*S.I.G.*,³ 838 = Smallwood 72), τοῦ ἔθν[ους τ]ο[ὺς] ἡγεμόνας, " the authorities of the province," whom the ship captain regularly transported. Hadrian must have meant the proconsul and the latter's legate. With a similar phrase in the Columbia *apokrimata*,[1] line 17, ὁ ἡγούμενος τοῦ ἔθνους, Severus and Caracalla meant the governor (prefect) of Egypt. In *Gerasa* 161 (A.D. 293-305) the governor is called ὁ διασημότατος ἡγούμε[ν]ος τῆς ἐπαρχείου. See also *S.E.G.*, XVII, 759, line 29, for the governor of Syria as the ἡγούμενος. Ad. Wilhelm, *Neue Beiträge*, V, pp. 36-38 (*Sitzungsb. Wien*, CCXIV, 4, 1932) presents other examples. Alexander Severus, cited in Digest, XIX, 1, 25, says τοῖς ἐπιτρόποις καὶ τοῖς ἡγουμένοις τῶν ἐθνῶν, which implies that the procurators were not subsumed under the *hegoumenoi.* Here, accordingly, Marcus Aurelius seems to mean the proconsul of Achaia and the latter's legate (compare J. H. Oliver, *The Ruling Power*, pp. 963 f., Case I).

Lines 44-46: The reference must still be to one aspect of the case which Aelius Praxagoras appealed from the court of Gavinius Saturninus. The Athenians have

---

[1] H. C. Youtie and A. A. Schiller, *Chronique d'Égypte*, XXX, 1965, p. 333.

asked for a pardon on the grounds of the father's age and loneliness, not on the son's innocence. The petition is neither refused nor granted but temporarily shelved. The first adjective in line 46 [.]φείλιμον can hardly be anything but a variant spelling of ὠφέλιμον (compare ἐφείεσθω for ἐφέσθω in line 39), since the adjectives ὀφέλλιμος and ὀφέλσιμος, the only ones derived from ὄφελος, are attested only in verse.

Line 46: ἐκ τῆς νή[σο]υ εἰς ἣν εἰσεφυγαδεύετο. See Marcianus in Digest, XLVIII, 19, 4, beginning *Relegati sive in insulam deportati* and ending *et nemo potest commeatum remeatumve dare exuli, nisi imperator, ex aliqua causa*; also Ulpian in Digest, XLVIII, 22, 6: *Inter poenas est etiam insulae deportatio, quae poena adimit civitatem Romanam.* In Institutes I, 16, 2 the second of the three types of *capitis deminutio* is defined as follows: *Minor sive media est capitis deminutio, cum civitas quidem amittitur, libertas vero retinetur, sed status hominis commutatur. quod accidit ei, cui aqua et igni interdictum fuerit, vel ei, qui in insulam deportatus est.* The man here mentioned is presumably the subject of Fragment C, lines 4-11, on Plaque I.

Line 47, Agathocles: For his son Agathocles, who was ephebe in 169/70 and prytanis around A.D. 200, see *I.G.*, II², 2097 and 1813.

Lines 47-48: The equivalent of expenses incurred through the embassies shall be repaid to Agathocles. Compare the conclusion of various imperial letters like that of Hadrian to the Gerusia of Ephesus, *S.I.G.*³, 833 = Smallwood 452, ὁ πρεσβεύων ἦν Κασκέλλιος [Πον]τικός, ὧι τὸ ἐφόδιον δοθήτω, εἴ γε μὴ προῖκα ὑπέ[σχε]το πρεσβεύσειν, and that of Hadrian to Stratonicea Hadrianopolis in Lydia, *S.I.G.*³, 837 = Smallwood 453, ἐπρέσβευσεν Κλ. Κάνδιδος, ὧι τὸ ἐφόδιον δοθήτω, εἰ μὴ προῖκα ὑπέσχηται. Whereas in these Hadrianic cases and in two more at Coronea in *I.G.*, VII, 2870 (Antoninus Pius) the city is instructed to reimburse the ambassador for travel expenses there and back, the term ἡ διὰ τὰς πρεσβείας ἀξίωσις covers both travel and a sojourn of long duration. A Spartan inscription, No. 2 below, honors an ambassador with the words συνθύτης ἰς Νέαν πόλιν ὑπερχρονίαν μὴ λαβών.

Line 49: The case of Aelius Ameinias, otherwise unknown, came on Plaque I.

Lines 50-52. For Aelius Praxagoras, Claudius Demostratus, Aelius Themison see the cases mentioned in line 1. For Sentius Attalus and Clement son of Clement see the cases cited in lines 7-8. Valerius Mamertinus was their opponent in line 9. For Ladicus son of Polyaenus see the case cited in line 15. For the case of Nostimus son of Dionysius see line 30 rather than lines 27-28. The case of Popilius Pius came in lines 31-35. Euodus son of Onesimus is mentioned on C, line 8. We have no mention of the Claudius Chrysippus who in line 8 was bracketed with Sentius Attalus and Clement son of Clement in the cases against Valerius Mamertinus. These were apparently two or three separate cases against Mamertinus, and Claudius Chrysippus lost his case. With the phrase ἐπὶ ταῖς δίκαις ταῖς παρ' ἐμοὶ λεχθείσαις compare Caracalla in *S.E.G.*, XVII, No. 759, ἐλέχθη παρὰ τῷ ἡγουμένῳ.

Lines 52-53: For the word περιγεγράφθ[αι] see line 9. The case of Epigonus (son of Epictetus) is given in lines 20-23, that of Athenodorus (son of Agrippa) in lines 23-27.

Line 53: διαγνώσεως. For the *cognitio* procedure see Max Kaser, *Das römische Zivilprozess*, Munich, 1966, pp. 339-409.

Lines 53-54: ἐδ[ήλω]|σα πρὸ ἀποφάσεως. Compare line 87, δεδηλῶσθαι δι' ὧν ἀπεφηνάμην. The instructions would be a formal statement such as the emperor made in the case of Epigonus vs. Eudemus in lines 20-21, or in the case of Athenodorus vs. the agents of Herodes in lines 24-27.

Line 54: The *iudex* is Ofillius Ingenuus of C, line 15.

Line 58: τὸ παρ' αὐτοῖς ἔκκριτον συνέδριο[ν. In *I.G.*, II², 3606, the epigram commemorating the official reception of Herodes Atticus on his return, the Areopagus is called βουλὴ κεκριμένη Κεκρόπων. The Aurelius Heras monument, No. **51** *infra*, suggests that the phrase " select synedrion " was a familiar description of the Panhellenion.

Lines 58-59: The date at which the emperor tried to weed out of the Areopagus socially undesirable members cannot be fixed with certainty beyond citing the *terminus post quem* of early 169 when Marcus became sole emperor. Against the assumption that it coincided with his visit to Athens we have a reference in line 67 to a letter of his on this question. Since the new system was tried for a time, the letter must have preceded the visit to Athens. Two passages in Philostratus, *V.S.*, II, 1 give a clue. The first will be found in Philostratus, p. 58 Kayser, p. 144 Wright. In a speech which Marcus doubtless read Herodes bitterly attacked the freedmen of his father as having curried favor with the Athenians at his own expense. Again Philostratus, II, 1, p. 69 Kayser, p. 172 Wright, says that at the trial of Herodes at Sirmium Marcus turned his anger against the freedmen of Herodes. It is not improbable that Marcus was in A.D. 174 finally moved to reduce the influence of freedmen at Athens. The example of Augustus, who cleansed the Roman Senate of unworthy members, caused Marcus to make a special effort with the Areopagus. Even the phrase πρὸς τὸ παλαιὸν ἔθος recalls the declared aim in Suetonius, *Augustus* 35: *Senatorum affluentem numerum deformi et incondita turba . . . ad modum pristinum et splendorem redegit duabus lectionibus.* See p. 48.

Line 60: τοὺς ἀπὸ τῆς τριγονίας ἐξετασθέντας. Compare the early Hellenistic law at Halicarnassus, Sokolowski, *Lois sacrées de l'Asie Mineure*, 73: [ὁ] πριάμε[νο]ς [τὴ]ν ἱερητείαν τῆς Ἀρτέμιδος τῆς Περγαίας πα[ρέ]ξεται ἱέρειαν ἀστὴν ἐξ ἀστῶν ἀμφοτέρων ἐπὶ [τρεῖ]ς γενεὰς γεγενημένην κ[αὶ] πρὸς πατρὸς καὶ πρὸς [μη]τρός. In the *Ath. Pol.*, 55 the would-be archon is first asked τίς σοι πατὴρ καὶ πόθεν τῶν δήμων, καὶ τίς πατρὸς πατήρ, καὶ τίς μήτηρ, καὶ τίς μητρὸς πατὴρ καὶ πόθεν τῶν δήμων. In the time of Marcus Aurelius the rhetorician Pollux, *Onomasticon*, VIII, 85 (ed. Bethe) wrote, ἐκαλεῖτο δέ τις θεσμοθετῶν ἀνάκρισις, εἰ Ἀθηναῖοί εἰσιν ἑκατέρωθεν ἐκ τριγονίας καὶ τῶν δήμων πόθεν. The word τριγονία is classical Attic, but it probably became more com-

mon after Marcus Aurelius used it. Themistius, Or. 8, p. 137 Dindorf, wrote καὶ
πολλοὶ τῶν εὐπατριδῶν τὰ σκῆπτρα ἐκ τριγονίας διαδεξάμενοι. Marcus Aurelius, however, in this inscription does not use the word to mean free birth on *both* sides of the
family; rather he means the man himself, his father and his paternal grandfather to
judge from lines 64-66.

Lines 60-61: The phrase καὶ νῦν ἔτι (e.g. Cassius Dio, XL, 14, 4) or ἔτι καὶ νῦν
(e.g. Demosthenes, II, 30 and Aristotle, *Ath. Pol.*, 22, 2) is very common.

The ruthless separation of freedmen from men of good birth proved impossible.
One is reminded of the debate in the Senate in A.D. 56 according to Tacitus, *Ann.*,
XIII, 27: *si separarentur libertini, manifestam fore penuriam ingenuorum.*

Line 61: "the things that happened through the interference of fortune," τὰ
συμβάντα διὰ τὴν τύχην. See Marcus Aurelius, X, 33, 4, "Nothing harms the city
that does not harm the law. Now none of what are called strokes of bad luck harms
the law," with Farquharson's commentary. Good laws, because of occasional mis-
fortune such as plague and other disasters due to chance (not to one's own folly),
should undergo temporary adjustments but not be abandoned. For events uncon-
nected with the nature of the polis and with political teleology see the interesting
remarks of James Day and M. Chambers, *Aristotle's History of Athenian Democracy*
(U. Calif. Pub. History, LXXIII), 1962, pp. 42-50. On τὰ συμβάντα see also Demosthenes, IV, 39.

Line 63: φιλανθρωπίαι, the attitude of civilized men, which in this case embraces
consideration for the past and concern for the future. See the primary material and
bibliography cited by J. Kabiersch, *Untersuchungen zu dem Begriff der Philanthropia
bei dem Kaiser Julian* (= Klassisch-philologische Studien, Heft 21), 1960, H. Mar-
tin, Jr., "The Concept of *Philanthropia* in Plutarch's *Lives*," A.J.P., LXXXII,
1961, pp. 164-175, and H. Hunger, "Φιλανθρωπία: Eine griechische Wortprägung
auf ihrem Wege von Aischylos bis Theodoros Metochites," *Wiener Anzeiger*, C,
1963, pp. 1-20.

Line 63: "make once and for all a viable settlement (αὐτάρκως ἱδρῦσαι) for the
future." For political αὐτάρκεια see Aristotle, *Politics*, IV, 1291a14-15. *Autarkeia*
implies the presence, in the city, of all the elements necessary for survival and stability.
If aristocracy were weakened, the emperor supposes that the constitution would cease
to be a mixed (stable) constitution.

Lines 64-66: The emperor relaxes the three-generation rule in such a way that
it will suffice for the present that the man himself and his father be of free birth.
Nothing is said about the man's mother. In the future, however, it will be necessary
for both γονεῖς of the man to be freeborn. The question arises whether γονεῖς means
"father and mother" or "father and paternal grandfather." The latter must be the
true meaning because the mother would have been mentioned with the father in the
clause running from line 64 to 65, if it were an ancient Athenian type of τριγονία

ἑκατέρωθεν being reduced to two generations. In A.D. 23 or earlier the regulation concerning the use of the gold ring of a Roman knight was formulated partly on the basis of a three-generation rule which applied to the father and the paternal grandfather alone, as we know from Pliny, *N.H.*, XXXIII, 2, 8, 32: *constitutum, ne cui ius esset nisi qui ingenuus ipse, ingenuo patre, avo paterno HS* $\overline{CCCC}$ *census fuisset et lege Iulia theatrali in quattuordecim ordinibus sedisset?* [2]

Among references to the three-generation rule at Rome is Suetonius, *Vitellius* 2: *P. Vitellius domo Nuceria, sive ille stirpis antiquae sive pudendis parentibus atque avis, eques certe Romanus et rerum Augusti procurator.* The implication of the phrase *pudendis parentibus atque avis* is an absence of the three-generation qualification on both sides of the family for the father of the emperor Vitellius. What was ideally expected in the case of an emperor need not have been a rule for senators, much less for knights. Plutarch, *Pompey*, 13, 11 says that Fabius Rullianus expelled from the Roman Senate certain rich men who were sons of freedmen. That does not mean that Rullianus had no objection to grandsons of freedmen. Plutarch, I think, found the expulsion proper. Plutarch, *Flamininus*, 18, 1 reports acceptance of all who had free γονεῖς into citizenship. The most important reference to the three generation rule for Roman senators occurs in Suetonius, *Divus Claudius*, 24, 1:

> Latum clavum, quamvis initio affirmasset non lecturum se senatorem nisi civis R. abnepotem, etiam libertini filio tribuit, sed sub condicione si prius ab equite R. adoptatus esset; ac sic quoque reprehensionem verens, et Appium Caecum censorem, generis sui proauctorem, libertinorum filios in senatum adlegisse docuit, ignarus, temporibus Appi et deinceps aliquandiu " libertinos " dictos non ipsos, qui manu emitterentur, sed ingenuos ex his procreatos.

Tacitus, *Ann.*, XI, 24, 7, as Orelli suggests, may reflect the speech made on this or a similar occasion. Finally, L. R. Taylor, *The Voting Districts of the Roman Republic* (Papers and Monographs of the American Academy in Rome, XX), 1960, Ch. 10, " The Urban Tribes and the Registration of Freedmen," brings together interesting material.

Marcus Aurelius probably knew Aristotle's lost work Περὶ εὐγενείας and Plutarch's lost essay of the same title. Stobaeus, IV, 29 has a whole chapter of extracts from dramatists and philosophers on the theme that *eugeneia* is not what city codes represent it but a quality of the soul whether or not inherited. The comment of Menander's character,

ὃς ἂν εὖ γεγονὼς ᾖ τῇ φύσει πρὸς τἀγαθά,
κἂν Αἰθίοψ ᾖ, μῆτερ, ἐστὶν εὐγενής

[2] On this passage of Pliny see A. Stein, *Der römische Ritterstand*, Munich, 1927, p. 27; A. M. Duff, *Freedmen in the Early Roman Empire*, Oxford, 1928, Appendix II; Cl. Nicolet, *L'ordre équestre à l'epoque républicaine* (= Bibl. Écoles Françaises d' Athènes et de Rome, CCVII), 1966, pp. 140-142.

(lines 11-12 in fr. 612 Koerte-Thierfelder), expresses the protest perfectly, but none of all this literature has here affected the author of our document, who speaks, not like a philosopher, but like a practical statesman in the tradition of Augustus.[3]

In the cities of the Roman Empire the disqualifying ancestry was of two sorts, freedmen and barbarians. The first-generation citizens who because of some distinction became Augustales (but not decurions) were in Northern Italy newly enfranchised Celts and, as everywhere, freedmen. The emphasis on *eugeneia* in Herodian's version of the speech of Pupienus Maximus (VIII, 7, 4) was due to the barbarian origin which should have disqualified Maximinus as a candidate for emperor. Maximinus, though free-born, was not in a Roman sense *ingenuus*. At Athens free barbarians posed no problem. Marcus Aurelius in this case thought only of servile extraction. In the choice of the more ambiguous word εὐγενής as a translation of the clear *ingenuus* Marcus was certainly not reacting against philosophers. If he was reacting against anyone, it was against those who used stylistic barbarisms. Roman officials had been translating the Latin word *ingenuus* into Greek as ἐγγενής. For instance, a governor of Egypt in the first century speaks of ἐγγενεῖς Ἀλεξανδρεῖς when he means freeborn Alexandrian citizens perhaps.[4] In the second century the same translation word turns up in the *Gnomon* of the Idioslogos, where it clearly means *ingenua*. The usage doubtless offended purists like Herodes. The word εὐγενής sounded less barbarous. There was no simple Greek equivalent of *ingenuus*,[5] and the need to find a convenient translation for a Latin term may be very significant. This translation, which many modern scholars have not understood, caught on. Speaking of legislation in 18 B.C., Cassius Dio, LIV, 16, 2 says: " And since among the *ingenui* (τοῦ εὐγενοῦς) there were far more males than females, Augustus allowed all who wished, except the senators, to marry freedwomen, and ordered that their offspring should be held legitimate " (Loeb translation except that εὐγενοῦς is there preposterously mistranslated as " nobility," which does not suit Dio's own context nor conform with the evidence in Digest, XXIII, 2, 23: *Lege Papia cavetur omnibus ingenuis praeter senatores eorumque liberos libertinam*

---

[3] This character of the government of Marcus did not escape A. Garzetti, *L'impero da Tiberio agli Antonini*, Bologna, 1960, pp. 530 and 538, and certain others, but this is an unusually clear example.

[4] So rightly G. Chalon, *L'Édit de Tiberius Julius Alexander* (Bibliotheca Helvetica Romana, V), 1964, p. 162, note 17, except that this is not an alternative explanation. Tib. Alexander thereby certainly excluded the Jews. The Jews of Alexandria, though they had a kind of citizenship, were of a status inferior to that of the local *ingenui*.

[5] Of course it could be expressed in Greek less simply. In *Politics*, IV, 6, 1292b35-37 Aristotle speaks of a kind of democracy in which everyone to whose birth there is no objection is eligible to participate in the government but does not actually participate unless he can find leisure: ἔστι γὰρ καὶ πᾶσιν ἐξεῖναι τοῖς ἀνυπευθύνοις κατὰ τὸ γένος, μετέχειν μέντοι δυναμένους σχολάζειν. Aristotle's terminology ἀνυπεύθυνος—the term occurs also in IV, 4, 1292a1-2—means of free birth but perhaps free birth from citizen father and citizen mother.

uxorem habere licere [cited as from Celsus]). Again Cassius Dio, LV, 31, 1, οὐκ εὐγενεῖς μόνον ἀλλὰ καὶ ἐξελευθέρους (as soldiers). Modestinus in Institutes, XXVII, 1, 1, 4: ἀπελευθερικοῖς ὀρφανοῖς εὐγενεῖς οὐ δώσουσιν οἱ ἄρχοντες ἐπιτρόπους.

But it should be added that the meaning " of birth good enough to hold sacred or public office," though not attested for εὐγενής in the *GEL*, can be found in Demosthenes, LVII, which shows a contrast between those citizens who were not of sufficiently pure origin (LVII, 55: ὅσοι μὴ καθαρῶς ἦσαν πολῖται) and those who were of perfectly good birth, ἐν τοῖς εὐγενεστάτοις (LVII, 46 and 62, where εὐγενέστατος clearly has nothing to do with nobility, but means *civis optimo iure*). Isocrates, *Areopagiticus*, 37 says that (in the time of the ancestors) only those who were of good birth could belong to the Areopagus (ἧς οὐχ οἷόν τ᾽ ἦν μετασχεῖν πλὴν τοῖς καλῶς γεγονόσι).

Line 67: " infiltrated themselves," ἑαυτοὺς ἐνβεβληκόσιν. We are not told how they could do this, but Aristotle's comment (*Ath. Pol.*, 7, 30) that the thetes were *theoretically* excluded from the archonship suggests that before assuming an archonship the candidate made some sort of false statement and that it had become customary or common to accept the statement without proof or even when it was known to be false, especially where a benefaction was involved. Then if the archonship was performed without scandal, the ex-archon became an Areopagite. Proof is now to be demanded, not necessarily before an archonship, but at the review, before the ex-archon is accepted into the Areopagus.

Lines 67-68: The phrase μετὰ τὴν ἐπ[ιστο]|λὴν ἐ⟨μ⟩ὴν ἑτέραν is restored on the basis of the phrase πρὸ τῆς ἐπιστολῆς in the next sentence (line 68) and should be interpreted as a reference to another letter, one to which lines 58-60 refer.

Lines 68-69: Apparently cases concerning the eligibility of a man for membership in the Areopagus from the standpoint of his father's free birth did not come before the whole Areopagus itself, which might be expected to judge the qualifications of its own members. There were, it says, jury courts that could be assigned for that purpose (οὐδενὸς δικαστηρ[ίου]| τῶν ἐπὶ τοῦτο[ι]ς ἀποδοθῆναι δυναμένων). There is some indication (see Ch. II) that these were small Athenian courts whether empaneled with Areopagites alone or with a mixture of Areopagites and non-Areopagites, but we do not know. Other types of courts could be imagined, even from abroad, because, as *S.E.G.*, XI, 491 (Sparta) and other inscriptions show, the practice of international arbitration continued and jurors were often sent from one city to another. With the use of the word μενεῖ in line 69 compare Plutarch, *Pericles*, 37, 4, οἱ δὲ μείναντες ἐν τῇ πολιτείᾳ καὶ κριθέντες Ἀθηναῖοι, and Trajan to Pliny, X, 115, *Mihi hoc temperamentum eius placuit, ut ex praeterito nihil novaremus, sed manerent quamvis contra legem adsciti . . . , in futurum autem*, etc.

Lines 74-76: " lesser posts and honors." While those ineligibles who withdraw voluntarily suffer a loss of *dignitas* but no *capitis deminutio*, those who stay on until they are thrown out suffer *capitis deminutio minima*. The distinction appears clearly in Institutes, I, 16, 5: *Quibus autem dignitas magis quam status permutatur, capite non minuuntur: et ideo senatu motos capite non minui constat.* Those thrown out, on the other hand, become ἐλάττους ἐν τῷ μετιέναι τὰς καταδεεστέρας τάξεις καὶ τιμάς, ineligible for candidacy to the lesser posts and honors, but they retain not only their freedom but even their citizenship. From Aristotle, *Ath. Pol.*, 26, 2 it is known that until the sixth year after the death of Ephialtes eligibility for office rested at Athens on a distinction of census classes. The nine archons were chosen from the Pentacosiomedimni and the Knights; the Zeugitae were not eligible for an archonship but were eligible for the lower offices which Aristotle called τὰς ἐγκυκλίους. An inscription from Xanthus, *I.G.R.*, III, 623, distinguishes between curial or buleutic magistracies and demotic or plebeian magistracies. On cities of Bithynia Pliny, *Ep.*, X, 79, 2 says: *Secutum est dein edictum divi Augusti, quo permisit minores magistratus ab annis duobus et viginti capere.* At Rome major and minor magistracies are distinguished by Sallust, *Bell. Cat.*, 30, 7, *decrevere uti . . . Romae per totam urbem vigiliae haberentur eisque minores magistratus praeessent,* and by Aulus Gellius (citing Messala), *N.A.*, XIII, 15, 4: *Minoribus creatis magistratibus tributis comitiis, magistratus maiores centuriatis comitiis fiunt, sed iustus curiata datur lege.*[6] The reading τὰς μεγάλας ἀρχὰς ἀπένειμεν, proposed by von Fritz for *Ath. Pol.*, 7, 3, has now been verified by M. Chambers, *T.A.P.A.*, XCVI, 1965, pp. 34 f. Note also *Ath. Pol.*, 4, 2, ἀρχὰς ἐλάττους. See further pp. 55-56 *infra*.

Lines 79-81: The sense is clear from lines 99-101, and the restoration ε[ὗ γε]γονένα[ι] is justified by the phrase πα]τὴρ εὐγενής, which in line 65 means well-born in the sense of freeborn, and εὗ γεγονότων in line 66.

Lines 81-87 seem to concern two types of litigation, private suits between individuals of two groupings (though the word μερῶν in line 81 can be interpreted either as parties in a law suit[7] or as groups), and public suits against former officials who had handled public moneys without accounting for them. The two types are connected and have some common factor, perhaps the quarrel of Herodes Atticus and the Athenians with ramifications in the Peloponnese. In line 82 the new word ἀντε[ι]σπράτ[τ]ωσιν probably translates the Latin *contra vindicare*, and if so, we probably have a reference to *in iure cessio*. Accordingly, it seems easier to connect the relative pronoun οἵπερ with ἐκείνους than with τοῖς προνοουμένοις. The private suits brought by either side will be judged by (Ofillius) Ingenuus, who is empowered to settle also uncontested claims for those in charge of the estates of Herodes Atticus. Ingenuus does not have sufficient rank to judge a Roman senator, let alone consular. The public cases, on the other hand, come before the Quintilii, who represent the

---

[6] Convinced that the last five words are out of place in the manuscripts, I have shifted them from their traditional position just after *magistratus*. For *iustus* (sc. *magistratus*) see A. Magdelain, *Recherches sur l'imperium: La loi curiate et les auspices d'investiture,* Paris, 1967, pp. 14-17.

[7] W. Litewski, *R.I.D.A.*, XIV, 1967, pp. 310-380.

emperor on a higher level. With the phrase ἔχουσιν δικασ[τάς] in line 83 compare
P. Mil. Vogliano, II, No. 47 = *C.P.J.*, No. 435, ἔχει δικα[σ]τὴ[ν] ὑπὸ Καίσαρος
ἐπὶ τοῦτο πεμφθέντα. Lines 83-87 should be compared with an imperial letter at
Ephesus, published by J. Keil, *Jahreshefte*, XXVII, 1932, Beiblatt, cols. 21-25.

Line 84: For *syndikoi* see Aelius Aristides, L (Keil), 92, and the references
cited by David Magie, *Roman Rule in Asia Minor,* Princeton University Press, 1950,
pp. 1517 f., and, at Athens, Hadrian's Oil Law, *S.E.G.*, XV, 108 (= Oliver, *The
Ruling Power*, p. 961), lines 55-57: ἐὰν δὲ ἐκκαλέσηταί τις ἢ ἐμὲ ἢ τὸν ἀνθύπατον, χειρο-
τονείτω cυνδίκους ὁ δῆμος. Fr. De Martino, *Storia della costituzione Romana*, IV, 2,
p. 758 defines *syndikoi* as " representatives appointed from time to time to take up
business of the city with the emperor or governor."

Lines 87-88: ἕκαστα π[ρ]οϊδόμην ο[ὐ διὰ] | π[αρ]ουσίας μᾶλλον ἢ φροντίδος.
Augustus in the fifth edict at Cyrene says ὅσην φροντίδα ποιούμεθα, but he never
went to the Cyrenaica in person. The legate of Moesia writes to the Histrians in
A.D. 67 or 68 that everything will be all right πάντων φροντίζοντος τοῦ θειοτάτου [νῦν
αὐτοκράτο]ρος ἡμῶν, though Nero never visited Moesia.[8] The παρουσία is contrasted
with the kind of forethought and care a province receives from an absent emperor. At
Tegea two documents are dated ἀπὸ τῆς θεοῦ Ἀδριανοῦ ἰς τὴν Ἑλλάδα παρουσίας, *I.G.*,
V (2), 50 and 52. At Athens the presence of Hadrian was remembered as something quite different from the best intentions of any absent emperor. The *Vita Marci*
8, 5, which has a similar treatment of *cura* and *praesentia*, justifies the restoration
[παρ]ουσίας. Also Sallust, *Bell. Jug.*, 100, 3: *omnia providere, apud omnis adesse*. In
Demosthenes, III, 3 there is a contrast between the phrases πολλῆς φροντίδος καὶ
βουλῆς δεῖται (on the part of the Athenians) and ἐξ ὧν παρὼν καὶ ἀκούων σύνοιδα. Jean
Béranger, *Recherches sur l'aspect idéologique du principat*, pp. 186-217 has a good
section on *cura*. Herodian, *Ab excessu divi Marci* uses the phrase διὰ φροντίδος in
III, 2, 4, VIII, 2, 5 and VIII, 7, 6.

Lines 87-94 reflect the quarrel of Herodes Atticus[9] with the Athenians. To

---

[8] J. H. Oliver, " Texts A and B of the *Horothesia* Dossier at Istros," *Greek, Roman and
Byzantine Studies*, VI, 1965, p. 148, line 33.

[9] Herodes Atticus, *PIR*[2] C 803, of whom the chief modern study is that of Paul Graindor,
Un milliardaire antique: Hérode Atticus et sa famille, Cairo, 1930. Three metrical inscriptions
have subsequently come to light. One, the epitaph of an infant child of Herodes, was published by
W. Peek, *Ath. Mitt.*, LXVII, 1942, pp. 136-139, No. 306 (= *Gr. Vers.*, 1613 = *Griechische Grabge-
dichte*, 356). Another, published by D. J. Geagan " A New Herodes Epigram from Marathon,"
Ath. Mitt., LXXIX, 1964, pp. 149-156, reads:

1-2   " Ἀ μάκαρ ὅστις ἔδειμε νέην πόλιν, | οὔν[ο]μα δ' αὐτὴν
            Ῥηγίλλης καλέων, ζώει ἀγαλλόμενος."
   4   " Ζώω δ' ἀχ[ν]ύμενος τό μοι οἰκία ταῦτα τέτυκται
            νόσφ[ι] φίλης ἀλόχου καὶ δόμος ἡμιτελής.
         ὡς ἄρα τοι θνητοῖσι θεοὶ βιοτὴν κεράσαντ[ες]
         χά[ρ]ματα τ' ἠδ' ἀνίας γείτονας ἀμφὶς ἔχο[υν]."

judge from line 91 the reconciliation had not yet taken place, but the emperor, addressing himself here to the Athenians, indicates his strong desire to learn of a reconciliation. Marcus Aurelius has not only heard the charges at Sirmium where Herodes Atticus was accused by Aelius Praxagoras, Valerius Mamertinus and Claudius Demo-

The third is *Corinth*, VIII, iii, 128 which reads somewhat as follows:

['Ρηγίλλης τ]όδ' ἄγαλμα, φυὴν δ' ἐχάραξε τεχνείτης
[πᾶσαν σ]ωφροσύνην ἐς λίθον ἀραμένην·
['Αττικ]ὸς Ἡρώδης μέγας ὤπασεν, ἔξοχος ἄλλων,
[παντ]οίης ἀρετῆς εἰς ἄκρον εἰκόμενος,
5   [ὃν π]όσιν Ἑλλήνων ἔλαχεν περίβωτον ἀπάντων,
[κΑὔ]σονα δ' αὖτε πάιν, ἄνθος 'Αχαιάδος.
['Ρηγίλ]λα, ἡ βουλή σε, Τύχην ὡς εἰλάσκουσα,
[ἐν λαμπ]ρῷ τεμένι στήσατο λαϊνέην.

In line 6 J. and L. Robert, *Bull. ép.* 1966, No. 186 proposed [Αὔ]σονα, which may be too short but improves the sense. J. Bousquet, " Regilla à Corinthe," *B.C.H.*, LXXXVIII, 1964, pp. 609-613 proposed [ἐν λαμπ]ρῷ τεμένι for line 8. The writer once considered [εἰν ἱε]ρῷ, but will accept Bousquet's restoration. Also the excellent emendation π⟨ά⟩ιν (παῖδα) for πλιν in line 6 is due to Bousquet. Another fragment of *I.G.*, II², 4780 has been published by M. Mitsos, 'Αρχ. Δελτίον, XXII, 1967, Χρονικά, p. 14, No. 1, so that it now reads:

Κλαύδ[ιος Σεου]ῆρος
δὶς ὕπατος, [κ]ηδεστὴς
Αὐτοκράτο[ρ]ος 'Αντω
νίνου Γερμ[α]νικοῦ.
5   ὁ ἀναθεὶς τῇ θεῷ ['Ηρ]
[ώδ]ης 'Αττι[κ]οῦ

On p. 15, No. 5, Mitsos publishes a new fragment of *I.G.*, II², 3384, which he thinks was erected by Herodes but which I assign to his father, by restoring the name as[Τ]ιβέριο[ς Κλαύδιος | 'Α]ττικός. Three other new texts are:

Hesp., XXVI, 1957, p. 220, No. 78, Κείβικα Βάρβαρον | ὕπατον | Ἡρώδης 'Αττικοῦ Μαραθώνιος | ὁ φίλος | ψηφισαμένης | τῆς πόλεως.

Hesp., XXX, 1961, p. 272, No. 107, Ἡρώδης 'Α[ττικοῦ] | Μαραθώνιο[ς Φάβιον | Φ]αβιαν[όν – –
Hesp., XXXV, 1966, p. 249, No. 10, – – | ῥήτ[ορα | – –] Ἡρώδη[– – – | τὸν] ἑαυτο[ῦ φίλον – – |
– – κα]θηγητ[ήν – –.

J. H. Oliver, *The Athenian Expounders*, pp. 102-119 argued that in *I.G.*, II², 4072 and other texts the word ἐξηγητοῦ applied to Herodes was an Atticistic rendering of a Roman priesthood (*XVvir s. f.*). Herodes and his quarrels receive due attention from G. W. Bowersock, *Greek Sophists*, e. g. pp. 92-100, and R. Bogaert, *Banques et banquiers dans les cités grecques*, Leyden, 1968, pp. 84 f. and 338 f.

The discourse Περὶ Πολιτείας, which has come down under the name of Herodes in the Crippsianus and its copies, has been carefully reedited in the *Serie dei Classici Greci e Latini*, VIII, Florence, 1968, by Umberto Albini, who argues cogently that it cannot be a work of the fifth century B.C., admits that it might belong to the second century after Christ, but claims that it is not good enough for Herodes Atticus. I fail to see why then it should have been attributed to Herodes. Wealth and position brought the young man, son of a consular, immediate recognition. We hope that his later reputation, high for three generations, rested on better works than this but remember that Polemo's extant orations hardly justify the enthusiasm of Philostratus. For the view that it is a work of the fifth century see now Ap. Dascalakis, *The Hellenism of the Ancient Macedonians*, Thessalonica, 1965, pp. 236-249, who attributes it to an Athenian sophist residing in Thessaly or more probably to a Thessalian, around 404 B.C.

stratus, as we learn from Philostratus, *V. S.*, II, 1, pp. 67 and 71 Kayser, but he has received an ambassador and investigated specific charges. Whereas the overall charge according to Philostratus was that Herodes enslaved the Athenians, the emperor according to Philostratus put the blame for certain wrongs on the freedmen of Herodes, not on Herodes himself. The " epistle " supports Philostratus in showing the high regard Marcus Aurelius had for Herodes Atticus, to whom he wrote also privately. The reference in lines 92-93 is to more, I think, than the great benefactions which Herodes had already performed as cosmete, high priest and so forth. To alleviate the economic tyranny about which the " Athenians " complained, he seems to have made some great concessions which are not mentioned by Philostratus, who does, however, tell the story of the sophist's early refusal to honor his father's *fideicommissa* in respect to the Athenians. At the time of this " epistle " Herodes was still in self-imposed exile at Oricum in Epirus. In lines 88-89 we seem to have a new word συνευφ[ροσύ]|νια (like ἐγκαίνια, ἐπιφέρνια and ἱεροσύνια). The reading is not certain, but the suffix was one of the most common throughout the history of the Greek language, as C. D. Buck and W. Petersen, *A Reverse Index of Greek Nouns and Adjectives*, p. 43, point out. With the whole phrase σ. περί τε τὰ θεῖα καὶ τὰ ἀνθρώπινα ἔχειν, then, compare Demosthenes, LVII, 3, τῶν ὑμετέρων ἱερῶν καὶ κοινῶν μετεῖχον. Herodian, *Ab excessu divi Marci* has several parallels: I, 16, 2 on the New Year's festival at Rome, κοινωνίᾳ τῶν γῆς καὶ θαλάττης καλῶν εὐφραίνουσιν αὐτούς, still better II, 7, 9-10 on Niger who was ready to συμπανηγυρίζειν with the Antio-chenes and to give them leisure ἐς τὸ ἑορτάζειν καὶ εὐφραίνεσθαι, and II, 8, 9, (Niger) τοῖς Ἀντιοχεῦσι συνευφραίνετο ἑορταῖς καὶ θέαις ἐπιδιδοὺς ἑαυτόν. With the phrase σὺν τῆι εὐκλεεῖ περὶ τὴν παιδείαν σπουδῆι in line 89 compare *I. G. Bulg.*, III, 1573, a Spartan dedication in honor of a sophist, τῆς τε ἄλλης ἀρετῆς συνπάσης ἔνεκεν καὶ τῆς περὶ [π]αιδείαν καὶ λόγους σπουδῆς. In the epistle of the Areopagus to the Aezanitae concerning Ulpius Eurycles (*O.G.I.S.*, 505) occur the expressions τῆς περὶ τὰ κάλ-λιστα καὶ σεμνότατα σπουδῆς and τῆς περὶ παιδείαν φιλοτιμίας. Herodian, I, 13, 7 has τῆς περὶ τὰ καλὰ σπουδῆς. With the phrases of lines 89-91, τῆς πρό[τερον]|γν[ωτ]ῆς εἰς αὐτοὺς εὐποΐας . . . τῆς πρότερον περὶ ἀλλ[ήλ]ους ο[ἰκει]|ότητος compare Isocrates, *Philippus*, 37, αἱ γὰρ ἐν τοῖς παροῦσι καιροῖς εὐεργεσίαι λήθην ἐμποιοῦσι τῶν πρότερον εἰς ἀλλήλους πεπλημμελημένων. Isocrates, *Philippus*, 38 and 41, using the words διαλλάξειεν and διαλλάξαι, calls on Philip to effect a reconciliation in Greece, and this passage, together with Demosthenes, IX, 41, καὶ οὐδὲν ἐμοῦ προσδεῖσθε μάρτυρος, was at least faintly in the emperor's recollection, as he wrote δι' ἣν οὐδὲ⟨ν⟩ ἐμοῦ διαλλακτοῦ δέονται. The emperor speaks in the role of the *prostates* and conciliator which Iso-crates hoped that Philip would become. The restoration at the end of line 92 depends upon a reading in line 93, ἐξ[ῆν], after which the particle ἄν might easily have been dropped.

Lines 97-98: εἴ τινες ἐκ πατέρων ἀπε[λευ]|θέρων γεγονότες τῆς βουλῆς τῶν Πεντακοσίων ἐξανέστησαν. The first letter had been worded in a manner that introduced an ambiguity at Athens. One spoke ordinarily of *decuriones* (or *curiales*) and *plebeii*, of βουλευταί and δημόται as in *T.A.M.*, II, 176 (Sidyma, A.D. 185-192). At Ephesus, for example, one entered the " Council " for life just as at Athens one entered the Areopagus. The words βουλή and βουλευταί, as employed by the emperor in his first letter, referred to the Areopagus and its members, but some Athenians may have worried lest it included also the Council of the Five Hundred and its members.

Lines 98-99: τούτοις ἐπανιέναι πάλιν εἰς τὴν [ἐξέ]|τασιν. Syllabic division eliminates any restoration like κατάστασιν and imposes [ἐξέ]|τασιν. It has been granted to these men to return again to the list of those eligible for the lesser posts and honors. Like those who withdraw voluntarily from the Areopagus they are to suffer no *deminutio capitis*. Their names are not to be stricken from the census rolls. The word ἐξέτασις (cf. Xenophon, *Hell.*, II, 4, 8) belongs to the *sermo publicus* of Athens. It occurs above on Plaque I, fragment F. Cassius Dio, LIV, 26, 3, ἐξέτασις αὖθις τῶν βουλευτῶν ἐγένετο, referred to a *lectio* of the Roman Senate, but the linguistic parallel applies perfectly. Cassius Dio, LII, 42, 1, τὴν βουλὴν ἐξήτασε, likewise concerns the Roman Senate. Plutarch, *Aemilius Paulus*, 38, 9, after speaking of the way Paulus as censor treated the Senate, says, " And in regard to the selection of the knights (περὶ τὴν τῶν ἱππέων ἐξέτασιν) he showed a similar moderation." The *exetasis* is primarily an examination but secondarily a list based on an examination, a group of eligible men. This secondary meaning lies behind the word συνεξετάζεσθαι, " to be an associate," in Demosthenes and Lucian. Also Cassius Dio, XLIII, 21, 4 uses *exetasis* to mean *recensus*.

Lines 99-102: *Cod. Iust.*, IX, 21 says: *Lex Visellia* (A.D. 24) *libertinae condicionis homines persequitur, si ea quae ingenuorum sunt circa honores et dignitates ausi fuerint attemptare vel decurionatum adripere, nisi iure aureorum anulorum impetrato a principe sustentatur.* The son of a freedman was eligible to serve in the Athenian Council of the Five Hundred, but not the freedman himself. *Libertorum ingenia servilia*, says Tacitus, *Ann.*, II, 12, 4. He comments in the *Germania* 25. Compare lines 79-81.

TRANSLATION OF PLAQUE II = E

[On appeal suits which] Aelius Praxagoras, Claudius Demostratus, Aelius Themison brought against Aelius Dionysius: To be entitled – – – ought to hear, it was decided that it suffices that the elections when held at the right time – – – of these men, I did not consider it necessary for him to undergo – – – what not at all at Athens – – – the following period of time in order that nothing be left ambiguous. I very much desire that those holding a torchbearership or any other voluntary priesthood remember to prepay, as ordained by law, the food honorarium of the priesthood which they already have. If a man is called [by] the demos, there will be no case against him if he does not prepay his prior contributions before he gets the appointment; once elected, however, he too will lay down his prepayment.

Line 7

On appeal suits which Sentius Attalus and Clement son of Clement and Claudius Chrysippus brought, suits from the jury court and from the king archon, Claudius Eupraxides, against Valerius Mamertinus shall have been concluded. Since Mamertinus, who is a Eumolpid, obtained neither of his parents from the clan of the Ceryces, so lacks the only means by which it has been permitted to those from either of these [two] clans to transfer to the other, he shall refrain from seeking the office of sacred herald. The elections shall be held all over again among the others, both those who have already gone to court and those who will now wish to be candidates, in accord with the laws of the Athenians. Mamertinus shall not be removed from the number of Eumolpidae, and he shall recover his priesthood. The decision which ripened in me in this case after I had formed an opinion from the present trial will not let that which is likely to confuse the traditional, carefully guarded procedures slip by.

Line 15

Ladicus son of Polyaenus, he who has appealed a case against Sophanes son of Sophanes from the court of Julius Damostratus the archon of the Panhellenes, seems [to have been away] at the appointed time [when] it is permissible for actions to be brought against the Panhellenes elect. Although the customary period after the election has taken place had expired, he was summoned to trial and was disqualified, according to the prescription of my deified grandfather, on the grounds that he had even then not attained the legal age and had held no previous office. He has, in our judgment, made an appeal without justification.

Line 20

Epigonus son of Epictetus, he who appealed from Julius Damostratus in the case against Eudemus son of Aphrodisius, will stand trial in the court of my Quintilii concerning his membership in the Panhellenion, and in fact he himself asked to be sent to their court, for it is clear that much of the work that devolves upon me in the affairs at the review session is completed by them.

Line 23

Athenodorus son of Agrippa, he who had appealed from Papius Rufus the archon of the Panhellenes of the previous quadriennium in a case against the administrators of the estates of the vir clarissimus Claudius Herodes: Since he presented neither the minutes of the Panhellenes nor the published result of the investigation, he will argue his case in the court of my Quintilii, in order that after so long he shall not have to wait for the opportune moments in which it will be possible for me to judge the cases which need a decision precisely at the time of our military activity.

Line 27

Nostimus son of Dionysius did not prove that he had become Areopagite according to (the wording of) the laws, but if it is legally possible in this (synedrion) as in the Council of the Areopagus for him to be added to the roll, the Quintilii will [determine]. Why he could be ejected from membership in the synedrion of the Panhellenes [was not before me?] when I was judging his appeal made in the case against Euphras son of Nicon.

Line 30

For Popilius [Pius], who has a claim to the citizenship of the Athenians, it will remain as the Aeropagites decided. For it is necessary that security [of status] be available [to him] and to all others who, following because of fear of the opponent the option granted to them, presented their own proofs of citizenship to the Areopagites. In the future precautions shall be taken and an examination shall be made in a man's case according to the laws and the ancestral customs to see if he has [the qualification] from descent.

Line 35

The appeal which Aelius Praxagoras made from Gavinius Saturninus: At the trial the so-called codicils in the (false) name of Pratolaus were produced and the investigation took place. (Praxagoras), it appears, was justified. If, however, anyone within two months after the reading of this epistle at Athens should wish [to take action], either publicly or privately, concerning the gift which (the codicils) reserved for the city, let it be permitted to the same, within a carefully respected term of two months more, to approach my Quintilii with reference to the [point at issue]. But if he should fail to act in this interval, he would not, I hope, interpose or resume an action. Praxagoras shall return into possession of these estates and shall receive from the viri clarissimi Quintilii an arbiter concerning the crops. As for the estates which were said to have been left to the vir clarissimus Herodes Atticus, to these he will already have returned. Concerning these crops Ingenuus will judge. And if Praxagoras finds fault with the slowness of transfer, (an action) will be introduced by the provincial authorities. As for the petition of the [Athe]nians—since it concerned the age of the father and the fact that he had been the only one left in the family—I shall go into it if I can. [Perhaps] it would be helpful for him to be recalled during the examination of the affair from the island to which he was relegated but to stay away from the borders of Attica from then on.

Line 47

To Agathocles son of Agathocles for the ambassadorial services which he is performing at my court: The claim shall indeed be paid. To his fatherland and to the synedrion of the Areopagites the deposits for the appealed suits which the administrators of the estates of the vir clarissimus Herodes brought against Aelius Ameinias, likewise deposits for appealed suits which Aelius Praxagoras, Claudius Demostratus, Aelius Themison, Sentius Attalus, Clement son of Clement, Valerius Mamertinus, Ladicus son of Polyaenus, Euodus son of Onesimus, Nostimus son of Dionysius, Popilius Pius brought at the trials pleaded in my court, shall be refunded. That the appeals of Epigonus and Athenodorus have been concluded I am not yet ready to announce. As for other appeals which may not have been included in this *cognitio*, if any have occurred concerning which I gave no pre-judicial instructions, they shall have been cancelled, to be examined before the *iudex* by the same rules as they were going to be examined (in this court), also when no appeal is being made, and Ingenuus shall report to me whose cases they are if any. If after the decision any suits have been brought, he himself will decide them in the proper order.

Line 57

How much interest I take in protecting the reputation of Athens, so that she remain in possession of her ancient dignity, has been made sufficiently clear, I think, and particularly so when I tried to lead the city's own select synedrion back to the ancient custom, according to which they received into the Areopagus only those tested by the three-generation rule. And would there were an abundance of the good old families so that it might be possible for me even now to stand by our decision! But since the Athenians have to allow for the things that happened through the interference of fortune, especially situations which, to my knowledge, made many other cities seek relief in court, and since accordingly the Athenians need to relax some rules in humanity toward the past and of other matters to make once and for all a settlement viable for the future, I go this far in meeting their wishes: I shall grant to the Athenians that as for the time that has passed one look to this only, whether a man has a father of good birth, and if one of these members of the Areopagus is shown to have been expelled on account of the three-generation rule, he shall recover his rank, but that from here on one look to the qualification from the good birth of both a man's ancestors. For those who after my other letter have infiltrated themselves into the Areopagus though they are of freedman fathers, it will suffice that they have recognized their folly in time. If, however, a man born of a freedman father had become a member before my letter and was not expelled by any court of those juries available to be assigned for these cases, he shall remain.

Line 69

All who after our letter were either expelled from the Council of the Areopagus because the grandfather had been a freedman or for this reason voluntarily withdrew are debarred from [having] the honor (of belonging to the Areopagus). On the other hand, those who on account of the aforesaid regulations will step down from the synedrion must not, as a consequence of such action, be discouraged at all from the pursuit of the other honors and posts. If any have been enrolled contrary to our injunctions, men who are not permitted to sit in the Areopagus after the decision now published, they shall remove themselves within a year. Whoever continues to remain even after our prohibitions, or gains entrance against the regulations that have been publicized, shall be placed in the same category as those expelled by the jury court and consequently disqualified also in the pursuit of the lesser posts and honors.

Line 77

If any Areopagites unable to meet the three-generation rule are found to be today among the Panhellenes, they shall not be expelled from the synedrion (of the Panhellenes) on this account, but for the future no Areopagite other than those who can enter the elections with the three-generation quality shall be enrolled among the Panhellenes. As for what concerns the Council of the Five Hundred it is enough that it has been arranged for this corporation that those on each occasion enrolled be themselves of good birth.

Line 81

Ingenuus himself for the claims of each of the parties shall be the judge, and he shall give judgment also for the caretakers of the estates of the vir clarissimus against people who make no reasonable countervindication. Those who have managed the public finances of the city and owe accountings shall have as judges my Quintilii, in whose court the advocates of the Athenians will see to it that they complete their sums. Ingenuus will hold court at Eleusis and in Piraeus for the Athenians who need trial, in each place at whatever time he chooses; for the Lacedaemonians he will assign a locality in the neighboring towns according to what is most convenient after his own decision.

Line 87

It has, I think, been made clear through my formal statements that [absent in body] rather than in mind I attended to each matter. I gave thought in order that in the future it might be possible for Herodes at the side of the Athenians with his famous zeal for education and culture to share the good cheer at their religious and secular festivities, and that the Athenians, mindful of his formerly well-known beneficence toward them, might renew the confidence of their formerly mutual friendship, for which they do not at all need me as a reconciler. What resentment in anybody's mind would still be lingering there afterwards if the reminder in these charges were expunged? Now that in all matters good care of the Athenians has been worked out, [would it not be possible] for them to love my Herodes, who is also their own, since no other conflict of importance any longer remains?

Well, this is a reflection I had after all these orders had been drafted in the Hellenic tongue concerning the cases brought to trial. I added it because it was omitted in the formal statement I made; it could be inferred from my verdict, though admittedly [missing from] the wording of my statement, but it needed some additional explanation.

Line 96

In order that nothing may provide a [new] controversy, it has seemed proper that this too be clearly defined: If any born from freedmen fathers have resigned from the Council of the Five Hundred, let it be recognized as having been granted to them, on the same terms as to those who resigned from the Areopagus, to be included again in the list. Let the members of the Council of the Five Hundred show that they themselves have been born in freedom. For not those from freedmen fathers but those alone who have themselves been freed are necessarily excluded. This ruling which has been precisely formulated concerning them applies also to the future.

AUTHOR AND DATE

The author of the document uses the first person singular. He is clearly the emperor, because no one but the emperor could give orders, as the writer does, affecting the governing authorities of the province. A reference in line 19 to his deified grandfather in connection with rules concerning the Panhellenion can only be a reference to Hadrian. Hence the emperor, who has no co-emperor, must be Marcus Aurelius. If there were any doubt about this, the frequent reference to " my Quintilii " would dispel it, also the tone in which the author speaks of Herodes Atticus. The *Vita Marci* 10 says of Marcus, *Iudiciariae rei singularem diligentiam adhibuit*, and this inscription would support it. Marcus ceased to be sole emperor on 27 November 177.

The year 169 when Marcus became sole emperor seems far behind, because Marcus had already written an earlier letter (E, lines 66-68) as sole emperor and because the trial at Sirmium in which the quarrel of Herodes Atticus and the Athenians had culminated cannot well be dated before 173, as we shall see. The quarrel was now senseless, and the emperor (E, lines 91-94) calls for an end. Undoubtedly the Athenians were prepared to comply and to avoid the emperor's displeasure. Hence the document can be dated shortly before the return of Herodes Atticus from self-imposed exile.

The word [παρ]ουσίας in line 97 cannot serve as proof that the document post-dates the visit of the emperor in the summer of A.D. 176 (*Vita Marci* 27, 1 and *I.G.*, II², 3620), when Marcus was initiated into the Mysteries. The essential question is the date at which Herodes returned to Athens. Unmentioned by Philostratus, the triumphal return is recorded in an epigram now best consulted in *I.G.*, II², 3606,[10] of which we here present a translation:

> Blessed were you, O Marathon, just now, and an object of care to men more than before, as you looked upon glorious Alcaides, who returned from the Sarmatian nomads at the outermost edge of the world, whither he had followed the warlike, far-traveled emperor of the Ausonians. Him Bacchus Eiraphiotes, the ivy-bearing son of Zeus, himself conducted to his famous fatherland, his own priest. Behind came the two life-giving goddesses in escort. Athena, protectress of the city, met them as they were approaching the sacred Rheitoi, which are two Chalcidic rivers, and Thria, where sea and stream join at the shore. She was leading the people, all the citizens gathered together, first the priests with unbound, flowing hair, in full regalia, all resplendent, and behind them the priestesses, who had wisely loving Aphrodite with them; next to them the glorious boys' class busy with song, a lusty choir for Olympian Zeus; behind them the young students of manhood, sons of the Athenians, ephebes gleaming in bronze, youths whom he himself, when they were still mourning (Theseus') forgetfulness of father Aegeus, separated from the black raiment of atonement and clothed in shining garb at his own expense, the gift of costumes fastened with amber clasps over the shoulder; behind them the select council of the Cecropians, standing out in precedence, marched all together, the higher corporation, named for Ares, while the other, of lesser rank, followed behind it. They all arrayed themselves in newly washed, white cloaks. Close to them strode forward all the rest of the people, denizens and strangers and [even slaves]. No watchman was left [in the halls], no boy, no fair-skinned maiden, [but all were gathered] to receive Herodes – – – as when a mother embraces her child – – – from afar – – –

Philostratus not only does not mention the *hypapantesis* of Herodes but does not credit the emperor with pressure upon the Athenians to receive Herodes so royally.

Graindor [11] dates the return close to the revolt of Avidius Cassius. The revolt occurred in 175, and Herodes wrote to Avidius Cassius, "You went mad." [12] Graindor thinks the letter was written from Athens, and perhaps it was. In 176, according to Philostratus, Marcus wrote to Herodes as if Herodes were already in Athens and expressed a hope to have him as his mystagogue at the initiation (August or September). Herodes is known to have died at the age of 76, about A.D. 177 according to Graindor. That would make Herodes 25 years old in 126/7 when he was archon. There is no new evidence to contradict this reconstruction of the sequence of events.

Accordingly, we conclude that Herodes returned before A.D. 176, probably in 175, and that the new document from the Roman Market Place must be dated before 176, probably in 174/5 before the revolt of Avidius Cassius. It follows that the emperor was still on the Danube.

---

[10] Add the restoration λευ[κόχρως proposed by Graindor, *Hérode Atticus*, p. 236 and overlooked by Kirchner. In line 20 read ἀκειομένο⟨υ⟩s, and see P. Roussel, *R.É.A.*, XLIII, 1941, pp. 163-165. E. Kantorowicz, "The King's Advent," *Art Bull.*, XXVI, 1944, pp. 204-231 treats this kind of reception.

[11] P. Graindor, *Hérode Atticus*, pp. 127-130.

[12] Graindor supposes that Avidius Cassius had written to Herodes as to an enemy of Marcus. News of the royal reception which Herodes had received at Athens may have led Avidius Cassius to overrate the influence of Herodes, political as well as economic.

There is one other indication of date. The documents at Aezani concerning Ulpius Eurycles, Nos. **28-30** *infra*, reveal that a new archon of the Panhellenes took office in A.D. 157. Two archons of the Panhellenion are mentioned in the inscription from the Roman Market Place, Julius Damostratus mentioned in E 16 and 20 as in office when the emperor was writing, and Papius Rufus mentioned in E 23-24 as archon of the previous term of four years. If a new archon took office in A. D. 157, Julius Damostratus must have taken office in A.D. 173. For when the emperor wrote, Julius Damostratus had been in office long enough so that appeals had been made of cases already tried in his court. His first year was 173/4. The emperor could conceivably be writing late in 173/4, but the year 174/5 has from this evidence a better chance of being the right date. The cases tried by Julius Damostratus concerned the credentials of newly elected Panhellenes, and one case from the previous archonship still remained unsettled, so that we cannot be too far from the year 173. The year 175/6 would seem too late.

Thus from two indications, the evidence from the career of Herodes Atticus and the evidence from the archonship of the Panhellenes, we are drawn to a date in the year 174/5.

TYPE OF DOCUMENT

In lines 66-67 ($\mu\epsilon\tau\grave{\alpha}$ $\tau\grave{\eta}\nu$ $\grave{\epsilon}\pi[\iota\sigma\tau o]|\lambda\grave{\eta}\nu$ $\grave{\epsilon}\langle\mu\rangle\grave{\eta}\nu$ $\grave{\epsilon}\tau\acute{\epsilon}\rho\alpha\nu$), in line 68 ($\pi\rho\grave{o}$ $\tau\hat{\eta}s$ $\grave{\epsilon}\pi\iota$-$\sigma\tau o\lambda\hat{\eta}s$), in line 69 ($\mu\epsilon\tau\grave{\alpha}$ $\tau\grave{\alpha}$ $\grave{\eta}\mu\acute{\epsilon}\tau\epsilon\rho\alpha$ $\gamma\rho\acute{\alpha}\mu\mu\alpha\tau\alpha$), in lines 72-73 ($\grave{\epsilon}\nu\alpha\nu\tau\acute{\iota}o\nu$ $\tauο\hat{\iota}s$ $\grave{\upsilon}\phi'$ $\grave{\eta}\mu\hat{\omega}\nu$ $\grave{\epsilon}[\pi\epsilon]|\sigma\tau\alpha\lambda\mu\acute{\epsilon}\nuο\iota s$), the emperor implies that the document falls under the category *epistula*. In fact, he says so explicitly.

Modern scholars distinguish an *epistula* from an *edictum*, because the *epistula* begins with a greeting and closes with a salutation, whereas the *edictum*, though it may have been used as a letter to whom it might concern (without specified recipients), was couched in the form of the traditional edict. Nevertheless, neither this document nor certain other " edicts " were edicts in content.

The communication of Marcus Aurelius closes without the salutation $\epsilon\grave{\upsilon}\tau\upsilon\chi\epsilon\hat{\iota}\tau\epsilon$ customary in an epistle. The second person is never used, so that the document, if it is one document (as it seems to be), hardly resembles an epistle to specific recipients. This document, which contains instruction for the Athenians, for the Panhellenes and for Roman officials of the province, presents a single document in the form of an edict but really a letter to whom it may concern.

Perfect parallels for our document will be found in *S.E.G.*, IX, 3 = Ehrenberg and Jones 311, which contains five such communications and a *senatus consultum*. The five communications are the five so-called Cyrene " Edicts " of Augustus. Modern scholars, particularly De Visscher, have recognized that the Cyrene " Edicts " were not edicts as previously understood; that is, they were edicts in form but not in content. They did not give orders. Augustus never calls these communications *diatagmata* and the classification " edict " is entirely that of modern scholars. In " Edict " V Augustus seems to call " Edict " V a *programma*, but that term signifies a communication like a covering letter for the *senatus consultum* and would not apply to the first four " edicts." There is no reason why the Cyrene " Edicts " should not have been called *epistulae* even in the time of Augustus. Such communications may later have passed through the office of the *ab epistulis*, while true edicts may later have passed through another secretarial branch, in so far as such communications as these were not entirely the work of the emperor himself or of the emperor and his special (senatorial) advisers. The Cyrene " Edicts " were probably worded by Greek secretaries (in contrast to the crude literalness of the *senatus consultum*), but our " epistle " of Marcus Aurelius seems to be, especially in lines 87-97, in large part the emperor's own composition and wording, though different in style from the *Meditations*.

The edict form for an epistle seems to have been used when more than one recipient entitled to an epistle would have had to be addressed. Cyrene " Edict " V was sent " to the provinces." " Edict " IV was addressed to all the Greek cities of Cyrenaica, likewise " Edicts " III, II and I. Nero's edict in *S.I.G.*³, 814 was a mere invitation sent to all the cities of Achaia. In our " epistle " of Marcus Aurelius the edict form is used because both the city of the Athenians and the Panhellenion were addressed, if not also certain cities in the Peloponnese. Otherwise he would have had to write separate letters to all the parties concerned, just as the emperor Titus had to write to the governor of Baetica as well as to the city of Munigua, when the latter appealed *ex sententia Semproni Fusci* in the case against Servilius Pollio.[13] On the other hand, why did Claudius cast his famous letter to the Alexandrians,[14] *P. Lond.* 1912, in the form of an epistle, in which he addressed not only the *politai* of Alexandria but also the Alexandrian *politeuma* of the Jews? Here only the city rated an epistle. The Jewish factions of Alexandria were certainly not entitled to an epistle. The emperor may have felt that the Jews of Alexandria had a share in the city and that accordingly the whole text was addressed to one recipient community through its authorities, but perhaps it is unnecessary to find a justification in theory for an addition which Claudius personally wished to make in the already drafted epistle.

The line between an epistle to specific recipients and an epistle in edict form to whom it may concern was not sharply drawn. There was one bureau *ab epistulis* for both epistles and edicts. A bureau or official secretary *ab edictis* did not exist, and

---

[13] Text published by H. Nesselhauf, *Madrider Mitteilungen*, I, 1960, pp. 148-154, available also through A. d'Ors, *S.D.H.I.*, XXVI, 1960, p. 506 and A. Merlin, *Année épigraphique*, 1962, No. 288.

[14] Originally well published by H. I. Bell, *Jews and Christians in Egypt*, London, 1924, pp. 1-37, republished with a remarkable thoroughness and good sense in 1960 by V. A. Tcherikover and A. Fuks, *C.P.J.*, 153, available also in E. M. Smallwood, *Documents Illustrating the Principates of Gaius, Claudius and Nero*, Cambridge Univ. Press, 1967, No. 370. All of lines 73-104 seem to be a personal addition by Claudius himself.

the secretary *ab epistulis*[15] is never called *ab epistulis et edictis* because many edicts which the emperor published were themselves epistles in character and differed considerably from the *edicta magistratuum* which they resembled in form.

Ulpian, *libro primo ad edictum*, refers to an epistle directed by Marcus Aurelius and Commodus to a wide group of recipients:

est etiam generalis epistula divorum Marci et Commodi, qua declaratur et praesides et magistratus et milites stationarios dominum adiuvare debere inquirendis fugitivis.[16]

It would appear that our document, which the emperor himself despite its form called an *epistula,* resembles what Ulpian described as a *generalis epistula.* It was not quite the same.

APPEALS TO THE EMPEROR

The first fifty-six lines of Plaque II concern appeals to the emperor either by defendants or by plaintiffs. Some of these have not yet been decided, others have. In one case he says that he has not yet reached the point of declaring that they have been concluded, τὰς ἐκκλήτους περιγεγράφθ[αι οὐ]δέπ[ω] φθάνω προειπών (lines 52-53), but in two cases where he decides in favor of the appellant he says that the cases on appeal shall be considered as having been concluded, περιγεγράψονται (lines 9 and 54). In one case where he decides against the appellant he says ἀδίκως [ἐφει]κένα[ι δ]οκεῖ, " he seems to have appealed on grounds without merit " (lines 19-20). The noun ἐφέσεις occurs in lines 2 and 53, and the participle ἐφεικώς in line 24. The other terminology comes from ἐκκαλέομαι: ἔκκλητοι (δίκαι) ἃς ἐποιήσαντο (lines 1, 7, 48 and 49) or ἔκκλητος ἣν ἐποιήσατο (lines 30 and 35), ἐκκλήτου δίκης (line 55), and ἐκκεκλημένος (line 15) or ἐκκαλεσάμενος (line 20).

Among the powers and honors decreed for Octavian in 30 B.C. Cassius Dio, LI, 17, 7 lists right after the tribunician power ἔκκλητόν τε δικάζειν καὶ ψῆφόν τινα αὐτοῦ ἐν πᾶσι τοῖς δικαστηρίοις ὥσπερ Ἀθηνᾶς φέρεσθαι. Peter Garnsey[17] suggests that " there is a connection between the *tribunicia potestas* of Augustus and the *auxilium* which he evidently gave to citizens and non-citizens alike." Since neither Augustus himself nor Tacitus mentions the *appellatio* and the *calculus Minervae*, they cannot have been very important then.[18] The *appellatio,* however, became very important, as the em-

---

[15] For the at first occasional division of the secretariat into one *ab epistulis Latinis* and one *ab epistulis Graecis* see G. B. Townend, " The Post *ab episulis* in the Second Century," *Historia,* X, 1961, pp. 375-381. For the contemporary *ab epistulis Graecis*, either Vibianus Tertullus or Alexander " Clay-Plato," see Chr. Habicht, *Alt. v. Perg.,* VIII, 3, pp. 66-67, No. 28.

[16] Digest, XI, 4. The passage is discussed by R. Orestano, *Il potere normativo degli imperatori e le costituzioni imperiali,* Rome, 1937, pp. 74-81.

[17] *J.R.S.,* LVI, 1966, pp. 185 f.

[18] So Fr. De Martino, *Storia della Costituzione Romana,* IV, Naples, 1962, p. 453.

perors on request intervened more frequently in cases where the public interest seemed to be involved. The appellants did not have to have Roman citizenship. In a senatorial province intervention (on request) was based on the emperor's *maius imperium*, and everywhere on his *auctoritas*. Orestano [19] points out that Suetonius, *Aug.* 33 in speaking of *appellationes* meant any call upon the emperor to decide a case in first or second instance. The word had not yet been restricted to the technical meaning " appeal." The same is true of ἔκκλητος δίκη in our inscription.

In lines 7-9 it is stated who appeals and *a quo* and against what adversary. Likewise in each of the other cases. This causes no surprise in view of Ulpian *libro primo de appellationibus* (Digest, XLIX, 1, 1, 4): *Libelli qui dantur appellatorii ita sunt concipiendi, ut habeant scriptum et a quo dati sunt, hoc est qui appellet, et adversus quem et a qua sententia.*

The most interesting novelty of these cases transferred on request to the emperor is that the city of Athens and the synedrion of the Areopagus have put up security (lines 48-53) to have the cases tried by the emperor himself or his representatives. The city stands between the appellant and the fiscus. Just as *decemviri* or *vigintiviri* or the regular treasury in a city advance the taxes owed to Rome and so relieve the central government from dealing with the individual taxpayer, the city apparently arranges for real or cash security in certain appeals made by individuals and deals itself with the latter. Deposits guaranteed the appearance of the parties. Where the cases have been settled, the deposits made by the winners are restored to the city and the Areopagus, perhaps some to the city and others to the Areopagus. There must have been deposits made by the losers too,[20] and these covered the costs of the trial in the emperor's court.

Line 1 mentions three plaintiffs and one defendant, Aelius Dionysius. Whether we have one case or two or three concerning the same man, the affairs of this defendant and the thoughts they evoke occupy lines 1-7. The trial seems to have concerned the contribution which a new priest was expected to make ahead of time. It is probably the defendant who has demanded trial before the emperor. Since no lower court is mentioned, the emperor may be judging as a court of the first instance. The emperor upholds the necessity of the prepayment, and the deposits of the three plaintiffs are those returned to the city.

Line 8 mentions three plaintiffs, one defendant, and perhaps two lower courts. Since the deposit of one plaintiff, Claudius Chrysippus, was not repaid to the city, we infer that two or three separate cases against the defendant Valerius Mamertinus

---

[19] R. Orestano, *L'appello civile in diritto Romano*, 2nd ed., pp. 196-200.

[20] In fact, the *pecuniae periculum* in any *appellatio* to the emperor is attested by Tacitus, *Annals*, XIV, 28. The emperor Titus in a letter to Munigua cited by A. d'Ors, *S.D.H.I.*, XXVI, 1960, p. 506 and published by H. Nesselhauf, *Madrider Mitteilungen*, I, 1960, pp. 148-154, mentions the *poenam iniustae appellationis*. See also W. Litewski, *R.I.D.A.*, 3e série, XV, 1968, pp. 217-222.

are the subject of lines 7-15. In one case, or in the two first cases, Sentius Attalus and Clement son of Clement bring an action or two actions against Mamertinus on the grounds that he has illegally passed from the genos of the Eumolpidae to the genos of the Ceryces and therefore his election to the office of sacred herald, reserved for Ceryces, is illegal. The emperor finds for the plaintiffs and orders Mamertinus to stop trying for this office and calls for a new election open to any qualified candidate. In the action brought by Claudius Chrysippus against Mamertinus the plaintiff argued that Mamertinus no longer belonged to the Eumolpidae and should not recover the Eumolpid priesthood he had previously held. The emperor finds for the defendant. The deposit made by Claudius Chrysippus is not returned to the city, while the deposit made by Valerius Mamertinus is listed indeed in line 51 among those to be repaid.

All these cases in lines 1-15 concern Athenian priesthoods. Appeals concerning priesthoods are envisaged in the edict of an unknown emperor on *BGU* II 628 recto: [21] *Appella[ti]ones vero quae ad magistratus et sacerdotia et alios honores pertinebant habe[ant] formam tem[po]ris sui.*

The quarrel of Herodes Atticus and the " Athenians " was the most important local question. Since these trials of men prominent in Philostratus as enemies of Herodes probably reflect this quarrel, we infer that their adversaries were friends of Herodes, to wit: Aelius Dionysius (line 1), Sentius Attalus (lines 7-8), Clement son of Clement (line 8), and Claudius Chrysippus (line 8). Herodes was a powerful member of the clan of the Ceryces, and it is easy to believe that the encroachment of a well-known enemy of Herodes had something to do with the attempt to undermine Herodes.

The case of Athenodorus son of Agrippa (lines 23-27) against the administrators of the estates of Herodes was a case involving the material interests of Herodes Atticus. It is surprising that it came before the court of the Panhellenes rather than that of a Roman official; the Panhellenes upheld the agents of Herodes. The case shows that the records of the trial were the *hypomnemata* of the Panhellenes and that the archon presided rather than decided himself. It took place under the previous archon between 169 and 173, probably near the end of this period when the domination of Herodes Atticus at Athens collapsed. In assigning the case to the Quintilii so that Athenodorus, who had not sent on to the emperor the necessary documents, would not have to wait until the emperor was free, Marcus forestalled delays by the detestable freedmen of Herodes.

The other cases in lines 15-35 were appeals by men who had been refused a

---

[21] Mitteis, *Chrest.*, no. 371; Riccobono, *F.I.R.A.*, I², no. 91. On the date see A. A. Schiller, " The First Edict of BGU II 628 Recto," *The Classical Tradition: Literary and Historical Studies in Honor of Harry Caplan*, Cornell University Press, 1966, pp. 293-312, who says late second or early third.

seat in the Panhellenion after a trial in the court of the archon of the Panhellenes, to wit:

Ladicus son of Polyaenus (lines 15-20), who had been refused a seat on the grounds that he was not of legal age and had not held office previously as Hadrian had prescribed. He has argued that the trial was illegal because the time had expired, but the emperor upholds the decision of the court.

Epigonus son of Epictetus (lines 20-23), who had asked that the appeal be heard in the court of the Quintilii. The emperor grants the request without prejudice.

Nostimus son of Dionysius (lines 27-30), whose seat was being challenged on the ground that the office he had held at Athens was not a regular magistracy. The emperor, who in a previous appeal by Nostimus had not ruled on this issue, assigns the case to the Quintilii.

Popilius Pius (lines 30-35), whose seat was being challenged on the ground that he could not prove his Athenian citizenship in a manner that would satisfy the court of the Panhellenes. He had proved it to the satisfaction of the Areopagites, and the emperor rules that their decision sufficed and prescribes that proof of citizenship should always conform with the custom in the city of the defendant.

The three last cases, accordingly, are those appeals for which the emperor refused a *cognitio*.

Lines 35-47 concern an inheritance case with a criminal background. The appeal by Aelius Praxagoras from the decision of (the *procurator hereditatium*) Gavinius Saturninus is upheld concerning the codicils attributed to Pratolaus. Perhaps the codicils were not *testamento confirmati* (compare Pliny, *Ep.*, II, 16 with Sherwin-White's commentary) or were downright false (compare Pliny, *Ep.*, VI, 31, 5). No civilian adversary is mentioned, because the beneficiary of the codicils would have been the city of Athens. Counterclaims may be brought in the court of the Quintilii, but the emperor permits Praxagoras to enter into possession of the estates. The Quintilii will choose someone to arbitrate concerning the crops on these estates (which Praxagoras had not worked). As for the crops of the estates which were said to have been left to Herodes and to which Praxagoras will already have returned, Ingenuus will judge instead of someone appointed by the Quintilii, who were on bad terms with Herodes. The Athenians have requested that the son (of somebody) be allowed to return from the island, to which he had been relegated, because of the age of the father and because he was the only son. The emperor cannot yet take the time for this matter. However, he allows the son to be brought back temporarily during the investigation.

The situation remains obscure, but the writer would tentatively reconstruct it as follows: The son of somebody had forged a testament leaving estates to his father and to the most powerful local magnate, Herodes Atticus, and a gift to the city; the decision of Gavinius Saturninus may have concerned the city's right to inherit a legacy mentioned merely in the codicils; then criminal charges were successfully brought against the forger, and he was relegated to an island; the condemnation of the forger opened the way to an appeal from the decision of Gavinius Saturninus. In so reconstructing the situation, we think that the name of Herodes was introduced to make it more difficult to reject the testament as false. The gift of the city in the codicils had the same purpose, namely to strengthen the position of the forger's father. The subject was not entirely closed because someone might yet produce real evidence that the codicils themselves were authentic and had been confirmed in the original testament.

Lines 47-52 list those entitled to some payment or refund in connection with the above cases. Agathocles has served as ambassador and deserves the appropriate remuneration. In lines 49 and 50 the ἐγγύαι τῶν ἐκκλήτων δικῶν, which seem to be the deposits of the winners, are to be given back to the *patris* of Agathocles and to the synedrion of the Areopagites. The *patris* of Agathocles and of the litigants is of course the *civitas libera* of Athens, the polis. The trials involving priesthoods surely concern the polis as a whole, and it is noteworthy that an Athenian inscription, *Hesperia*, XXIX, 1960, pp. 29-32, No. 37, reinterpreted in *Colloque International sur les empereurs romains d'Espagne*, Paris, 1965, pp. 126-129, refers to sums reckoned in denarii ἃ ἡ πόλις ἐκ τοῦ ὀ[π]ισθοδόμου and ἀπὸ ἱερᾶς διατάξεω[ς]. One can speak of money going to, or coming from, the polis. The Areopagus is no treasury of the polis, but it may like any other corporation have had some funds of its own. It is our impression that the questions about membership in the Panhellenion were questions about Areopagites, and this would explain why some of the deposits were returned to the Areopagus. It is not likely that all reimbursements went to the polis and the Areopagus jointly; the Areopagus had no reason to receive deposits made by candidates for priesthoods, but there may have been a good reason in the case of trials concerning elections to the Panhellenion. No amounts are specified.

Lines 52-57 concern the two cases that are not yet finished and the disposition of other cases which may arise as a result of the hearing.

The emperor does not have to hold a trial concerning each appeal. In the case of Popilius Pius, who had been refused a seat in the Panhellenion on the ground that he could not represent Athens because he was not really an Athenian citizen, the emperor decided in favor of Pius without a trial. This case is not reported ἔκκλητος ἣν ἐποιήσατο Ποπίλιος Πεῖος. Only cases for which a *cognitio* actually occurred in the emperor's court are reported as ἔκκλητοι ἃς ἐποιήσαντο so and so, and they are so reported whether the appellant won or lost his case.

In the cases where the emperor delegates the decision to the Quintilii or even to Ingenuus it must be assumed that the judges will make a final decision not subject to appeal, because of what Ulpian *libro primo de appellationibus* (Digest, XLIX, 2, 1, 4) says: *Interdum imperator ita solet iudicem dare, ne liceret ab eo provocare, ut scio saepissime a divo Marco iudices datos.*

For general information and bibliography the writer refers the reader to W. Litewski, " Die römische Appellation in Zivilsachen," *R.I.D.A.*, 3ᵉ série, XII, 1965, pp. 347-436, XIII, 1966, pp. 231-323, XIV, 1967, pp. 301-403, and XV, 1968, pp. 143-351; J. M. Kelly, *Princeps Iudex, Eine Untersuchung zur Entwicklung und zu den Grundlagen der kaiserlichen Gerichtsbarkeit* (Forschungen zum römischen Recht, IX), Weimar, 1957; W. Kunkel, " Die Funktion des Konsiliums . . . im Kaisergericht," *Z.S.S.*, LXXXV, 1968, pp. 253-329. Kunkel now places the change from the utmost publicity to a secret discussion in the consilium in the time of Antoninus Pius or Marcus Aurelius.

There is a clause in the *Sententiae Pauli*, V, 26, 1 which deserves emphasis even after Garnsey's remarks in *J.R.S.*, LVI: *lege Iulia de vi publica damnatur qui aliqua potestate praeditus civem Romanum antea ad populum nunc ad imperatorem appellantem necaverit*, etc. The appeal to the emperor replaces the appeal to the People. Actually the emperor is a monarch, but theoretically the state is in balance between the aristocratic and the democratic element. *Senatus populusque Romanus* still expresses the theory behind the Roman state, but the enlarged *populus* functions no longer through the *comitia* but through the emperor, who was supposed to preserve the balance. In chapter III, note 1, we shall discuss the statement of Philostratus that when Herodes Atticus tried to bring the Athenian leaders to trial before the Senate, they fled to the emperor confiding in his more democratic sentiments. Aelius Aristides, Roman Oration 90, calls the emperor " the Ephor and Prytanis . . . from whom it is possible for the People to get what they want and for the Few to have the magistracies and influence."

CHAPTER II

CONSTITUTIONAL AND SOCIAL IMPLICATIONS

PRIESTHOODS

In the section lines 4-7 a distinction is made between men who volunteer for the priesthood of the *dadouchos* and for other, presumably less important, priesthoods and men who are being called to office by the Demos. The first question that arises is whether the same offices are meant in each case or two different sets of offices are involved. Was the office of *dadouchos* always voluntary but sometimes disputed and assigned by vote of the Demos? Elections are mentioned immediately afterwards. On the other hand, Foucart[1] argued that the hierophant and *dadouchos* were chosen by lot. He did so because of the Patmos scholion on Demosthenes[2] which reads: καὶ γένος ἕκαστον ἄνδρας εἶχε τριάκοντα τοὺς εἰς τὰ γένη τεταγμένους, οἵτινες γεννῆται ἐκαλοῦντο, ὧν αἱ ἱερωσύναι ἑκάστοις προσήκουσαι ἐκληροῦντο, οἷον Εὐμολπίδαι καὶ Κήρυκες καὶ Ἐτεοβουτάδαι. Aristotle was cited as the source of this scholion, which without the last six words occurs elsewhere. On p. 47 Foucart, struck by evidence that the office of *dadouchos* tended to remain in the same family, suggested that one placed in the sortition urn only the names of those who presented themselves as candidates.

> Dès lors, il est facile de concevoir que les Kéryces aient pu, par une abstention volontaire, laisser aux membres d'une branche, plus riche ou plus influente, une sorte de possession exclusive de la dadouchie. Mais il n'y avait pas là hérédité, et, à un moment donné, d'autres branches pouvaient revendiquer leurs droits et concourir au tirage au sort, qui restait la règle.

Roussel, *Mélanges Bidez*, p. 831 inferred from the decree in honor of the *dadouchos* Themistocles that the priesthood passed from father to son by heredity but that according to recognized rules it passed to another member of the family, if the sons of the deceased *dadouchos* were not of age to fill the office.

In the case of ancient aristocratic priesthoods the use of the lot may have been a passing phenomenon and may at all times have been evaded at the Eleusinian sanctuary by voluntary abstentions. In the Roman Period neither city archonships nor priesthoods of the Ceryces are filled by lot. For the priesthoods from the Ceryces lines 4-15 show that election had replaced sortition and strongly suggest that sortition was a legitimate means or expedient only during the fifth and fourth centuries

---

[1] P. Foucart, "Les grands mystères d'Éleusis," *Mémoires de l'Académie des Inscriptions et Belles-Lettres*, XXXVII, 1900, pp. 24 f., 47. A study of Eleusinian priesthoods by Kevin Clinton is forthcoming.

[2] Sakellion, *B.C.H.*, I, 1877, p. 152.

with occasional brief reversions later. But lines 4-7 show that election was not the usual way of filling these offices which are described as voluntary priesthoods. In the decree in honor of the *dadouchos* Themistocles, lines 37 ff. it is said that he inherited from his father and other ancestors his eligibility and the priesthood derived there-from (παρειληφότα τὴν εὐγένειαν καὶ τὴν ἀπ᾽ αὐτῆς ἱερεωσύνην παρὰ . . .). This suggests that the son had a right to the office held by his ancestors and that he normally succeeded if no impediment existed and if he volunteered. But if he were too young or were excluded by some disgrace or were unwilling to make the necessary gift of grain, the *trophion* which appears for the first time on Plaque II, lines 4-7, then the opportunity for other candidates to present their names arose and in such cases the appointment was more often contested and decided by election.

THE *HOMOPHYLOI* CONCEPT

The Areopagus has been well treated by B. Keil and D. J. Geagan, so that we need not repeat information familiar to many readers. The inscription from the Roman Market Place, however, brings new information. First it is clear from lines 27-28 that a man who performed some special service for the city, rather than the traditional archonship, could, if not otherwise disqualified, be accepted now in the Areopagus. This would be a departure from the letter of the law but not from the spirit. Secondly, we encounter in this inscription the three-generation rule and so the ancient concept of *homophyloi*.

The *GEL*, *s.v.* ὅμοιος, II rightly defines the ὅμοιοι as " all citizens who had equal right to hold state offices."

In the early Athenian state the only citizens who were permitted to hold archon-ships were the eupatridae. The sixth century in a development marked particularly by the reforms of Solon and Cleisthenes raised other Athenians to the same potential position, first of all, the *gennetai*, whom Wade-Gery convincingly identified as chiefly commoners and whom the writer equates with holders of ordinary land (as distinct from reservations and marginal lands). The reputed division of the people into 360 " clans " (γένη), each contributing thirty men, would then concern the holders of ordinary land and would be intelligible as a reform which the gradual shift to a hoplite army at some time imposed. The *gennetai* were at one time the " foster-brothers," ὁμογάλακτες, as we learn from Philochorus, frag. 35 Jacoby, and had a status above that of other commoners. The *homogalaktes*, as it seems to me, were the eupatridae plus the *geomoroi* commoners. The slogan of reformers in the time of Cleisthenes was μὴ φυλοκρινεῖν. According to Herodotus, V, 66 he had taken into partnership the demos, which in this context ought to mean, I think, the landless Athenian *demiourgoi* (as distinct from the *geomoroi* and other landholders), not just a few rich men but all the poor *demiourgoi*. These were men little involved, if at all, in the dissensions of the three regional factions of landholders. Many Athenians were still debarred from the highest public office because of an insufficient patrimony or census, but no longer did access to political office depend on eupatrid or homogalactic or land-holder status.

The Athenians were supposed to be originally autochthonous and later homophy-lous with each other. The word *homophylos* might be extended to include all Hellenes, but it more properly applied to those of the same stock or status within an ethnos or city. Thus Thucydides, I, 102, 3 says that the Lacedaemonians considered the Athen-ians *allophyloi*, that is, not *homophyloi* with themselves.

In the Crown Oration 181-187 we have what purports to be a decree of Demos-thenes but is more likely to be a composition by some rhetor of Asia Minor in the second or first century B.C.[2a] For our purposes the authorship does not matter too much. Philip is denounced in section 185 as an *allophylos anthropos*, unfit to rule over Hellenes. In 186 it continues: ἔτι δὲ οὐδὲ ἀλλότριον ἡγεῖται εἶναι ὁ Ἀθηναίων δῆμος τὸν Θηβαίων δῆμον οὔτε τῇ συγγενείᾳ οὔτε τῷ ὁμοφύλῳ. " The Demos of the Athenians does not consider the Demos of the Thebans alien to it either in its blood or in its status."

To return to the specific question of high public office, even the census require-ment seems to have been practically abolished by the generation after the Persian invasion according to Plutarch, *Aristides*, 22, 1 and Aristotle, *Ath. Pol.*, 26, 2, but with all the religious and traditional duties incumbent upon the archons there can have been no temptation to appoint *allophyloi* to these higher posts. In the crises of the Peloponnesian War and subsequent disturbances a substantial number of *allo-phyloi* received Athenian citizenship. The best known case is that of the Plataeans. [Demosthenes], LIX, 104 refers to this with the words μετέδοτε τῆς πολιτείας. The Athenians did give them citizenship but did not declare them *homophyloi*. On the contrary, Aristotle, *Ath. Pol.*, 55, 3 attests that care was taken to exclude new citizens from the archonships by requiring proof of three generations of citizenship on each side of the family. And since the Areopagus was recruited from ex-archons, no new citizens entered the select synedrion of the Areopagus. The slaves who were en-franchised in 407/6 were classified as " Plataeans " according to Hellanicus (*F.Gr. Hist.*, 323a, F 25) and to Aristophanes, *Frogs*, 694. Aristophanes disliked having ex-slaves and their sons as fellow-citizens. In *Frogs*, 727-732 he contrasts the εὐγενεῖς who have Hellenic virtues and education with the rascals from rascals who are slaves.

The evolution which Mathieu[3] envisaged for the citizenship of *allophyloi* at Athens was the following: after 427 the Plataeans were made Athenian citizens but excluded from the archonship; after 403 the number of naturalized Athenians in-

[2a] See T. Larsen, *Papyri Graecae Haunienses*, Copenhagen, 1942, pp. 14-28.

[3] See p. 115 of G. Mathieu, " La Réorganisation du corps civique athénien à la fin du Vᵉ siècle," *R.E.G.*, XL, 1927, pp. 65-116. For citizenship, see also A. Diller, " Scrutiny and Appeal in Athenian Citizenship," *Cl. Phil.*, XXX, 1935, pp. 302-311.

creased, but at the same time so had the feeling against them; so a general ruling was made which, if strictly interpreted, no longer admitted to the archonships and priesthoods any but the grandsons of those naturalized, the Plataeans retaining their special status; in the fourth century the law subsisted but custom mitigated its severity and in practice all the sons of those naturalized were treated as if they were sons of Plataeans. I doubt that the sons of ex-slaves were ever eligible for archonships and important priesthoods. The three-generation rule was, I think, aimed at them. But otherwise the evolution may well have been as Mathieu inferred. The most important references are these:

[Demosthenes], LIX, 106 on the citizenship of Plataeans: ἔπειτα καὶ τὸν νόμον διωρίσατο ἐν τῷ ψηφίσματι πρὸς αὐτούς (sc. τοὺς φάσκοντας Πλαταιέας εἶναι) εὐθέως ὑπέρ τε τῆς πόλεως καὶ τῶν θεῶν, {καὶ} μὴ ἐξεῖναι αὐτῶν μηδενὶ τῶν ἐννέα ἀρχόντων λαχεῖν μηδὲ ἱερωσύνης μηδεμιᾶς, τοῖς δ᾽ ἐκ τούτων, ἂν ὦσιν ἐξ ἀστῆς γυναικὸς καὶ ἐγγυητῆς κατὰ τὸν νόμον.

Aristotle, *Ath. Pol.*, 55, 3 on the testing of prospective archons: ἐ[πε]ρωτῶσιν δ᾽, ὅταν δοκιμάζωσιν, πρῶτον μὲν "τίς σοι πατὴρ καὶ πόθεν τῶν δήμων, καὶ τίς πατρὸς πατήρ, καὶ τίς μήτηρ, καὶ τίς μητρὸς πατὴρ καὶ πόθεν τῶν δήμων;"

This kind of discrimination was by no means limited to Athens; rather it was probably the usual custom of Greek cities. But at Rome the story of the Claudian gens, as told by Dionysius of Halicarnassus, *Roman Antiquities*, V, 40, perpetuated the tradition of a new citizen being made immediately eligible for the highest offices in the person of their Sabine ancestor who was εὐγενὴς καὶ χρήμασι δυνατός.

It is hardly necessary to remind the reader that Aelius Aristides knew well the distinction made by Athenians in the case of the Plataeans, to whose Athenian grant of citizenship he refers in the Panathenaic Oration, section 53, and the implications of the word τριγονία in the Attic orators. It is also clear that he knew that many aristocratic Greeks under the Roman emperors were enrolled in the Roman Senate or Senatorial Order and thus declared eligible for the highest offices in the Roman state. This made a great impression upon him, and in the famous passage where he praises the Roman generosity and wisdom in the extension of their citizenship he compares the Romans with the Greeks to the latters' disadvantage and says (Roman Oration, section 59) that " you proclaimed the superior element everywhere as πολιτικὸν ἢ καὶ ὁμόφυλον." That is, they became citizens or even citizens entitled to hold the highest offices,[4] fit to rule even over Romans. Aristides avoided precise legal terms. By ὁμόφυλον he meant more than citizenship, certainly *ingenuitas*, perhaps even *trigonia*.

---

[4] The Greek text makes perfect sense as it stands, but C. A. Behr, *Aelius Aristides and the Sacred Tales*, Amsterdam, 1968, p. 5, note 7, resorts to an emendation ⟨εἰ⟩ καὶ ὁμόφυλον and paraphrases his emended text: " The more powerful are given Roman citizenship (or a part in the Roman government) even if they keep their own city's franchise." But the word ὁμόφυλον cannot

When individual benefactors received Athenian citizenship in the Classical Period they were normally allowed to choose the tribe, deme and phratry in which they were to be enrolled. The phratries were subdivided into *gene* (the *thiasoi* need not concern us). Membership in the tribe and deme seem to have sufficed, at least at first, though membership in the phratry brought the right to hold certain priesthoods and to participate in certain religious and social events for which membership in tribe and deme was not enough. Cleisthenes did not disturb the phratries. To what extent non-membership in a phratry was used against a man cannot be traced, but at the end of the upheavals during and just after the Peloponnesian War, the phratries too had to be reorganized, if we may judge from the so-called Demotonid Decrees which Wade-Gery identified as decrees of the Dekeleeis who were a mere fraction of the phratry.[5]

It is convenient to picture Athenian citizenship as a dual institution, partly a membership in the Cleisthenean tribes and demes, partly a membership in pre-Cleisthenean phratries and *gene*. All Athenians were in the Cleisthenean city, most or only many (according to the period) were in the pre-Cleisthenean organization. In the first century B.C. the pre-Cleisthenean organization received some special blessing from Delphi and, perhaps after some redistribution, became politically very important.[6] The phratries no longer appear but the *gene* do. The full-fledged citizens now belong not only to the Cleisthenean organization[7] but to the " Solonian " *gene*, and non-membership in the pre-Cleisthenean organization effectively barred a man before A.D. 161 not only from state priesthoods, but from active citizenship as well.

This aspect should be borne in mind, but we now return to the two above cited passages, [Demosthenes], LIX, 106 and Aristotle, *Ath. Pol.*, 55, 3. In Aristotle's day the standards had been raised so that three generations of citizenship were required on both sides of an archon's family, whereas in the year indicated by [Demosthenes], LIX an archon could conceivably have three generations on only one side of his family, that of his mother. Whether or not an archon of that sort was denied access to the Areopagus we cannot say.

The new inscription from the Roman Market Place shows that in the second century after Christ Athens still made a distinction between citizens who were en-

have the meaning " keep their own city's franchise." Behr's emendation makes Aelius Aristides say, " You proclaimed the superior element everywhere as Roman citizens if they were also of the same stock as the Romans." Against another unnecessary emendation I have defended and explained the text of Roman Oration 65 in *La Parola del Passato*, CXVIII, 1968, pp. 50-52.

[5] H. T. Wade-Gery, " Studies in the Structure of Attic Society: I, Demotionidai," *Class. Quarterly*, XXV, 1931, pp. 129-143 (= *Essays in Greek History*, pp. 116-134).

[6] The writer's theory is based partly on the inscription reedited by B. D. Meritt, *Hesperia*, IX, 1940, pp. 86-96, No. 17, partly on references to the *gene* in Philostratus, *V.S.*, II, 1, 3 (p. 57 Kayser, p. 144 Wright) and in Aelius Aristides, *Panathenaic*, section 261.

[7] The Cleisthenean organization is here visualized as the ten original tribes and whatever post-Cleisthenean tribes were carved out of them.

titled to hold the highest offices and citizens who were not, but that the old three-generation rule had been revised to mean three generations of " good " birth on the paternal side instead of three generations of citizenship on both sides of the family. The emperor calls it an ancient custom. Is he effacing the difference between the three-generation rule of the fourth century B.C. and that of the Roman Period? Quite possibly he has subsumed both types under the phrase παλαιὸν ἔθος of line 59. We still have the problem of tracing the great constitutional alteration which substituted for the old a new type of three-generation requirement such as Augustus, or rather Octavian, applied or reapplied to the Roman Senate. For in advising those with a freedman father to resign from the Areopagus or face expulsion with a penalty Marcus Aurelius was following the example of the divine Augustus, who according to Cassius Dio, LII, 42, 1-3 and LIV, 13-14 purged the Roman Senate of unworthy members in 29 B.C. and again in 19/18 B.C. On the former occasion Octavian, who undertook the censorship along with Agrippa, " persuaded about fifty to withdraw voluntarily from the Senate, then later he forced one hundred and forty others to imitate their example; he deprived none of them of civic rights, but he published the names of the second batch, whereas the first batch, because they did not dilly-dally but obeyed him promptly, he spared from the disgrace of being publicly listed." The ineligible senators were those of non-senatorial family who had been appointed without first being of the Equestrian Order or who had been appointed from those *equites* with a freedman father, as one may infer from what Cassius Dio, XLIII, 47, 3 relates about Julius Caesar, who in 45 B.C. packed the Senate, not just with new men, but with new men from the ranks or of freedman stock indiscriminately, μηδὲν διακρίνων μήτ᾽ εἴ τις στρατιώτης μήτ᾽ εἴ τις ἀπελευθέρου παῖς ἦν.[8] Thus Octavian cleaned up the mess which the Civil Wars allegedly induced Julius Caesar (and perhaps others) to create. Similarly Marcus has an alleged mess to clean up after Lucius Verus, as we shall argue in Chapter III.

The latest occasion when the new type of three-generation rule could have been introduced at Athens was in the recodification of the laws from Draco and Solon under Hadrian, but to the writer it seems unlikely that Hadrian would have introduced so important a change if Augustus had not already done so in 21 B.C. at the time that he, Augustus, had intervened to prevent the sale of Athenian citizenship (Cassius Dio, LIV, 7, 2: καὶ ἀπηγόρευσέ σφισι μηδένα πολίτην ἀργυρίου ποιεῖσθαι).

---

[8] In case one harbors a suspicion that Dio Cassius with the evils of the reign of Maximinus Thrax in mind has given to the senators admitted by Julius Caesar an anachronistic color, we remind the reader of Suetonius, *Divus Augustus* 35: *Senatorum affluentem numerum deformi et incondita turba . . . ad modum pristinum et splendorem redegit duabus lectionibus.* The military followers promoted to the Senate from the ranks constituted an *incondita turba*; those of slave or freedman antecedents were a *deformis turba*. We are not suggesting that all Caesar's appointments fell in one or the other of these disreputable categories, merely that certain of his appointments could be so criticized.

This was certainly an important turning point in the history of citizenship at Athens. The sale of citizenship, attested elsewhere as early as the fourth century B.C., continued in certain Greek cities even after Augustus.[9]

These two opportunities, namely in A.D. 125 and in 21 B.C., were not the only occasions of great change. Surely the citizen rolls required much revision after Sulla's capture of Athens. The more respectable metics were now enrolled as citizens, if not earlier. Athens had lost many families in the dreadful years 88-84 B.C.

One can go back even further, to the fourth quarter or second half of the second century B.C. This was the period when Delos and the Piraeus attracted many business men from all over and brought, at least to a few, great prosperity for a while. The political ideas that inspired certain *equites* in Italy had their reflection in many circles at Athens. The rich men of Athens were international, though a few old families may have retained the real power. In earlier times citizenship was rarely given. Now it became much more common, particularly through the ephebate.[10] From 119/8 through 39/8 B.C. something like ten ephebic catalogues attest the presence of numerous foreigners in the ephebate at Athens. Concomitantly the long list of decrees which from the fifth to the second century B.C. gave a single grant of citizenship or right to acquire real estate now came to an end.[11] Citizenship was no longer a rare privilege. In fact, Polybius, XXX, 20 attests the change in the official attitude at Athens. At Priene too there were foreigners in the ephebate, and ex-ephebes, if not yet citizens, were at least a privileged group.[12]

While the ephebate became more important as the door to citizenship in a more truly international Hellenic society, the prejudice against lowering the bar for slaves and their offspring was not at all removed. Sons of slaves with the connivance of others did infiltrate themselves, but they were not entitled to citizenship acquired under false pretenses and could be stripped of their privileges. This we know from the epistle of Claudius to the Alexandrians in A.D. 41.[13] The emperor reassures the Alexandrians; he guarantees the citizenship of Alexandria to all those who have completed the ephebic training, with a reservation in the cases of any who have been born from slaves and infiltrated themselves.

In summary the new type of three-generation rule may have been introduced as early as the second century B.C., been interrupted in the popular uprising of the

[9] Evidence is collected and earlier literature cited by L. Robert, *Hellenica*, I, 1940, pp. 38-42. See also D. Magie, *Roman Rule in Asia Minor*, pp. 919 f.

[10] O. W. Reinmuth, "The Ephebate and Citizenship in Attica," *T.A.P.A.*, LXXIX, 1948, pp. 211-231, and Chrysis Pélékidis, *Histoire de l'ephébie attique des origines à 31 avant Jésus-Christ* (École Française d' Athènes, *Travaux et Mémoires*, XIII), Paris, 1962, pp. 183-209.

[11] Excellent study by Jan Pečírka, *The Formula for the Grant of Enktesis in Attic Inscriptions* (Acta Universitatis Carolinae philosophica et historica, Monograph XV), Prague, 1966.

[12] *Inschriften von Priene*, 123, second or first century B.C.

[13] See above p. 36, note 14.

Mithradatic Period, been restored by Sulla, been lost and restored again, and finally solidified at the desire of Augustus. Or it may have been introduced once and for all by Augustus. Other moments for its introduction cannot be excluded entirely, but the Augustan Period and the second century B.C. are more likely times.

Is it not possible that two of the most common privileges of cities belonging to Greek confederacies, namely *enktesis* and *epigamia*, were now assumed as existing within the great alliance of cities and federal states under the hegemony of the Romans, the alliance which we rightly call the Roman Empire but which Greeks in the time of Augustus were encouraged to visualize in terms of Hellenistic aspirations? The words of Aelius Aristides, Roman Oration 102, γάμους τε κοινοὺς ποιήσαντες, and 105, γάμων νόμῳ γιγνομένων, seem to allude to *epigamia*. If *epigamia*[14] was

---

[14] Intermarriage was common from the second century B.C. on. The following examples drawn from Attica alone are accompanied by Kirchner's conjectural dating:

I.G., II²,				
7883, aetat. imperat.,	Athenian	married to a woman of	Ancyra
7922, s. I p.,	Antiochene	" " " "	" "
7961, s. I a./s. I p.,	Athenian	" " " "	" Aegina
7981, s. I/II,	Antiochene	" " " "	" Aenos
8088, post a. 317/6,	Athenian	" " " "	" Amphissa
8092, s. II a.,	"	" " " "	" Andros
8167, aetat. imperat.,	"	" " " "	" Antioch
8171, fin. s. I a./init. s. I p.,	"	" " " "	" "
8173, s. I a.,	Seleuceian	" " " "	" "
8178, s. I p,,	Athenian	" " " "	" "
8208, aetat. Rom.,	"	" " " "	" "
8209, undated,	Apamean	" " " "	" "
8298, s. I a.,	Heraclean	" " " "	" "
8321, s. I p.,	Athenian	" " " "	" "
8358, s. I p.,	Sidonian	" " " "	" Arados
8377, s. II a.,	Athenian	" " " "	" Argos
8390, s. I p.,	Antiochene	" " " "	" Ascalon
8407, s. I p.,	Athenian	" " " "	" Berytus
8447, ante med. s. II p.,	Apamean	" " " "	" Byzantium
8481, undated,	Athenian	" " " "	" Edessa
8485, s. I a.,	"	" " " "	" Epidamnus
8503, s. I p.,	"	" " " "	" Eumeneia
8521, s. I p.,	Antiochene	" " " "	" Ephesus
8527, post fin. s. IV a.,	Athenian	" " " "	" Elis
8549, s. I p.,	"	" " " "	" Heraclea
8578, s. I a.,	"	" " " "	" "
8579, aetat. Rom.,	"	" " " "	" "
8581, s. II a.,	"	" " " "	" "
8587, s. I a.,	Laodicean	" " " "	" "
8588, s. II a.,	Ephesian	" " " "	" "
8606, undated,	Athenian	" " " "	" "

8609, s. II/I,	Athenian	"	" "	"	"	"	
8628, init. s. I p.,	Maronean	"	" "	"	"	"	
8671, s. III/II,	Ancyran	"	" "	"	"	"	
8686, s. I a./s. I p.	Antiochene	"	" "	"	"	"	
8688, aetat. Rom.	Athenian	"	" "	"	"	"	
8693, s. II a.,	"	"	" "	"	"	"	
8695, aetat. Rom.,	"	"	" "	"	"	"	
8728, c. s. II/I,	Mede	"	" "	"	"	"	
8734, s. I a.,	Termessian	"	" "	"	"	"	
8735, s. I p.,	Athenian	"	" "	"	"	"	
8757, s. I a.,	"	"	" "	"	"	"	
8768, post fin. s. IV a.,	"	"	" "	"	"	"	
8773, undated,	"	"	" "	"	"	"	
8781, s. I p.,	"	"	" "	"	"	"	
8785, s. I p.,	"	"	" "	"	"	"	
8793, s. I p.,	Maronean	"	" "	"	"	"	
8818, s. II/I a.,	Plataean	"	" "	"	"	"	
8820, aetat. Rom.,	Cibyran	"	" "	"	"	"	
8855, post med. s. IV a.,	Epirote	"	" "	"	"	Thebes	
8875, post fin. s. IV a.,	Athenian	"	" "	"	"	"	
8887, s. I a.,	Milesian	"	" "	"	"	"	
9018, post med. s. IV a.,	Heraclean	"	" "	"	"	Cius	
9027, s. II a.,	Athenian	"	" "	"	"	Cibyra	
9052, init. s. II a.,	Corinthian	"	" "	"	"	Sicyon	
9054, s. II a.,	Athenian	"	" "	"	"	Corinth	
9065, s. I p.,	"	"	" "	"	"	"	
9082, s. I/II,	"	"	" "	"	"	Coronea	
9101, s. I a./s. I p.,	Alexandrian	"	" "	"	"	Cyzicus	
9146, s. I a.,	Corinthian	"	" "	Lacedaemonian woman			
9150, s. II/I,	Athenian	"	"	"	"		
9152, s. III a.,	"	"	"	Laconian woman			
9182, s. I/II,	"	"	"	woman of Laodicea			
9195, aetat. Rom.,	"	"	" "	"	"	"	
9198, s. II a.,	"	"	" "	"	Lappa		
9217, s. II a.,	"	"	"	Locrian woman			
9238, s. II a.,	Lacedaemonian	"	"	Magnesian woman			
9260, s. I p.,	Heraclean	"	"	Macedonian woman			
9316, aetat. imperat.,	"	"	"	woman of Megara			
9362, s. I a.,	Athenian	"	"	Milesian woman			
9363, fin. s. I p.,	"	"	" "	"	"		
9444, s. I p.,	"	"	" "	"	"		
9448, init. s. I p.,	"	"	" "	"	"		
9450, aetat. Rom.,	"	"	" "	"	"		
9470, undated,	Antiochene	"	" "	"	"		
9504, "	Athenian	"	" "	"	"		
9531, "	"	"	" "	"	"		
9543, s. I a./s. I p.,	"	"	" "	"	"		

9642, s. II/I,	Athenian	"	" "	"		"
9662, s. III/II,	"	"	" "	"		"
9664, s. I p.,	"	"	" "	"		"
9665, s. I a.,	Plataean	"	" "	"		"
9669, s. II/I,	Athenian	"	" "	"		"
9678a, s. I a.,	"	"	" "	"		"
9679, s. II a.,	"	"	" "	"		"
9683, med. s. I p.,	"	"	" "	"		"
9699, s. I p.,	"	"	" "	"		"
9718, s. II p.,	"	"	" "	"		"
9721, med. s. I p.,	"	"	" "	"		"
9735, s. II/III,	Milesian	"	" an Athenian			"
9747, s. I p.,	Athenian	"	" a Milesian			"
9764, aetat. imperat.,	"	"	" "	"		"
9783, aetat. Rom.,	"	"	" "	"		"
9787, s. II p.,	"	"	" "	"		"
9797, fin. s. I a./init. s. I p.,	"	"	" "	"		"
9805, s. II/I,	Athenian	"	" "	"		"
9813, s. I p.,	"	"	" "	"		"
9815, s. I/II p.,	Milesian	"	" an Athenian			"
9820, aetat. Rom.,	Alexandrian	"	" a Milesian			"
9821, s. I p.,	Athenian	"	" "	"		"
9830, s. II a.,	Laodicean	"	" "	"		"
9838, s. II/I,	Athenian	"	" "	"		"
9864, undated,	"	"	" "	"		"
9878, s. I a.,	"	"	" "	"		"
9881, init. s. I p.,	"	"	" "	"		"
9888, s. II a.,	Antiochene	"	" "	"		"
9895, s. II a.,	Athenian	"	" "	"		"
9900, s. I/II,	"	"	" "	"		"
9914, s. I a.,	"	"	" "	"		"
9959/60, aetat. imperat,.	"	"	" "	"		"
9968, s. II a.,	"	"	" "	woman of		Mytilene
9975, med. s. II a.,	"	"	" "	"	"	Myrina
10123, s. I p.,	"	"	" "	"	"	Ptolemais
10138, s. I p.,	Milesian	"	" "	"	"	Rhodes
10198, init. s. I p.,	Athenian	"	" "	"	"	Salamis
10204, s. II a.,	"	"	" "	"	"	"
10206, c. s. II a.,	"	"	" "	"	"	"
10216, init. s. I p.,	"	"	" "	"	"	"
10235, init. s. I p.,	"	son	" "	"	"	Sardis
10250, s. I a.,	"	married	"	"	"	Seleuceia
10275/6, s. I p.,	"	"	" "	"	"	Sidon
10282, s. I p.,	Callatian	"	" "	"	"	"
10284, s. II/I,	Athenian	"	" "	"	"	"
10304, s. II a.,	"	"	" "	"	"	Sicyon
10307, s. I a./s. I p.,	"	"	" "	"	"	"
10368, s. II p.,	Scyrian	"	" an Athenian woman			
10372, s. I p.,	Athenian	"	" a woman of Smyrna			

recognized or tolerated, the old three-generation rule of citizenship on both sides of the family needed replacement, especially since the most prominent citizens were those most likely to marry abroad.[14a] Also grants of Roman citizenship to Greeks made the old type of *trigonia* and the old law of property obsolete, since the cities could not discriminate against the friends of Rome.

Perhaps the eponymates held by foreigners provide a clue to the date when the old type of *trigonia* disappeared. At Athens the earliest foreigners among archons so far known or so far recognized are the Spartan C. Julius Laco and the Thracian Cotys under Augustus, and King Rhoematalcas in A.D. 36/7.[15]

Aristotle recognized the existence of a political criterion known as εὐγένεια, which he defines as nothing more than the qualification of old wealth and excellence. In discussing types of civic constitutions he rules out *eugeneia* as a criterion on which the control of the city government could be primarily based, in *Politics*, IV, 8, 1294a15-25, which reads as follows:

> Now in most cities the form called polity exists, where the fusion goes no further than the attempt to unite the freedom of the poor and the wealth of the rich, for it is more or less true that in most cases the latter seem to occupy the place of the *kaloi kagathoi*, and no wonder when there are three qualifications which are rival criteria for the quality of those eligible to rule in the city, namely mere freedom, wealth, excellence (the fourth, which men call *eugeneia*, is not separate from the two last: for *eugeneia* is just ancient wealth plus ἀρετή). Therefore, it is clear that the fusion of the two groups, the rich and the poor, is to be called a polity, and the union of all three comes closer to being an aristocracy than any of the others except the true, prime aristocracy.

The Athenian constitution of the Roman Period, accordingly, was what Aristotle in the *Politics*, IV, 15, 1300a40-b1 called a polity with aristocratic leanings or regard for merit (πολιτικὸν ἀριστοκρατικῶς), except that the word *eugeneia* has undergone a semantic change. The Athenian constitution had the form of a balanced mixed constitution with the Areopagites as the aristocratic or oligarchic element and with the democratic element residing in the Council and Demos. The emperor's role was

10373, init. s. I p.,	"	"	" "	"	"	"
10408, s. I p.,	"	"	" "	"	"	Tanagra
10412a, s. II/I,	"	"	" "	"	"	Tarentum
10439, s. I a.,	"	"	" "	"	"	Termessus
10452, s. II a.,	"	"	" "	"	"	Tolophon
10459, s. I p.,	"	"	" "	"	"	Tralles
10464, c. s. I p.,	Tyanan	"	" an Athenian woman			
10469, undated,	Athenian	"	" a woman of Tyre			
10513, s. II/I,	"	"	" "	"	"	Oreos

[14a] For intermarriage among the aristocracy of Roman Greece see *I.G.*, II², 3704 and 4071, J. Bousquet, *B.C.H.*, LXXXVII, 1963, pp. 198-206, and the better edition of *I.G.*, IV², 86 by W. Peek, *Abh. Ak. Wiss. Leipzig*, LX, 2, 1969, p. 30.

[15] P. Graindor, *Chronologie des archontes sous l'empire* (Acad. roy. de Belgique, Classe des Lettres . . . , *Mémoires* . . . 4°, VIII, 1921), Nos. 19, 26 and 39.

to keep either element from usurping the place of the other and so starting the baleful succession of constitutional forms which the proper checks and balance precluded. It is not the mixed constitution known from Polybius and Cicero as one of three elements but that mixture of only two elements which Aristotle and others discerned,[15a] and which apparently became an influence upon Augustus, Hadrian and Marcus Aurelius.

The inscription from the Roman Market Place attests furthermore that the new type of *trigonia* based on three generations of good (= free) birth existed in many other Greek cities and perhaps in all. For in many other Greek cities, says Marcus Aurelius (line 62), not in Athens alone, it had recently broken down. The old type of *trigonia*, attested by *S.I.G.*³, 1015 = Sokolowski, *Lois sacrées de l'Asie Mineure*, 73, still existed in the third century B.C. at Halicarnassus.

Lines 76-79 of the inscription from the Roman Market Place show that the new type of *trigonia* was required also of the Panhellenes. Here Marcus Aurelius was surely not the first to formulate the rule. The three-generation requirement undoubtedly went back to the beginning of the Panhellenion in or near A.D. 132, and thus we can connect it with Hadrian in two ways, in his revision of the laws from Draco and Solon in 125 and in his foundation of the Panhellenion in or near 132. The writer believes that the new type of *trigonia* was something that Hadrian inherited, because the imposition of a three-generation rule seems out of character for Hadrian but in keeping with the social legislation of Augustus. Admittedly indication of the paternal grandfather became much more common after 125 in the inscriptions of Asia Minor and even at Sparta as in *S.E.G.*, XI, 491, so that three generations of known public figures were sometimes advertised; but the Menogenes documents of *Sardis*, VII, 1, 8 from the time of Augustus were just as particular. Hadrian would probably not have gone out of his way to penalize the sons of freedmen and would not have wished to antagonize important elements in the Greek cities, if a pre-existing rule or endorsement of the revered Augustus had not fixed his course. He could hardly have set aside a standard recommended by Augustus.

We come back to Augustus or rather to the ultimate victory of the conservative program in the time of Augustus. For we must allow the probability that the new type of three-generation rule existed in some places as early as the second century B.C.

At Rome itself there was no law against the election of a freedman's son as late as 304 B.C. when Cn. Flavius Cn.f. served as curule aedile. The need for any kind of three-generation rule had not previously been felt. In that same year, nevertheless, Fabius Rullianus as censor had the sons of freedmen expelled from the Roman Senate.[16] The sons of freedmen could be elected to office, if they had the necessary

---

[15a] G. J. D. Aalders, " Die Mischverfassung und ihre historische Dokumentation in den *Politica* des Aristoteles," *Entretiens Hardt*, XI, 1965, pp. 199-244.

[16] Plutarch, *Pompey*, 13, 11.

backing, but they were debarred from the Senate. The same was true in the time of Nero.[17]

Was the three-generation rule in Athens limited during the Age of the Antonines to the Areopagus? Did it apply like the old type to all the archonships? Without the three-generation qualification a man was normally ineligible for appointment to the Areopagus. But could he be appointed archon eponymous, or one of the three highest archons, or a thesmothete? The emperor mentions only the office of Areopagite as beyond a man's reach without the *trigonia*, and he says that the lesser posts and honors are open to him. In Classical Athens the archonships were always distinguished from the lesser posts, but the lesser posts in the language of Marcus Aurelius could conceivably include six of the archonships. If, however, in the absence of evidence to the contrary we stay with the interpretation that the higher offices were even now the nine (or at least the three chief) archonships and the Areopagus to which they prepared a man's entry, we may explain the emperor's insistence on the purity of the Areopagus and his silence about the archonships themselves by pointing out that this epistle was the second on the subject and that any question concerning the archonships themselves had been settled in the first epistle. The residual problem concerned the status of ex-archons both at Athens and elsewhere. The ambition for which rich men paid was not just to fill an archonship but to become an ex-archon of a higher grade.

The sons to whom the emperor guaranteed access to the lesser offices if they resigned from the Areopagus were men who presumably achieved entry into the Areopagus by holding the generalship or the post of herald of the Council and Demos.[18]

Civic institutions and their *summae honorariae* were reflected in the ephebic organization. From the ephebic catalogues, *I.G.*, II², 2059, 2085, 2113, 2119, 2130, 2193, 2203, 2208, 2235, 2237, 2239 and 2243, one sees which non-Areopagitic posts in the government of the city commanded the highest respect at Athens under the Antonines and Severi, because these titles were given to ephebes irregularly in a way which suggests recognition for donations of varying amounts. The title of archon enjoyed the highest prestige, but the general and herald usually preceded the basileus and polemarch. In one case, *I.G.*, II², 2208, there were two generals and two heralds and a polemarch, but no archon or basileus. The thought arises that only the boys with *trigonia* were eligible for the archonships, but boys without *trigonia* could become general and herald. The general and the herald normally paid at a higher rate to take precedence among the ephebes over the basileus and the polemarch. Thesmothetae, *agoranomoi* and *astynomoi* are occasionally listed and presumably represent smaller

---

[17] Suetonius, *Nero*, 15.

[18] For the hoplite general and the herald of the Council and Demos see D. J. Geagan, *The Athenian Constitution after Sulla* (*Hesperia*, Supplement XII), 1967, pp. 18-31 and 104-106.

donations. Here again one suspects a distinction between boys with *trigonia* who were eligible for the post of thesmothete (*I.G.*, II², 2235 has only one thesmothete) and boys without *trigonia*.

Men without *trigonia* who slipped into the Areopagus past the legal barrier did so presumably after serving as general or herald at great expense, but one possible route may have been through the office of thesmothete, because the Areopagus according to Geagan's calculations (*op. cit.*, pp. 56 f.) consisted of many more than the ex-archons from the three chief archonships, though less than one might expect if every ex-thesmothete was included. Perhaps one criterion for admission to the Areopagus was payment of a satisfactory *summa honoraria*. This or a high death rate would explain why only two-thirds of the likely ex-archons appear to have qualified.

An honorary classification as Areopagite might bring the right to a special seat at public functions and to other marks of respect without giving a man the right to attend sessions of the Areopagus and to vote on proposals. This need not concern us. It can probably be recognized in a monument like *I.G.*, XIV, 1102 for an athlete, M. Aurelius Asclepiades called Hermodorus, Ἀθηναῖος βουλευτὴς καὶ ἄλλων πόλεων πολλῶν πολείτης καὶ βουλευτής, and in *Insch. v. Olympia*, 464 for a sophist.

The two types of *trigonia* differed as follows:

1. The old Hellenic type referred to three generations of citizenship, while the new or Roman type referred to three generations of good (= free) birth.

2. The old Hellenic type referred expressly to both sides of the family, while the new or Roman type was formulated with reference to the paternal side alone.

3. The old Hellenic type referred to archonships and priesthoods (without mention of the Areopagus), while the new or Roman type seems more concerned with the status of ex-magistrates, and with the preservation of an aristocratic element in the constitution.

In the fourth century it was said that Cleisthenes introduced the custom of using the demotic in order to eliminate the difference in nomenclature between *neopolitai* and citizens of old stock (*Ath. Pol.*, 21). Perhaps without commiting ourselves to this interpretation of his purpose we may use the statement to argue that in the reforms *neopolitai* were not differentiated from *homophyloi*. Μὴ φυλοκρινεῖν, the cry of his supporters, may have meant primarily or secondarily that there should exist no legal category of *neopolitai* (*allophyloi*).[19]

---

[19] P. Lévêque and P. Vidal-Naquet, *Clisthène l'Athénien*, Paris, 1964, p. 13, note 1, write: " L'expression ne nous paraît pas faire allusion aux tribus de Clisthène, comme le pensent les traducteurs, mais aux anciennes tribus qui ne jouent plus désormais de rôle politique." But it does not refer to tribes (*phylai*), because Cleisthenes did indeed divide the city into tribes. The verb is based

The new type of three-generation rule (i.e. on the paternal side alone) may have seemed like a return to the Laws of Solon. Down to the time of Pericles there was never any doubt that Cleisthenes the Alcmaeonid or any other aristocrat born from an aristocratic mother like Agariste of Sicyon or even a Thracian, if she was a princess, was well born and so had the right to hold office. The case of Themistocles differed because his mother was not well born, at least not in the same sense. Plutarch, *Themistocles*, 1 explains that Themistocles was νόθος πρὸς μητρός, and he speaks of the contrast between *nothoi* and εὖ γεγονότες. Cleisthenes apparently put the *nothoi* on the citizen rolls, where they remained until the law of Pericles. Evidence on the status of *nothoi* is lacking, but the writer thinks that in the fourth century many had the status of " Plataeans " at Athens, i.e. citizenship but not the right to high office. They were not in the phratries.

If we have correctly analyzed the eligibility of a man like Cleisthenes the Alcmaeonid, the three-generation rule of the new type could have been plausibly misrepresented as a mere return to ancestral practice. Cleisthenes derived from his father and paternal grandfather the *eugeneia* which made him eligible for high office at Athens. In the sixth century B.C. the custom of a suitable marriage guaranteed the quality of the maternal side.

In Latin the word *libertinus* originally meant " son of a freedman." At Rome, accordingly, there were once three kinds of citizens, namely *liberti*, *libertini*, and homophylous citizens.

We conclude this section with a reference to Cassius Dio, LII, 4, 1-2, who lets Agrippa imply that *homophyloi* are men " who have been reared in the same moral attitudes and been educated by similar laws " and can be expected to serve the fatherland whole-heartedly.

THE DEMOCRATIC ELEMENT

Some sort of a *lectio* determined who among the ordinary citizens were eligible for appointment to the Council of the Five Hundred. It was an honorable appointment for any citizen but it also involved expense. Certain criteria of sanity, age, wealth, morality, livelihood, and birth existed, but wealth may have been reckoned in land or agricultural revenues and may have been circumscribed by membership in religious organizations known as γένη (clans). There is no proof of a property quali-

on *phylon*, not *phyle*. James Day and Mortimer Chambers, *Aristotle's History of Athenian Democracy* (Univ. of California Publications in History, LXXIII), 1962, pp. 113 f. make the same assumption (false, in my opinion) that the verb is connected with *phylai*. On the contrary, it should mean " to separate *phyla*." What it came to mean later is something else again, but it never acquired a connection with the *phylai* into which a city was divided: " Do not make fussy distinctions of race or class." Despite some disagreement, however, I have profited generally from both books, and on Cleisthenes in particular from articles in *Historia* XII and XIII by D. M. Lewis, Kagan and Wüst.

fication, but reappearance of the same families has suggested this to Geagan and other scholars. A list of eligibles is called *recensus* in Latin, ἐξέτασις in Greek.

The inscription from the Roman Market Place, however, in lines 96-103 not only proves the existence of a list of eligibles; it shows that free birth was an absolute requirement for the Council. Since free birth was a requirement for decurions in general, this may not surprise anyone. It corresponds also to the rule for the Equestrian Order, except that the Equestrian Order represented the non-senatorial cream of the freeborn citizens throughout the world within the much larger group formed by *cives Romani*. The real surprise lies in the discovery that the sons and grandsons of freedmen were ineligible for membership in the Areopagus, although they were eligible for the Council of the Five Hundred and (if Roman citizens) for the Equestrian Order. The Areopagites were not just decurions; they were, though only on a small scale, comparable to Roman senators in the conception of an educated class which still thought in terms of city states. In *I.G.*, II², 3607 the Areopagites are called οἱ κράτιστοι Ἀρεοπαγεῖται.

Ever since A. Stein's *Der römische Ritterstand* we have been familiar with the phenomenon of the son of a Roman knight entering upon a senatorial career at the earliest age, and we have known that the son of a good freedman often entered the Equestrian Order, sometimes at a very early age indeed.[20] But it would be wrong to think of the able grandsons of freedmen becoming senators, though it doubtless happened in a very few, very irregular cases.[21]

Whereas in Rome ex-slaves automatically became citizens, we have no indication that in Greek cities freedmen ever received local citizenship automatically. On the contrary, what evidence we have shows that the freedmen constituted a separate group among the resident aliens. For instance, the Debtor Law at Ephesus, *S.I.G.*³, 742, in line 45 mentions separately the *exeleutheroi* (*ca.* 85 B.C.); at Pergamum *O.G.I.S.*, 338 = *I.G.R.*, IV, 289 shows *exeleutheroi* becoming resident aliens; at Syllium *I.G.R.*, III, 801 specifies distributions in descending order to various grades of citizens, then smaller amounts to " those freed with *vindicta*, those freed in a testament, and the resident aliens." At the time of Marcus Aurelius were there many of servile extraction on the list of Athenian citizens?

Aelius Aristides in the Panathenaic Discourse,[22] section 27 (p. 164 Dindorf) said to the Athenians, " you alone can boast of pure *eugeneia* and citizenship." Of course he remembers old claims of autochthonous origin and exaggerates the purity of the

---

[20] See the *eques annorum V* in an inscription published by P. Veyne, *B.C.H.*, XC, 1966, pp. 144-149.

[21] On Tacitus, *Annals*, XIII, 27, 1, *et plurimis equitum, plerisque senatoribus non aliunde originem trahi*, see Mary L. Gordon, *J.R.S.*, XXI, 1931, p. 65 and R. Syme, *Tacitus*, Oxford, 1958, pp. 612 f. It occurred more often on the mother's side.

[22] J. H. Oliver, *The Civilizing Power, A Study of the Panathenaic Discourse of Aelius Aristeides* (Trans. Amer. Philosoph. Society, LVIII, 1), 1968.

Athenians of A.D. 165-167. But a skilled orator like Aristides would have avoided the absurd. Aristides, who was born in A.D. 117,[23] may have been contrasting the Athenians whom he knew in his student days with the citizens of Ionian and Aeolian and new Asian cities of 167. He had not heard that large numbers of freedmen had been enrolled among the citizens of Athens. Perhaps large numbers had not been enrolled. We have no figures.

In a period when a considerable part of the well-to-do Athenian families had acquired Roman citizenship a good number of slaves will surely have been manumitted by Athenian masters who were Roman citizens and will thus have acquired Roman citizenship. Along with Roman citizenship a Roman citizen was expected to have some local citizenship. It is possible that this consideration along with considerations based on the prestige of the sponsoring patrons opened the door to ex-slaves at Athens and elsewhere. Surely freedmen with Roman citizenship could not for long be treated quite like freedmen without Roman citizenship. A profound change, therefore, took place at Athens and other Greek cities between Trajan's reign and that of Marcus Aurelius.

Even so, it is not likely that ex-slaves immediately acquired full status as citizens. If enfranchised at all, they will have acquired demotics, but they may have been excluded from the clans, into which the Demos was now divided for certain religious purposes. There was also a graduated census at Athens, and whoever kept the list of those eligible for the lesser posts and honors did not place the enfranchised freedmen on that list, as we know from lines 97-102.

The sons and grandsons of freedmen, however, were at Athens allowed to find an outlet for their ambition within the Council of the Five Hundred and the lesser offices, whatever that meant. The Herald of the Council and Demos and various other newly important posts may have served this purpose, whereas the archonships, at least the three highest archonships, were traditionally reserved for men from old families. The date at which the Herald of the Council and Demos was raised to a kind of parity with the Herald of the Areopagus need not be the date at which the new order began but was certainly very important.[24] On the other hand, the offices of Herald of the Council and Demos, Hoplite General and other important posts were by no means reserved for new families.

The " Athenians " had asked the emperor to relax the rules so that some of the men of servile descent might remain in the Areopagus and others perhaps enter it. Why? Whether or not the Areopagites themselves concurred in this opinion, the term " Athenians " seems to imply that men of servile descent made such important financial contributions that their enthusiastic support was indispensable to the city. The

[23] C. A. Behr, *A.J.P.*, XC, 1969, pp. 75-77.
[24] See S. Dow, *Prytaneis* . . . (*Hesperia*, Suppl. I), 1932, p. 17 and D. J. Geagan, *The Athenian Constitution after Sulla*, p. 104.

men of dubious antecedents may have contributed on a scale much greater than anyone except Herodes Atticus himself, who was no longer contributing. They were probably ready to pay more than noble Athenians for the same offices. In the years 167/8 and 169/70 no man could be found for the chief archonship,[25] and this in itself indicates the financial troubles of Athens.

The most ambitious study of the sons and grandsons of freedmen, that of Mary L. Gordon, " The Freedman's Son in Municipal Life," *J.R.S.*, XXI, 1931, pp. 65-77, restricts itself to Italy, where the sons of important freedmen often entered the council of port towns and small cities. She believed that they remained in commerce. So did Rostovtzeff. P. Veyne, on the other hand, emphasizes the urge of freedmen and their sons to imitate the local aristocracy whose wealth was in land; in a remarkable study, " Vie de Trimalcion," *Annales*, XVI, 1961, pp. 213-247, Veyne depicts the kind of career that Trimalchio had with a wealth of observations as to epigraphical and other evidence. Veyne does not fail to remind the reader that the *Satyricon* is a work of fiction but he generalizes from this case to deny that the freedmen gave rise to a continuing business class. The reader, however, will not forget that the *Satyricon* is indeed a work of fiction. The writer believes that here Petronius has telescoped three generations into one. For it seems more likely that business in the second century, if not also the first, remained in much the same hands with each successive generation of the freedman's descendants adapting themselves more and more to the style of the municipal and imperial aristocracies. Even the old aristocracy often engaged in money lending; the wealthy new families at Athens had presumably more than the frozen assets of landed estates to make them indispensable to their nobler fellow-citizen. Petronius found the freedman's desire to imitate the aristocracy an amusing trait and so exaggerated for comic effect this visible tendency. Veyne, who was writing before the publication of the inscription from the Roman Market Place,[26] makes many valuable observations on the psychology of the freedmen, corrects our interpretation of Trimalchio, but overstates his case.

One might say that the discrimination against the grandsons of freedmen was a peculiarity of Athens, if the emperor did not show that the age had inherited to its

---

[25] *Hesperia*, XI, 1942, p. 86 and XVIII, 1949, pp. 13 f.

[26] Also H. W. Pleket, " Technology and Society in the Graeco-Roman World," *Acta Historiae Neerlandica*, II, 1967, pp. 1-25, who on p. 20 rightly says, " the freedmen were the only group which, if it had found no social obstacles in its path, would have been able to evolve into a modern entrepreneurship." This is more accurate than the formulation of Carl Brinkmann, *Wirtschafts- und Sozialgeschichte*, 2nd ed., Göttingen, 1953, p. 31: " Umgekehrt wäre das gewerbliche Sklaven- element vielleicht das einzige gewesen, das zu einem antiken Unternehmertum getaugt hätte, wenn die übrigen Voraussetzungen für die Entstehung eines solchen gegeben gewesen wären. Aber das waren sie eben nicht." In my opinion entrepreneurs, though not of a modern type, did exist. See of course M. Rostovtzeff, *Social and Economic History of the Roman Empire*, Oxford, 1926; revised edition edited by P. Fraser, 1957.

discomfort the same discrimination in many other cities. Though commerce never became respectable, the wealth achieved through commerce commanded much respect, and it was through commerce and moneylending that new fortunes could be made. The poor man of free birth remained poor. The " Athenians " who combined against Herodes Atticus were old families in alliance with freedmen and their descendants. The wealth of old families owed much to an early alliance and intermarriage with Italian capitalists of free descent resident in Attica; a new alliance with merchants of servile extraction might in the second century support the old local régime, if statutory discrimination could be overlooked or set aside. Opposed to this were the pride of some influential families and the power of traditional education, which regarded commerce as a form of vice and the usual slave as a rascal. Tacitus (and the upper classes in general) had a strong prejudice against most freedmen and their sons, who were ready to profit from disorder, easily corrupted, and instinctively opportunistic. *Nam et hi malis temporibus partem se rei publicae faciunt,* says Tacitus, *Histories,* I, 76.

In the time of Trajan the sons and grandsons of freedmen, we think, were the rich men most likely to be enrolled in the councils of Bithynia if there were not enough candidates with the qualification of three generations of good birth. This is an inference: the actual words used by Pliny, *Ep.,* X, 79, 3 were that it was *aliquanto melius honestorum hominum liberos quam e plebe in curiam admitti.* The *honesti homines* at Athens were eligible for the Areopagus; the sons and grandsons of freedmen aspired to the Areopagus but apart from the bad years A.D. 161 to 174 they were not acceptable. On the other hand, they were always welcome in the Council of the Five Hundred, if financially qualified citizens and not disqualified in other ways. The sons and grandsons of freedmen were rather different in style of life from the *honesti* whom most of them sought to resemble. The absurd Trimalchio tried to live like a senator, but in reality most of them set their sights upon the urban or provincial aristocracy, and well before the fourth generation the gap had closed and they were indistinguishable.

The Athenian citizens who were not active in the Council of the Five Hundred or in office could participate in the Assembly. Many of these probably lacked the minimum property qualification for the Council; others were too young; a few were subject to penalties which kept them out of office. The whole group of these adult male citizens could be subsumed as οἱ ἐκκλησιάζοντες κατὰ τὰ νομ[ιζόμενα to judge from a letter of Marcus Aurelius and Commodus to the Athenians, Epistle I in the text which we shall present as No. 4.

Pliny, *Ep.,* X, 116, *solent totam bulen atque etiam e plebe non exiguum numerum vocare binosque denarios vel singulos dare* means that (in Bithynia) members of the local council and an important group *e plebe* were customarily invited to celebrations. All the active *honesti* and probably those *e plebe* who would come into consideration for election to the council if there were not enough *honesti* are, we think, included in the invitation. The entire *plebs* was not invited, and perhaps at Athens when Atticus the father of Herodes entertained the entire Demos " according to tribes and clans," not " tribes and demes," he may have been making a similar distinction. The Athenian people whom Aelius Aristides praises in the Panathenaic are organized in tribes and clans, not tribes and demes. The entire Demos at Athens was a smaller group than the entire Polis.

At Pogla a distinction was made among *bouleutai, ekklesiastai,* and plain *politai* who had no part in the Assembly. This appears in an inscription, *I.G.R.*, III, 409, published by M. Rostowzew, " Die Domäne von Pogla," *Jahresh.*, IV, 1901, Beiblatt, coll. 37-46, who inferred influence from Syllium, where *I.G.R.*, III, 800 and 801 attest a descending scale of donations for *bouleutai, geraioi, ekklesiastai,* and plain *politai,* below whom a group consisting of freedmen and *paroikoi* is mentioned. At Syllium and other Greek cities the word *politai* was being used to indicate a special group of non-citizens. Perhaps the word was first extended to include the privileged group of non-citizens and then became restricted in meaning, as the less ambiguous word *astoi* began to be more precise. A man from Syllium might call the Jews of Alexandria *politai* of Alexandria but he would never call them *astoi*. It is the word *astoi*, not *politai*, which we find in an epistle of Marcus Aurelius and Commodus to the Areopagus, Council of the Five Hundred and Demos of the Athenians (No. 4, below).

If the citizens of Athens are the *astoi*, the Polis might be the whole community of Athenians, both the *astoi* and all the privileged non-citizens who made up the community. On occasion the privileged non-citizens might ask and be permitted to join in honoring a benefactor, so that the honor came from the whole Polis instead of the Demos. Where the Polis seems to be contrasted with the Demos as on *I.G.*, II², 3571 but not on 3605, the situation may reflect a separate vote.

We now have evidence for three types of citizens in A.D. 175:

    1) those eligible for the Areopagus, the Council of the Five Hundred, and the higher offices;

    2) those eligible for the Council of the Five Hundred and the lower offices;

    3) those eligible only for the Assembly which served also as a court.

We may compare this with the evidence for public office around 470 B.C.:

    1) Pentacosiomedimni and Knights were eligible for archonships, Areopagus, and Council of the Five Hundred.

    2) Zeugitae were eligible for the lower offices and the Council of the Five Hundred.

    3) Thêtes were ineligible for office but participated in the Assembly.

The evidence for Zeugitae down to 452 B.C. will be found in Aristotle, *Ath. Pol.*, 26, 2. In the section on Solon's establishment of census classes Aristotle, *Ath. Pol.*, 7, 3 says: τοῖς δὲ τὸ θητικὸν τελοῦσιν ἐκκλησίας καὶ δικαστηρίων μετέδωκε μόνον.

One sees by this how important what passed for the constitution of Solon as revised by Cleisthenes remained for Roman Athens and how the changes imposed by new conditions were accommodated within the ancient frame. The basic rules established by Solon and the tribal system invented by Cleisthenes represented for the Athens of Hadrian and Marcus Aurelius the ancestral constitution, the model corrupted, in the opinion of conservatives, by the sortition of archons and then by the reforms of Ephialtes.

One more word on the position of Solon and Cleisthenes in the constitutional history of Athens. Solon was not just one of the Seven Sages; he not only created a tradition of fairness and compromise but he bequeathed the idea of a constitution with real checks and some balance. As Ferrara [27] recognized, Solon's constitution was not just something that writers of the fourth century fathered upon him. Cleisthenes, on the other hand, merely strengthened the democratic element so as to improve the balance. This was not a new constitution. The (popular) council and assembly already existed after Solon, but the new Council of the Five Hundred had much more importance because it was established as, or became after the Reforms of Ephialtes, a probouleutic corporation for a much more important assembly. The Council of the Four Hundred,[28] which presumably resembled the Popular Council at Chios, may not have been probouleutic at all. The Cleisthenean Reforms have more importance here to modern students than to ancient Athenians, who saw the essential part of the balance through popular participation as the creation of Solon. The modalities could be changed, wisely and effectively by Cleisthenes, unwisely and disastrously by later *prostatai* or demagogues, who cared little or nothing about balance. In the fourth century Solon's kinsman, Plato, made the checks and balance of a mixed constitution an ideal for political philosophers and many statesmen thereafter. In the second century after Christ the philosopher Juncus [29] speaks of the minimum age of an Athenian councillor as the age fixed by Solon, not because he thought that the Council of the Five (or Six) Hundred went back to Solon, but because he knew, or thought he knew, that the popular council was an invention of Solon at Athens. It is the *idea* of a second anchor that was important, not the precise shape.

[27] G. Ferrara, *La politica di Solone* (Istituto Italiano per gli Studi Storici, XVII), Naples, 1964, Ch. I.

[28] Many, perhaps most, modern scholars are inclined to deny the very existence of the Council of the Four Hundred, but the Athenians of the Roman Period thought of their Council (and Assembly) as dating from the Reforms of Solon.

[29] J. H. Oliver, *Hesperia*, XXXVI, 1967, p. 54.

DICASTERIES

In the Roman Period the Areopagus itself was one of the most important courts, and for certain cases the Council of the Five Hundred with or without the Assembly as we know from Hadrian's Oil Law, *S.E.G.*, XV, 108 (= Oliver, *The Ruling Power*, pp. 960 f.), and *I.G.*, II², 1103.

In addition to these there were dicasteries which were not necessarily the same as the dicasteries described by Aristotle. In fact, it seems highly unlikely that so democratic a feature of the Athenian constitution would have survived the changes of the time of Marius and Sulla, still less those of the Augustan Period. The evidence for dicasteries was very slight before the discovery of the inscription from the Roman Market Place. Lucian, *The Double Indictment*, 4 and 12 represents Justice empaneling dicasteries on the Areopagus with the promise that anyone who is dissatisfied can appeal to Zeus. The appeal to Zeus was clearly modeled on the appeal to the emperor, and if the Dialogue was composed when Lucian was about forty years old as he says in 32, and if there was only one emperor, that emperor was Marcus Aurelius. So the Dialogue has a bearing on the interpretation of our inscription, but it is hard to identify those elements which came from Lucian's reading of classical authors and those which came from the familiar Athens of Marcus Aurelius. The jurors were supposed to be ἐξ ἁπάντων 'Αθηναίων, to draw three obols for each case, and the juries to vary in size according to the amount involved. The jurors were chosen by lot and the first dicasteries empaneled in 13 consisted of seven, five, five, three and nine respectively and in 14 two more cases received eleven jurors each.[29a]

In the Augustan Period or shortly afterwards the catalogues *I.G.*, II², 1732 and 1733 show that four ἐπιμεληταὶ δικαστηρίων were appointed every year.

The third piece of evidence comes from 65 B.C. when Cicero, *Pro Balbo*, 30 spoke of Roman citizens at Athens serving *in numero iudicum atque Areopagitarum certa tribu certo numero*. The *iudices* were presumably *dikastai*, i.e. jurors for dicasteries, and it could be that in 65 B.C. courts called dicasteries were empaneled with Areopagites and non-Areopagites, the latter from a list of *iudices*. This is far from certain and not compelling evidence for the period of Marcus Aurelius, but the climate of ideas in the Roman Period may suggest that both at Rome and at Athens the lists of jurors had a similarity. The *equites* of the eighteen centuries provided the equestrian *iudices* at Rome.[30] The *homines politici* who at Athens sat periodically in the Council of the Five Hundred provided, I suspect, also the *dikastai*. One list of the eligible men between thirty and sixty would have served both purposes, offering

---

[29a] J. Delz, *Lukians Kenntnis der athenischen Antiquitäten*, Ch. X, " Areopag und Rechtswesen."

[30] See now Claude Nicolet, *L'Ordre équestre à l'époque républicaine* (Bibliothèque des Écoles Françaises d'Athènes et de Rome, CCVII), 1966 and L. R. Taylor, " Republican and Augustan Writers Enrolled in the Equestrian Centuries." *T.A.P.A.*, XCIX, 1968.

dikastai as well as *bouleutai*.[31] But this may not have been true for the Hadrianic Period. It is possible that all dicasts now had to be Areopagites. Favorinus, *Exil.*, 21, 53 through 22, 3 says:

> (*Arete* and *kakia*) are not distinguished in a court of law (ἐν δικαστηρίῳ). For to judge such cases would indeed be valuable, if the dicasts assigned recognition of *kakia* and recognition of *arete* with their perforated and their solid ballot. Rhadamanthys perhaps can find a way in Hades to do this, but the dicasts on the Areopagus (οἱ ἐν ᾽Αρείῳ πάγῳ δικασταί) cannot, nor the ephors in Lacedaemon, to mention those courts (δικαστήρια) which seem to be the most perfect in Greece.

Dicasteries are mentioned by Marcus Aurelius on E, lines 8, 68 and 75. One concerned an adoption, the other two references were to a court judging the eligibility of a man to be an Areopagite. The latter court surely consisted of Areopagites.

---

[31] The identity of the list of those eligible for the Council with the list of those eligible for the dicasteries can in my opinion be traced back to the fifth century. In the Athenian inscription concerning Chalcis, *I.G.*, I², 39 = Meiggs-Lewis, No. 52 = *A.T.L.*, D 17, it is the *boule* and the *dikastai* who are to take the oath at Athens. The establishment of this list goes back in some sense probably to Solon. For Roman feeling compare Livy, XXXIV, 51, 6 on Flamininus in Thessaly, *a censu maxime et senatum et iudices legit.*

CHAPTER III

JEALOUSY, WAR, REFORM AND INNOVATION

The new inscription contains the emperor's own appeal to the Athenians for a reconciliation with Herodes Atticus. About the famous quarrel itself we learn something else significant, namely that it was settled by great concessions on the part of Herodes. On the Quintilii, under whose "rule of Greece" the quarrel allegedly began and reached its climax, we have further information, so that we see more clearly how important they were.

THE QUINTILII

The main evidence on the quarrel between Herodes and the Athenians lies in Philostratus, *Lives of the Sophists*, II, 1, pp. 67-69 Kayser, pp. 166-172 Wright, and begins with a reference to the Quintilii, who were generally believed to have once had a disagreement with Herodes on a question of prizes at the Pythia.

> When these two men were both ruling Greece (τὼ ἄνδρε τούτω, ὁπότε ἄμφω τῆς Ἑλλάδος ἠρχέτην), the Athenians invited them to a meeting of the popular assembly. The Athenians shouted accusations of tyranny, pointing to Herodes and asking that their words be communicated to the ears of the emperor. The Quintilii felt some sympathy with the demos and without delay reported what they had heard. Herodes claimed that he was the victim of a plot on their part, that they were instilling suspicions against him into the Athenians. For it was after that meeting of the assembly that Demostratus and Praxagoras and Mamertinus and many others of their ilk, who opposed Herodes in city affairs, rose into action. Having indicted them as setting the demos against him, Herodes tried to lead them to the court in Rome (ἦγεν ἐπὶ τὴν ἡγεμονίαν),[1] but they secretly made off to the emperor Marcus, confiding in his more democratic nature and in the opportunity (afforded by suspicions against the friends of Lucius Verus).

[1] Some like Wright and Graindor think that the *hegemonia* meant the court of the proconsul, but G. F. Hertzberg, *Die Geschichte Griechenlands unter der Herrschaft der Römer*, II, Halle, 1868, p. 404, note 81a, more correctly interpreted the word as meaning " die Staatsregierung in Rom." So also Groag. The case is not discussed by J. Bleicken, *Senatsgericht und Kaisergericht* (*Abh. Ak. Wiss. Göttingen*, Phil.-hist. Kl., Dritte Folge, 53), 1962, nor by L. Wenger, *Die Quellen des römischen Rechts*, Vienna, 1953. In defense of Hertzberg's interpretation we may cite the, at this time, familiar phrase ἡγεμονὶς Ῥώμη. The bilingual inscription of Vibius Salutaris at Ephesus, *I.L.S.*, 7193 (= Smallwood, *Documents Illustrating the Principates of Nerva, Trajan and Hadrian*, No. 493), refers to silver statues, *unam urbis Romanae*, translated as μίαν ἡγεμονίδος Ῥώμης. An inscription of Lagina, published by Ch. Diehl and G. Cousin, *B.C.H.*, XI, 1887, p. 155, No. 61, honors a man, πρεσβεύσας καὶ ε[ἰς τὴν ἡγεμον]ίδα Ῥώμην πρὸς τὸν κύριο[ν] αὐτοκράτορα, while an inscription of Panamara, published by J. Hatzfeld, *B.C.H.*, LI, 1927, p. 108, No. 83, refers to an embassy εἰς τὴ]ν ἡγεμονίδ[α Ῥώμην. Therefore, it seems to the writer that the phrase ἐπὶ τὴν ἡγεμονίαν in Philostratus should be understood in the same way, " to the city of Rome," but it is possible

Graindor [2] and A. Stein [3] thought that the Quintilii "ruled Greece" as proconsul of Achaia and the proconsul's legate. Since the proconsul, so far as our evidence reaches, was always an ex-praetor and never an ex-consul, Graindor placed the date when the Quintilii "ruled Greece" in the period before their consulship (A.D. 151), Stein in 148-150. Groag,[4] however, refused to admit that the trial was twenty years or so later. Hence he preferred to think that the Quintilii ruled Greece as *consulares*, either under the *divi fratres* or at the beginning of the sole reign of Marcus Aurelius. Hanslik,[5] accordingly, dated their appointment in 169. We know of a rescript to the Quintilii from the *divi fratres* (cited below), but we do not need to connect it with this post.

The trial of Herodes Atticus before Marcus Aurelius at Sirmium occurred around 174 according to Graindor,[6] between 173 and 175 according to Groag, in 173 rather than 174 according to Zwikker.[7] Groag's argument for placing the Quintilii as "rulers of Greece" shortly before the trial seems valid, and so we conclude that they "ruled Greece" as *consulares*. When their "rule of Greece" came to an end we are not told. The whole question of their role is reopened by the discovery of the plaque from the Roman Market Place in which the Quintilii reappear as *consulares* and as representatives of the emperor. Furthermore, the position they occupied in 174/5 is not without relevance to the position they assumed in 177. The discussion ought to be extended to include the role which the Quintilii, the same Quintilii, played in the affairs of Illyricum shortly after the date of our new inscription according to Dio-Xiphilinus, LXXI, 33, 1 (cited below).

Passages which mention "the Quintilii" as if coordinated or paired as in our inscription have a special relevance. They are the following:

Digest, XXXVIII, 2, 16, 4 (from Ulpian): *divi fratres Quintiliis rescrip-serunt*.

that the spelling ἡγεμονίαν represents a corruption of either ἡγεμόνειαν or ἡγεμονίδα. Compare the phraseology in Lucian, *Eunuch*, 12, ἔγνωσαν ἀναπόμπιμον ἐς τὴν Ἰταλίαν ἐκπέμψαι τὴν δίκην. The Athenian enemies of Herodes who appear in Philostratus are like Herodes himself Roman citizens from Athens, a *civitas libera*. Since "the emperor's more democratic nature" implies his role as champion of the provincials against the oligarchy of the Senate, the trial that Herodes probably had in mind was a trial before the Senate, at Rome. It is safest to retain the reading ἡγεμονίαν and interpret it as ἡγεμονικὴν πόλιν, a phrase used for Rome by Dionysius of Halicarnassus, *Antiq.*, IV, 24.

[2] P. Graindor, *Un milliardaire antique, Hérode Atticus et sa famille*, Cairo, 1930, pp. 111-113.

[3] *PIR²*, II, 1936, p. 178.

[4] Edmund Groag, *Die römischen Reichsbeamten von Achaia bis auf Diokletian* (*Akad. Wiss. Wien, Schriften der Balkankommission*, Antiquarische Abt., IX), 1939, col. 130.

[5] R. Hanslik, *R.-E.*, XLVII, 1963, col. 984, s.v. "Quintilius (22)."

[6] *Op. cit.*, pp. 126, 144.

[7] W. Zwikker, *Studien zur Markussäule*, I (Allard Pierson Stichting, Archaeologisch-historische Bijdragen, VIII), Amsterdam, 1941, pp. 198 ff., because mention by Philostratus of the three year old child of Marcus Aurelius seems to him to fit 173 better than 174.

The basic passage is Dio-Xiphilinus, LXXI, 33, 1 (Boissevain, III, p. 273) on Marcus Aurelius in A.D. 178: ἐπειδὴ δὲ τὰ Σκυθικὰ αὖθις αὐτοῦ ἐδεήθη, γυναῖκα τῷ υἱεῖ θᾶττον δι᾽ αὐτὰ ἢ ἐβούλετο Κρισπῖναν συνῴκισεν· οἱ γὰρ Κυιντίλιοι οὐκ ἐδυνήθησαν, καίπερ δύο τε ὄντες καὶ φρόνημα καὶ ἀνδρίαν ἐμπειρίαν τε πολλὴν ἔχοντες, τὸν πόλεμον παῦσαι, καὶ διὰ τοῦτ᾽ ἀναγκαίως αὐτοὶ οἱ αὐτοκράτορες ἐξεστράτευσαν.

Dio-Xiphilinus, LXXII, 5, 3-4 (Boissevain, III, p. 286) on A.D. 183: ἐφόνευσε δὲ καὶ τοὺς Κυιντιλίους, τόν τε Κονδιανὸν καὶ τὸν Μάξιμον· μεγάλην γὰρ εἶχον δόξαν ἐπὶ παιδείᾳ καὶ ἐπὶ στρατηγίᾳ καὶ ὁμοφροσύνῃ καὶ πλούτῳ. ἐκ γὰρ δὴ τῶν προσόντων σφίσιν ὑπωπτεύοντο καλῶν, εἰ καὶ μηδὲν νεώτερον ἐνενόουν, ἄχθεσθαι τοῖς παροῦσι. καὶ οὕτως αὐτοί, ὥσπερ ἔζησαν ἅμα, οὕτω καὶ ἀπέθανον μεθ᾽ ἑνὸς τέκνου· διαπρεπέστατα γὰρ τῶν πώποτε ἐφίλησαν ἀλλήλους, καὶ οὐκ ἔστιν ὅτε οὐδὲ ἐν ταῖς ἀρχαῖς διεχωρίσθησαν. ἐγένοντο δὲ καὶ πολυκτήμονες καὶ παμπλούσιοι, καὶ ἦρχον ὁμοῦ καὶ παρήδρευον ἀλλήλοις.

Dio-Xiphilinus, LXXII, 7, 2: καὶ γὰρ καὶ οἱ Κυιντίλιοι ἀπηγχονήθησαν.

Philostratus, *V.S.*, II, 1, p. 67 Kayser, p. 166 Wright, on Herodes Atticus and the statues of his foster-sons: Κυιντιλίων δέ, ὁπότε ἦρχον τῆς Ἑλλάδος, αἰτιωμένων αὐτὸν ἐπὶ ταῖς τῶν μειρακίων τούτων εἰκόσιν ὡς περιτταῖς, " τί δὲ ὑμῖν " ἔφη " διενήνοχεν, εἰ ἐγὼ τοῖς ἐμοῖς ἐμπαίζω λιθαρίοις;" Ἦρξε δὲ αὐτῷ τῆς πρὸς τοὺς Κυιντιλίους διαφορᾶς, ὡς μὲν οἱ πολλοί φασι, Πυθικὴ πανήγυρις, ἐπειδὴ ἑτεροδόξως τῆς μουσικῆς ἠκροῶντο, ὡς δὲ ἔνιοι, τὰ παισθέντα περὶ αὐτῶν Ἡρώδῃ πρὸς Μᾶρκον· ὁρῶν γὰρ αὐτοὺς Τρῶας μέν, μεγάλων δὲ ἀξιουμένους παρὰ τοῦ βασιλέως " ἐγὼ " ἔφη " καὶ τὸν Δία μέμφομαι τὸν Ὁμηρικόν, ὅτι τοὺς Τρῶας φιλεῖ." ἡ δὲ ἀληθεστέρα αἰτία ἥδε· τὼ ἄνδρε τούτω, ὁπότε ἄμφω τῆς Ἑλλάδος ἠρχέτην, κτλ. (cited above in translation).

Philostratus, *V.S.*, II, 9, p. 87 Kayser, p. 216 Wright, Life of Aelius Aristides, on Marcus Aurelius at Smyrna: τὸν δὲ Ἀριστείδην οὔπω γιγνώσκων ἤρετο τοὺς Κυιντιλίους, μὴ ἐν τῷ ἀσπαζομένων ὁμίλῳ παρεωραμένος αὐτῷ ὁ ἀνὴρ εἴη, οἱ δὲ οὐδὲ αὐτοὶ ἔφασαν ἑωρακέναι αὐτόν, οὐ γὰρ ἂν παρεῖναι τὸ μὴ οὐ ξυστῆσαι, καὶ ἀφίκοντο τῆς ὑστεραίας τὸν Ἀριστείδην ἄμφω δορυφοροῦντες.

Ammianus Marcellinus, XXVIII, 4, 21 in an attack on conditions in Rome: *quidam ex his gregibus* (gambling clubs) *inveniuntur ita concordes ut Quintilios esse existimes fratres.*

Beginning with Ritterling [8] various scholars [9] have interpreted Dio, LXXI, 33, 1

---

[8] Emil Ritterling, " Die Statthalter der pannonischen Provinzen," *Archäologisch-epigraphische Mittheilungen aus Oesterreich-Ungarn*, XX, 1897, pp. 30-31, " Für beide würde eine pannonische Legation im J. 178 gut passen, ist aber jetzt durch ein einwandfreies Zeugnis nicht gesichert," and " Die legati pro praetore von Pannonia Inferior seit Trajan," *Archeologiai Ertesitö*, XLI, 1927, p. 291, with more conviction but still with a question mark, " um 177/78."

[9] For example, W. Reidinger, *Die Statthalter des ungeteilten Pannonien und Oberpannoniens von Augustus bis Diokletian* (*Antiquitas*, Reihe I, 2), Bonn, 1956, pp. 88 f.; A. Mócsy, *R.-E.*,

as referring not to the consuls of A.D. 151, who now appear in our new inscription, but to the younger Quintilii, cousins who were consuls respectively in 172 and 180 and who were never apparently employed as a pair. The two Quintilii in the year 177 took charge of negotiations in Illyricum after the victory and death of M. Bassaeus Rufus, who, as Dobiáš [10] has shown on the basis of *I.L.S.*, 1326, won a great victory in A.D. 177 at the end of summer or beginning of autumn. Smilda,[11] Groag,[12] and Dobiáš [13] confidently identified the Quintilii who took charge of negotiations in Illyricum in 177 or 178 as the consuls of 151. On the evidence they were justified, for any undifferentiated reference to the Quintilii as a pair is necessarily a reference to the famous *Quintilii fratres*.

In our inscription, lines 22-23, the emperor finds it necessary to say that the Quintilii were now relieving him of judicial business. Both our inscription and Dio, LXXI, 33, 1 speak of them as coordinated in a college of two, but we do not know what title they had, whether *correctores, praefecti* or *vicarii per Graeciam* or something else. Among other things they judged appeals *vice imperatoris* and represented the emperor in various ways. Groag, *Achaia*, I, cols. 128-131 leaned toward a subordination of one brother to the other as *corrector* and *comes*, but the wording of our inscription supports the coordination which Mommsen, *Staatsrecht*, II³, p. 852, note 1 proposed and which has usually been rejected because of a gratuitous comment about " Verkehrtheiten der Antoninischen Epoche." We see no reason why in a special case of a new type the emperor should not have appointed a college of two senatorial *vicarii* or *praefecti*, if he so wished. The principate itself had been reorganized in appearance as a college of two with the elevation of Lucius Verus.

Although we could conceive of the Quintilii being placed in charge of " Hellas " right after the return of Lucius Verus at the time when Avidius Cassius was placed in charge of the provinces in Asia, there is no trace of the Quintilii during the crisis of the invasion by the Costoboci who plundered Eleusis in 170. The Roman inscription *C.I.L.*, VI, 31856 = *I.L.S.*, 1327 shows a Roman procurator assuming command of

Suppl. IX, 1962, cols. 590, 592, *s.v.* Pannonia; R. Hanslik, *R.-E.*, XLVII, 1963, cols. 958 f., *s.vv.* Quintilius (23 and 26).

[10] Josef Dobiáš, " La seconda spedizione germanica degli imperatori Marco e Commodo alla luce delle iscrizioni," *Atti del III. Congresso Internazionale di Epigrafia Greca e Latina*, Rome, 1959, pp. 1-14.

[11] H. Smilda in the index to Boissevain's Dio, vol. IV, 1926, p. 553.

[12] *Achaia*, I, note 544.

[13] *Op. cit.*, pp. 5-6. In note 4 he contradicts Ritterling: " L'obiezione però che tutti e due i consoli dell'anno 151 sarebbero stati nel 177 già molto vecchi non vale; proprio in loro favore parla il fatto che Dione accentua la loro sapienza ed esperienza." Further bibliography will be found in Árpád Dobó, *Die Verwaltung der römischen Provinz Pannonien von Augustus bis Diocletianus*, Amsterdam, 1968, pp. 67 f., who makes Sex. Quintilius Condianus (cos. 151) legate of Lower Pannonia A.D. 176-179 and his brother or nephew (*sic*), Quintilius Maximus, legate of the consular province of Upper Pannonia.

the defense. This suggests that the Quintilii had not yet been appointed to rule " Hellas " and that the need in Achaia, Epirus and Macedonia for high-ranking Roman officials in whose political and military capacity the emperor had complete confidence now for the first time made itself felt. A special post in European Greece for the military crisis of 170/1 was then established under the Quintilii and lasted until the peace of 175. The Quintilii next accompanied Marcus on his tour of the Eastern provinces in 175 and 176 after the revolt of Avidius Cassius.

When war on the Danube broke out again in 177, Marcus Aurelius remembered only too well what had happened in the Asiatic provinces in 161 and in the European provinces in 169 and 170, and therefore he sent the Quintilii back to the neighborhood. It was not a military command. M. Bassaeus Rufus in the emperor's stead led the troops into battle, while the Quintilii relieved the emperor of administrative chores such as the hearing of cases on appeal. They were not separated, one in one province, the other in a different province. On the contrary, always working as a college of two *praefecti* or *vicarii* or something else, they replaced the emperor for much of his administrative labor in more than one province, in an area like a *dioecesis* of the Late Empire. This was the kind of assignment they had *in Graecia* in 174/5 and now again *in Illyrico* in 177/8. When Bassaeus Rufus died, the Quintilii *fratres* automatically assumed also the military command.

It has been convincingly argued, even proved,[14] that the Pannonias were in the time of Galerius, at least until the death of Constantius Chlorus, grouped with Illyricum and not with Italy. After the abdication of Diocletian and Maximian, *Caesares duo facti, Severus et Maximinus: Maximino datum est orientis imperium, Galerius sibi Illyricum, Thracias et Bithyniam tenuit. Severus suscepit Italiam et quidquid Herculius obtinebat* (*Exc. Val.*, ed. Moreau, Pars prior, III, 5). The importance for us lies in the existence of a military and administrative area called Illyricum which comprised the Pannonias and " Hellas." Also under the first tetrarchate the *dioecesis Pannoniarum* had belonged to the Eastern empire.

The position assigned to the old but still vigorous Quintilii by Marcus Aurelius was superficially not unlike that assigned to the aged Plutarch by Hadrian. George Syncellus, p. 659 Dindorf, includes among his notes for the reign of Hadrian: Πλούταρχος Χαιρωνεὺς φιλόσοφος ἐπιτροπεύειν Ἑλλάδος ὑπὸ τοῦ αὐτοκράτορος κατεστάθη γεραιός. The *Suda*, *s.v.* Πλούταρχος, 1793 Adler, says: Πλούταρχος Χαιρωνεὺς τῆς Βοιωτίας, γεγονὼς ἐπὶ τῶν Τραιανοῦ τοῦ Καίσαρος χρόνων καὶ ἐπίπροσθεν, μεταδοὺς δὲ αὐτῷ Τραιανὸς τῆς τῶν ὑπάτων ἀξίας προσέταξε μηδένα τῶν κατὰ τὴν Ἰλλυρίδα ἀρχόντων παρὲξ τῆς αὐτοῦ γνώμης τι διαπράττεσθαι. It is quite possible that the lexicographer mistook Traianus Hadrianus for Trajan, because the supervision exercised by Plutarch is

---

[14] Ingomar Weiler, " Huic Severo Pannoniae et Italiae urbes et Africae contigerunt (Exc. Val. IV, 9)," *Historia*, XIII, 1964, pp. 373-376.

surely that mentioned by Syncellus.[15] In neither case is the supervision limited to the province of Achaia. In one case the area is the larger area known as Hellas = Graecia, and in the other case the area is the larger area known as Illyris = Illyricum.[16] It is Hellas = Graecia which the Quintilii are said to have been " ruling " shortly before 173 and where we find them in 174/5. In 177 they were active in the merely praetorian province of Lower Pannonia. If the whole of what Illyris meant had been assigned to the Quintilii, the area included the Pannonias and the three provinces of Graecia. The term Illyris was proper for the Quintilii in 177 but improper for Plutarch, whose area corresponded to that of the Quintilii in 174/5.

We return to Herodes Atticus.

Two quarrels have become intertwined. One quarrel concerned the relations of Herodes Atticus with the Athenians.

Herodes Atticus came from an aristocratic priestly family on his father's or paternal grandfather's side and from a family with a name suggesting descent from Italian bankers and businessmen on his mother's side. His father had been immensely wealthy like his paternal grandfather, and he himself inherited senatorial rank and a position in the world along with a large part of the family fortune. He differed from his father and paternal grandfather in the objects of his ambition and in his neglect of business. He was financially far less competent and generally less practical but more artistic and more interested in reviving the ancient literary culture. As one of the leading figures of the period he should have for us a special interest. His vanity appears in inscriptions and even in Philostratus who dedicated the *Lives of the Sophists* to a man whom he took for a descendant of Herodes. In rhetorical talent he was well endowed during a period when rhetoric dominated education. The opposition to Herodes arose partly from envy and partly from resentment against his

[15] Ed. Groag, *Achaia*, I, Vienna, 1939, cols. 145-147 accepts the genuineness of both references and interprets the *Suda* to mean that Trajan or rather the Senate at the request of Trajan honored Plutarch with the *ornamenta consularia*; and he accepts the statement of Eusebius (source of George Syncellus) that Hadrian made Plutarch a procurator. K. Ziegler, *Plutarchos* (Stuttgart-Waldsee, 1949, separate publication of the article later published in *R.-E.*), cols. 22-23, inferred that Plutarch's friendship with Sosius Senecio brought him into personal contact with Trajan, who did something special for Plutarch, though what it was remains obscure. Ziegler accepts the statement by Eusebius only in part; he does not believe that Hadrian made him a procurator but he thinks that under Hadrian Plutarch received the possibility of political influence over a considerable area. The two notices, I think, are indeed to be taken seriously with Ziegler, Groag and even G. F. Hertzberg, *Die Geschichte Griechenlands unter der Herrschaft der Römer*, II, pp. 182 f., but probably need to be recognized as one report in two versions and certainly need to be compared with what we hear about the Quintilii. H. Dessau, *Hermes*, XLV, 1910, pp. 615-617 rejected both references as fantastic. For a similar confusion between Trajan and Hadrian see Dio, LXIX, 17, 3 with Syme's comment in *Gnomon*, XXV, 1957, p. 490, note 2. C. P. Jones, *J.R.S.*, LVI, 1966, pp. 63-66 argues that Plutarch died not later than A.D. 125.

[16] Compare the phraseology of *C. Th.*, VI, 4, 11: *per Achaiam, Macedoniam, totumque Illyricum.*

tyrannical spirit, because Herodes wished to cut a figure as a great benefactor like a beneficent Pisistratus and refused to interpret his father's *fideicommissa* like the Athenians who expected an end of the economic dependence of Athens on the wealth of Atticus.[17] The new inscription from the Roman Market Place suggests that in the end Herodes was forced to yield to public opinion and perhaps pressure from Marcus Aurelius and to offer some sort of compensation. The economic aspect of the quarrel appears in Philostratus less clearly than in the new inscription, lines 87-94.

This was the tyranny which the "Athenians" denounced, a type characteristic of the Roman Period. The melodramatic appeal to Marcus Aurelius in Philostratus, *Lives of the Sophists*, p. 68 Kayser, p. 168 Wright, "Save the Athenians," applied to this alleged economic tyranny.

The other quarrel was a quarrel between *consulares* jealous of their prestige. Who were the men of highest rank in Greece, socially, culturally, politically? The pretensions of Herodes Atticus, teacher and host of Lucius Verus, conflicted with the dignity of the Quintilii, who too were men of famous culture. The disagreement over prizes at the Pythia represented a public challenge and involved a loss of prestige. The great millionaire *consularis* Herodes Atticus was not accustomed to contradictions from the inferior proconsuls whom the Senate sent to Greece. The brothers Quintilii, who were friends of Marcus and of consular rank themselves, behaved differently. They did not defer to Herodes.

LUCIUS VERUS AND REFORM

The Greek city began as a republic of small landholders. By the standards of the Age of Marcus Aurelius even the nobles of the archaic period were small landholders and were eventually brought within the limits of a republic whose security depended primarily on local hoplites, who were not great landholders but who had the possibility of enough leisure for public activity. In Athens and certain other cities "extreme democracy" led to disaster and produced a reaction. The classical works of Plato and Aristotle assumed that the men worthy to be full citizens were landholders, not the aliens and ex-slaves who made money in commerce and services. Ancient religious rites and festivals connected with agriculture kept alive the dignity of farming as an activity worthy of the *homo politicus*. In the early period the wealthier members of a polis community were usually farmers, so that a contrast often found later did not exist. Aristotle did not count agriculture as chrematistic.

From the time of Plato much thought was given to the ethical foundations of a city. What sort of education was suitable for the future citizen? A laborer or a

---

[17] R. Bogaert, *Banques et banquiers dans les cités grecques*, Leyden, 1968, p. 85 infers from Philostratus that Herodes found various notes of indebtedness to his father in his father's estate and that he turned them over to several banks with instructions to deduct them from the five minas which Atticus had left to each citizen.

merchant did not need the kind of education the *homo politicus* had to have. Further-more, the dignity of labor depended on the contribution which the labor made to a citizen's *arete*. Agricultural labor was considered a splendid preparation for the rigors of military service and was highly respected if it was not carried out at someone else's order, but banausic occupations made no contributions to the moral and physical de-velopment of a true citizen. The life of a *homo oeconomicus* seemed unsuitable for a *homo politicus*. The ability to make money was not admired as ability *per se*, and if lucrative services contributed to *tryphe*, the luxury which Greek moralists deplored, they were positively disgraceful.[18]

Under the Roman Peace important changes occurred. Commerce unrestricted greatly increased, and the men who participated in commerce often became much richer and more important than the *homo oeconomicus* of an earlier period. In agri-culture, an abundance of slave labor permitted a growth of large estates at the expense of smaller estates in the first century after Christ.[19] Then in the second century the richest men of old lineage in Greek cities frequently received Roman citizenship, and their sons frequently entered the ranks of Roman senators or the imperial service. Thus the sons tended to be withdrawn from the service of their original cities. Fur-thermore, a decline in the number of slaves probably occurred in the second century, and a shortage of agricultural labor can be inferred from the settlement of barbarians within the empire by Marcus Aurelius. The profits of farming declined, while those of commerce increased.

Thus the underpinnings of the polis were loosened. The whole system came into danger because the cities depended on private outlays for much of the public expenses. Officeholders were unpaid at the top. Festivals were not supported by the public treasury, or the treasurer was supposed to fill the treasury from his own resources. Only rich men could serve properly as eponymous archon, gymnasiarch or agonothete, and the old land-owning families now had immunity or were no longer the wealthiest men of the community. With the accession of Marcus Aurelius and Lucius Verus

---

[18] These old attitudes continue into the Roman Period, as Dieter Nörr, " Zur sozialen und rechtlichen Bewertung der freien Arbeit in Rom," *Zeitschrift der Savigny-Stiftung*, LXXXII, 1965, pp. 67-105 argues. See also Francesco M. De Robertis, *Lavoro e lavoratori nel mondo romano*, Bari, 1963, and C. Nicolet, *L'ordre équestre à l'époque républicain*, Paris, 1966, pp. 360 f. and 500 f.

[19] Note the reference to slave and freedman in *S.E.G.*, XV, 108, Hadrian's Oil Law, cited by John Day, who, however, in his excellent *Economic History of Athens under Roman Domination*, New York, 1942, p. 159 comments that we have no information on agricultural laborers (for the period from Sulla to Augustus). On pp. 220 f. he says: " A few wealthy men, like Herodes Atticus, owned numerous slaves and, in addition, had numerous freedmen in their services. But we must conclude that slaves formed only a very inconsiderable part of the laboring population of Athens." Nevertheless, larger numbers could have been available in the Flavian and Trajanic Period. It is, however, not a question of slaves, but of freedmen from the time of Hadrian. For evidence that estates in the second century after Christ were indeed larger see Day, pp. 234 f., 250.

the problem which had been building up for a long while, suddenly, perhaps because of war, became critical.

Unlike the situation in the fourth century the *homo oeconomicus* was now probably wealthier than the *homo politicus*. If the city was to survive, new revenues were necessary. The wealth of the traders or sons and grandsons of traders could be enlisted for the city. Should this take the form of a sweeping aside of old ideals of civilization and public service? The cities had no sophisticated revenue service such as would enable them to collect a fair income tax even if the idea had occurred. The liturgy system could be altered but not replaced. The wealth of a millionaire like Herodes Atticus tended to escape the city entirely. The traders were eager to invest in land and cut a figure as landowners; unlike their predecessors, they could do so now, but the background of the traders was not the moral background of the traditional city. Some who did not think like Hellenes would scrap the whole ideal of the good city and eliminate the traditional distinction between the worthy and the unworthy to rule. Others would hang on to the ideal in the confidence that they knew what the city should be but yielded temporarily to fortune which had intervened. The modern man may think that institutions have to change because times change, but an ancient theorist would be far less apt to think that the ideal state changed with the times. The ideal state remained the same, even when τὰ συμβάντα forced temporary accommodations on the real city.

The new inscription from the Roman Market Place shows that many saw the solution in a break with the ideal polis of Plato and other Greco-Roman thinkers. Some thought of the break as temporary; others may have welcomed it as permanent and looked to new ideals which were not those of a world of city states; some had no ideals, only ambition. While certain struggles took on a cultural or religious character, those reflected in the inscription from the Roman Market Place arose from practical and theoretical considerations how best to keep the old cities in operation. Changes had to come and did come. But how successful were they and how far should they be pushed? Neither Marcus Aurelius nor Lucius Verus wished to sweep away the entire structure of the city state, but they differed in their assessments.

An accusation such as that by Herodes Atticus against Marcus Aurelius,[20] " This is what I get for showing hospitality to Lucius Verus, though it was you who sent him to me," suggests that a change of policy followed the return of Lucius Verus. The junior emperor had been on excellent terms with certain very wealthy men of the East. Documents at Gortyn and Eleusis bear out in the case of the Cretan millionaire Flavius Xenion [21] the loyalty and admiration for Lucius Verus. Resentment against the influence of these men and their agents may have had much to do with

---

[20] Philostratus, *V.S.*, p. 68 Kayser, p. 170 Wright.
[21] J. H. Oliver, " The Eleusinian Endowment," *Hesperia*, XXI, 1952, pp. 381-399. See No. **16** below.

the bad reputation which Lucius Verus certainly acquired, and the changes which followed his return may have had much to do with stories of the alleged disapproval of Marcus Aurelius. Perhaps, as Carrata Thomes [22] suggests, the rivalry of the two entourages eventually impaired relations between the two, at first harmonious, emperors.

On the other hand, the German invasions and the Plague may have produced a change in the attitude of Marcus Aurelius. It is possible that financial relief for the cities through a greater participation by families of servile origin was an attractive policy for a while and had the enthusiastic backing of Herodes Atticus, his Cretan friend Flavius Xenion, and Lucius Verus. The Greek cities had lost many families by promotion to the Equestrian and Senatorial Orders; precisely these important men from old Greek cities realized that the cities needed new men to take their place and supported their own favorites. With the Plague and the German invasion of Italy a wave of anxiety swept over the Roman leadership. These terrible events [23] were attributed to divine anger and among the scapegoats were Christians [24] and freedmen. Commerce still seemed a form of vice and other men's freedmen were traditionally rascals.[25] Reforms had let the sons and grandsons of freedmen (rather than freedmen themselves) into the government of old cities. Then came disaster, and along with the reaction came a sensational trial involving freedmen of Herodes Atticus before the emperor himself. In this climate the errors of judgment tended to be attributed to Lucius Verus who was already dead.

In the trial at Sirmium the Athenians attacked the freedmen of Herodes along with Herodes himself. The emperor, while he continued to love Herodes, felt resentment against the latter's freedmen.

Herodes himself had once attacked the freedmen of his father Claudius Atticus,[26] because they had induced Claudius Atticus to favor the Athenians at the expense of Herodes in his will. The sons and grandsons of those freedmen were hardly the ones

---

[22] Franco Carrata Thomes, *Il regno di Marco Aurelio*, Turin, 1953, p. 87.

[23] J. F. Gilliam, " The Plague under Marcus Aurelius," *A.J.P.*, LXXXII, 1961, pp. 225-251 writes on p. 249 that " after making due allowance for distortion and rhetorical convention, it is quite clear that there was a great and destructive epidemic under Marcus Aurelius." The psychological effect, it seems to me, was unusually great at the time because of the concomitance of other woes. See also S. Mazzarino, *Trattato di storia Romana*, Rome, 1956, p. 221, and F. Millar, *A Study of Cassius Dio*, Oxford, 1964, p. 13, note 4.

[24] W. H. C. Frend, *Martyrdom and Persecution in the Early Church*, Oxford, 1965, Ch. X, " The Years of Crisis, 165-180." J. H. Oliver and Robert E. A. Palmer, " Minutes of an Act of the Roman Senate," *Hesperia*, XXIV, 1955, pp. 320-349 submit that in A.D. 176 Marcus Aurelius yielded unwisely to arguments based on religion in the case of the *trinqui* in Gaul.

[25] P. W. Harsh, " The Intriguing Slave in Greek Comedy," *T.A.P.A.*, LXXXVI, 1955, pp. 135-142; S. Lauffer, " Die Sklaverei in der griechisch-römischen Welt," *Gymnasium*, LXVIII, 1961, p. 387.

[26] Philostratus, *V.S.*, II, 1, p. 58 Kayser, p. 144 Wright.

whom Herodes had wished to advance, but they may have been the men whom the enemies of Herodes had advanced. The " Athenians," which means or subsumes the enemies of Herodes, had protested against the emperor's order to throw the sons and grandsons of freedmen out of the Areopagus and had finally persuaded the emperor to allow the grandsons and even some sons to remain. Some sons or grandsons had, it appears from lines 66-68, entered the Areopagus after the emperor's first letter, that is, during the exile of Herodes and the domination of Athens by his enemies. Others from before the first letter were already there with the approval of the Athenians.

These are men of just the right age to be descended from the freedmen who aroused the indignation of the young Herodes by currying favor with the Athenians at his expense, and it would be safe to identify at least some of them as such. Since the emperor did not remain steadfast in his attempts to purify the Areopagus, it looks as if the reforms encouraged by Lucius Verus according to my interpretation still had some effect. At least they brought new people into the Areopagus, though not the people whom Herodes had wished.

In two dialogues Lucian transfers to heaven the problems of Greek cities. In Θεῶν Ἐκκλησία, 3, 4, 6 and 14 the criticism was made that many foreigners, both Greeks and barbarians, had infiltrated themselves into citizenship. Some of these were demigods, others still carried the marks of fire (surely an allusion to branded slaves). Many who were half mortal were not content that they themselves shared in the synedria of the gods but were fraudulently registering even their servants. *Zeus Trag.*, 7-9 deals with the civic assembly of the gods and the preferment there of barbarians who were coarse but made of gold or silver over Greek gods who were of superior *arete* but made of ivory, bronze or marble; Hermes says to Zeus, πλουτίνδην κελεύεις ἀλλὰ μὴ ἀριστίνδην καθίζειν, καὶ ἀπὸ τιμημάτων. The peace and prosperity which had been almost uninterrupted during the reigns of Hadrian and Antoninus Pius doubtless contributed to a shifting of wealth from the old families who controlled the Council of a Greek city to the new families engaged in commerce, the sons and grandsons of freedmen. We need not postulate much in the way of capitalism, but trade there certainly was and money lending too. Particularly the Greeks at this time saw an influx of wealth among people with whom Lucius Verus probably sympathized more than Marcus.

The *Vita Veri* draws a sharp contrast between the profligacy of Lucius Verus and the virtue of Marcus Aurelius. Undoubtedly Lucius Verus lived on a more extravagant scale and indulged in more pleasure, but in policy he usually followed the lead of Marcus Aurelius *ut legatus proconsuli vel praeses imperatori* (*V. Veri*, 4, 2). One area, however, found them far apart. *Libertis inhonestius indulsit*, says the *Vita*, 8, 6, *et multa sine fratre disposuit*.

For the contrast between the *divi fratres* the two most interesting references lie in the *Vita Veri*, 9, 3-6 and in the new inscription from the Roman Market Place at Athens. The former [27] reports that freedmen had great influence with Lucius Verus. Nothing about Lucius Verus is more significant than the information or story that he gave the widow of the consular Annius Libo, a first cousin of Marcus, to the freedman Agaclytus *invito Marco* to be his wife: *denique nuptiis a Vero celebratis Marcus convivio non interfuit.* The writer goes on to say in respect to other freedmen that Marcus cashiered them after the death of Verus: *quos omnes Marcus post mortem Veri specie honoris abiecit,* where *specie honoris* perhaps means " from an unmerited distinction of office."

It is against this background that the attempt of Marcus Aurelius to undo what Lucius Verus had encouraged should be studied. As we learn from the new inscription, he wrote to Athens and to other cities; at Athens he called for stringent regulation of the Areopagus. Three generations of good birth, at least in the paternal line, were required. But it proved hard or even impossible to impose this rule.

We may try to give dates. Lucius Verus was in the East from 162 to 165, and among the places he visited were Corinth and Athens: *et apud Corinthum et Athenas inter symphonias et cantica navigabat* (*S.H.A., Vita Veri*, 6, 9). In the years 167/8 and 169/70 Athens had been unable to find anyone to undertake the expense of the archonship (*Hesperia*, XI, 1942, p. 86). This attests a shortage of public funds, but a number of lesser benefactors came to the aid of their tribes during prytanies.[28] Between 162 and 166 Lucius Verus encouraged Athens and other cities to accept sons and grandsons of freedmen into high political office. Later as sole emperor, hence in 169 at the earliest, Marcus Aurelius took steps to discourage this practice. To Athens he sent his first letter on the subject before the revolt of Avidius Cassius, a letter known only from a reference in the new inscription from the Roman Market Place. Then in the year A.D. 174 he received an appeal from the Athenians to relax the rule. The Athenians were now suffering as a result of their quarrel with Herodes Atticus and needed whatever help they could get from well-to-do families.

After the death of Marcus Aurelius, or rather after the conspiracy of 182, the young Commodus became an enemy of certain conservative circles and adopted the liberal attitude toward social distinctions. The freedmen of his own entourage doubtless influenced the attitude toward freedmen and their sons everywhere.

[27] P. Lambrechts, " L'empereur Lucius Verus: Essai de réhabilitation," *L'antiquité classique,* III, 1934, pp. 173-201 demonstrates the prejudice of the *S.H.A.* against Lucius Verus but does not attack the validity of this anecdote. On which see, however, T. D. Barnes, " Hadrian and Lucius Verus," *J.R.S.*, LVII, 1967, pp. 65-79, on p. 73. The important article by Barnes brings out the value of the *Vita Veri*, i.e. its relative credibility. It is ironic that the son of Agaclytus married Vibia Aurelia Sabina, daughter of Marcus Aurelius, many years later, in the reign of Septimus Severus.

[28] J. H. Oliver, " Patrons Providing Financial Aid to the Tribes of Roman Athens," *A.J.P.*, LXX, 1949, pp. 299-308, 403.

In the time of Lucius Verus, however, the promotion of the sons and grandsons of freedmen was only part of the financial reforms which most of the Greek cities needed, and with these reforms the νεωτερισμοί, as they are called in two inscriptions at Sparta, may well be connected, if we assume that much the same problem existed in both cities.[29] The first text is that of C. Julius Arion, published by A. M. Woodward, *B.S.A.*, XXVII, 1926, pp. 234-236.

2.

Γάιος Ἰούλιος Ἀρίων, ἀριστίνδης, σύνδικος
ἐπὶ τὰ ἔθη, πρεσβευτὴς ἰς Ῥώμην
πρὸς τὸν ἐπὶ τῇ καθέδρᾳ τοῦ Αὐτο
κράτορος Καί(σαρος) Γά⟨ου⟩ιον Μάξιμον προῖκα,
5   συνθύτης ἰς Νέαν πόλιν ὑπερχρονί
αν μὴ λαβών, Πανέλλην, γερουσίας,
ἔφορος ἐπὶ τῶν νεωτερισμῶν, γερου
σίας τὸ β′, ταμίας ἐπὶ Σωκράτους

4 ΚΑΙΓΑΙΟΝ stone, Καί(σαρος) Γά⟨ου⟩ιον Groag (*Achaia*, I, col. 71, note 291).

Gavius Maximus (*PIR²*, G 104) served as praetorian prefect for twenty years under Antoninus Pius, but an embassy like this of C. Julius Arion would not have taken place at the beginning of this period. Rather this embassy took place in A.D. 157/8 or not long before. Some years later Arion became ephor in charge of the reforms or else, as Woodward later suggested, ephor first and then officer in charge of the reforms.

The date of the reforms was narrowed still further by A. M. Woodward, *B.S.A.*, XLIII, 1948, pp. 219-223 on the basis of *I.G.*, V (1), 44 which is known only from a copy by Fourmont and which reads as follows:

3.

Λυκεῖνος (Λυκείνου)Τι[β. Κλαυδίου Βρασίδα (?)]
συνέφηβος, ἱ[ππάρχης ἐπὶ – –, διαβέτης (?) ἐπὶ]
Μνάσωνος το[ῦ Λυσίππου, πράκτωρ τῶν ἀπὸ Εὐ]
ρυκλέους, σι[τώνης ἐπὶ – – – – – – –, στρατευ]
5   σάμενος τὰς εὐ[τυχεστάτας – – – – – – στρα]
τείας ἐπὶ Κλ. [Β]ρ[ασίδα (?) καὶ – – – –, καὶ]
τειμηθεὶς ⟨φ⟩αλ[άροις στρεπτοῖς, ἐπιμελητὴς]
[Κορ]ωνείας, λοχαγὸ[ς ἐπὶ – – –, – – – – – – –]
[γ]ερουσ[ί]ας ἐπὶ [– – – – – – – – – ἐπὶ τῶν]
10   [ν]εωτερισμῶν [– – – – – – – – – – – – – – –]
[νομ]οφύλαξ [ἐπὶ – – – – – – – – – – – – – – –]

[29] In line 63 Marcus Aurelius speaks of "many other cities."

$[\dots]\pi\alpha\tau\rho o[\,.\,]o\mu\omega[\,.\,\sigma\upsilon\sigma\tau\rho\alpha\tau\epsilon\upsilon\sigma\acute{\alpha}\mu\epsilon\nu o\varsigma\ K\alpha\acute{\iota}\sigma\alpha\rho\iota]$

$M\acute{\alpha}\rho\kappa\omega\ \acute{\epsilon}\gamma\ [K]o\acute{\iota}\lambda\eta\ [\Sigma\upsilon\rho\acute{\iota}\alpha - - - -,\ \acute{\epsilon}\pi\iota\mu\epsilon\lambda\eta\tau\grave{\eta}\varsigma]$

$\tau\hat{\eta}\varsigma\ \pi\acute{o}\lambda\epsilon[\omega\varsigma\ \acute{\epsilon}\pi\grave{\iota} - - - - - - - - - -,\ \pi\rho\acute{\epsilon}\sigma\beta\upsilon\varsigma]$

15 $\tau\hat{\eta}\varsigma\ \gamma\epsilon\rho o\upsilon[\sigma\acute{\iota}\alpha\varsigma\ \acute{\epsilon}\pi\grave{\iota} - - - - - - - - - - -,\ \acute{\epsilon}\pi\grave{\iota}]$

$\tau\hat{\omega}\nu\ \delta\iota\kappa\hat{\omega}\nu\ [\acute{\epsilon}\pi\grave{\iota} - - - - - - - - - - - - - \sigma\acute{\upsilon}\nu\alpha\rho]$

$\chi o\varsigma\ \pi\alpha\tau\rho o[\nu\acute{o}\mu\omega\nu - - - - - - - - - - - - - \tau\epsilon]$

$\tau\epsilon\iota\mu\alpha\mu\acute{\epsilon}\nu[o\varsigma - - - - - - - - - - - - - - -,\ \beta\acute{\iota}]$

$\delta\epsilon o\varsigma\ \acute{\epsilon}[\pi\grave{\iota}]\ II[- - - - - - - - - - - - - - - - - -]$

$[- -]$

1 Woodward. 2 ἐπὶ Kolbe, cetera Woodward. 3 το[ῦ et ἐπὶ Kolbe, Λυσίππου et Εὐ]|ρυκλέους Boeckh (*C.I.G.*, I, 1254), πράκτωρ τῶν ἀπὸ Woodward ut in *B.S.A.*, XXVI, 1923-5, p. 166, B 9. 4 σι[τώνης Woodward, πολιτευ- Boeckh, στρατευ-Kolbe. 5 Hiller von Gaertringen apud Kolbe. 6 Woodward. 7 ΤΑΛ Fourmont, ⟨φ⟩αλ[άροις Woodward, στρεπτοῖς Tod apud Woodward (cf. *I.L.S.* 2663), τα[ῖς μεγίσταις τιμαῖς Kolbe, ἐπιμελητὴς Boeckh. 8 ἐπὶ Kolbe, cetera Boeckh. 9 [γ]ερουσ[ί]ας Boeckh, ἐπὶ τῶν Woodward. 10 Hiller von Gaertringen et Wilhelm apud Kolbe. 11 Boeckh. 12 πατρο[ν]όμω Boeckh, [ἐπὶ] πατρο[ν]όμω Kolbe, στρατευσάμενος (?) σὺν Καίσαρι Woodward, συστρατευσάμενος Oliver. 13 ἐπιμελητὴς Kolbe, cetera Woodward. 14 πόλε[ως Boeckh, ἐπὶ et πρέσβυς Woodward. 15 γερου[σίας Boeckh, ἐπὶ Kolbe. 16 Kolbe. 17 πατρο[νόμων (?) Kolbe, τε]|τειμαμένος Woodward. 18-19 βί]|δεος [ἐπὶ] Boeckh.

As Woodward points out, the successful campaigns mentioned in lines 5-6 are those during two years of fighting against the Parthians, A.D. 163-165 (or 166). In line 13, however, Woodward has brilliantly identified a reference to the campaign following the overthrow of Avidius Cassius in Hollow Syria in 175/6. He continues:

> As, moreover, the subject of this *cursus* held three offices between the year of the νεωτερισμοί and his second period of eastern campaigning in 175-6, the *terminus ad quem* for the former must be put in 171-2. In other words, the possible date for the νεωτερισμοί has been narrowed down to the period 168-171/2.

The (constitutional) reforms at Sparta may have come before the death of Lucius Verus but certainly after his departure from Greece.

References to the protection or championing of the Lycurgan customs in *I.G.*, V (1), 560 which honors M. (not P.) Aurelius Chrysogonus, and in Woodward's new text of *I.G.*, V (1), 517 (*B.S.A.*, XLIII, 1948, p. 253) should be remembered in connection with these reforms. Are not many changes both rightly and wrongly presented as a return to the past? *I.G.*, V (1), 500 attests διδ]άσκαλοι οἱ ἀμ[φὶ τὰ Λυκούργει]α ἔθη under Marcus Aurelius and Lucius Verus, *I.G.*, V (1), 554 an ἐξηγητὴς τῶν Λυκουργείων ἐθῶ[ν] somewhat later.

The constitutional reforms, which were partly financial, were conceived probably in the time of the joint rule of Marcus Aurelius and Lucius Verus.[30] At Athens the latter still enjoyed great prestige when the Athenians were celebrating the victory

---

[30] See *Hesperia*, XXXII, 1963, p. 25, No. 26 for a fragment of a letter to Athens (= *S.E.G.*, XXI, 508).

of the brother-loving emperors.[31] The earlier letter, the one to which Marcus refers on EM 13366 (lines 66-67), could have been written after reforms had had a chance to work for a while. Certainly the trial of Herodes at Sirmium left Marcus Aurelius disgusted with the part played by freedmen at Athens and may well have been the moment (A.D. 173 or 174) when he wrote the earlier letter to the Athenians telling them to drive out of the Areopagus those who did not have the three-generation qualification, and to remove from the list of those eligible for the Council of the Five Hundred those who were themselves freedmen. Right after the death of Lucius Verus (the *terminus post quem* for a letter from Marcus as sole emperor) Marcus was so overwhelmed with more urgent problems that it is hard to think of him then as writing letters against the encroachment by men of servile extraction.

CHRONOLOGY

One might be tempted to connect reforms at Athens with the moment when Marcus Aurelius gave funds to establish at Athens state-supported chairs [32] of philosophy and a state-supported chair of rhetoric. For the latter Marcus personally selected Julius Theodotus,[33] while he appointed Herodes Atticus to preside as judge over the philosophers. Wright's translation of Philostratus, *Lives of the Sophists,* II, 2, p. 183, " assigned to Herodes the task of choosing " (προσέταξε ὁ Μᾶρκος τῷ Ἡρώδῃ κρῖναι) misleads the unwary. No important decision was supposed to be made without advice, and the magistrate was always supposed to be impartial. Therefore the philosopher basileus did not judge the philosophers, and to Herodes, the king of words, he assigned a task in which it was possible for Herodes to be impartial. Herodes probably had an assignment like a praetor or governor presiding over a court of jurors such as the court prescribed in the first " edict " of Augustus at Cyrene. Herodes was not invited to make arbitrary appointments but to conduct something like the contest mentioned by Lucian, *Eunuch,* 2. He would have been bound by the

---

[31] On altars erected at Eleusis and Athens see A. E. Raubitschek, *Hesperia,* XXXV, 1966, p. 250 except that the new altar from the Agora Excavations surely does not say Αὐτοκράτορσι διὰ εὐποδίας φιλαδέλφοις. His greatest admirers never credited Marcus Aurelius with fleetfootedness. The phrase, if Raubitschek's transcription is not too far off, should probably be read αὐτοκράτορσι διὰ συ(μ)πο⟨ν⟩ίας φιλαδέλφοις.

[32] According to P. Graindor, *Un milliardaire antique: Hérode Atticus et sa famille,* Cairo, 1930, p. 147, and H. I. Marrou, *Histoire de l'éducation dans l'antiquité,* 2nd ed., Paris, 1950, pp. 403, 561, there were four chairs of philosophy supported by the fiscus. According to F. H. L. Ahrens, *De Athenarum statu politico et literario inde ab Achaici foederis interitu usque ad Antoninorum tempora,* Göttingen, 1829, which I have not seen, and C. Barbagallo, *Lo stato e l'istruzione pubblica nell' Impero Romano,* Catania, 1911, p. 155 there were eight, because Lucian, *Eunuch,* 3 mentions the recent death of the ἕτερος Peripatetic. A. M. Harmon in the Loeb still translates " one of the two," but Marrou and others interpret it as " the second."

[33] *PIR²*, IV, p. 283, no. 599. J. H. Oliver, *The Athenian Expounders,* pp. 76-81, discusses the family to which Theodotus belonged.

vote of the jurors. The assignment gave honor to Herodes and was surely meant to compensate for the trial at Sirmium. That Herodes actually performed the task, which could have been carried out in 175 after the reconciliation, appears likely. Marcus himself undoubtedly consulted Athenian advisers before he appointed Theodotus.[34]

Dio-Xiphilinus, LXXII, 31, 3 (Boissevain, III, p. 272) assigns the establishment of the professorships unequivocally to the year 176. It is good evidence. The year 176, when Marcus visited Athens, has a further advantage in being a year when Marcus ruled alone. Would the grant of salaries from the fiscus have been attributed to one emperor if Lucius Verus were still alive? Probably not. And it could hardly have been afforded during a war. The writer sees no connection between the constitutional reforms and the establishment of the professorships, except that the period of the Parthian War produced a new awareness of the importance of Hellenism in the East and so was a period in which Athens and Sparta would have assumed a greater importance to thoughtful Romans and have occupied a special position in plans for the reconstruction of society. But that was just as true ten years later.

Furthermore, we know from Philostratus, *V.S.* II, 10, p. 92 Kayser, p. 230 Wright, that Adrian (*PIR*[2] H 4) had already come into possession of the sophistic chair when Marcus visited Athens in September 176. Therefore, we should not interpret Cassius Dio as meaning all the professorships. If Julius Theodotus was, as Philostratus says, the first to hold the sophistic chair with a salary from the fiscus, he must have been appointed earlier than 176, namely at the time Herodes Atticus withdrew to Oricum and the students at Athens were left without their professor, or even during the trial at Sirmium, as Naechster[35] has already proposed. The emperor came

[34] The whole question has been discussed by C. Barbagallo, *Lo stato e l'istruzione pubblica nell'Impero Romano*, Catania, 1911, pp. 152-162, who speaks of Herodes having the "choice" (*scelta*) and adds that regulations concerning future appointments were issued soon afterwards. He questions the date 176 and thinks it may have occurred earlier, but he correctly emphasizes the importance of what Marcus Aurelius did. John W. H. Walden, *The Universities of Ancient Greece*, New York, 1909, p. 135 has misunderstood the situation to such an extent that he speaks of Herodes as "in charge of the philosophical department of the University." It is a pity that Barbagallo had not seen the study by M. Naechster, *De Pollucis et Phrynichi controversiis*, Diss. Leipzig, 1908, especially pp. 33-46, who suggests that when Adrian was called to Rome and the state-supported sophistic chair (*ca.* 178) became vacant, the *ab epistulis* Cornelianus received from Marcus Aurelius and Commodus an assignment to choose the new incumbent, on the analogy of the assignment received by Herodes Atticus earlier. It was for this reason, according to Naechster's theory, that Phrynichus dedicated his *Ecloga* to Cornelianus, who, however, did not recommend Phrynichus for the chair but Pollux. Of course Philostratus, *V.S.*, II, 12, p. 97 Kayser, p. 240 Wright, assigns the choice of Pollux to Commodus, without mentioning Marcus Aurelius. Whether or not Cornelianus had any part in the appointment of Pollux cannot really be proved, but it is possible that he presided over a consilium or court and that the reference to the influence which Pollux had on Commodus reflected the gossip by disappointed partisans of other candidates.

[35] M. Naechster, *De Pollucis et Phrynichi controversiis*, p. 39, who dates the tenure of Theo-

to the rescue by establishing the state-supported sophistic chair either in 173 or 174. Two years later Adrian succeeded Theodotus. It is only the chairs of philosophy which were established in 176.

Recently Mazzarino [36] has carried Naechster's theory a little further, saying that the appointment of Theodotus was an intervention of the emperor against Herodes Atticus, now compromised as a friend of Lucius Verus. Theodotus had been a pupil of Lollianus. Then in 175 occurred the revolt of Avidius Cassius, and Marcus found that he needed Herodes. A reconciliation occurred in 175. Theodotus was dismissed, and Adrian, a pupil of Herodes, succeeded. Naechster emphasized the rivalries of sophists, Mazzarino the involvement of the emperors. Mazzarino's theory, influenced by his belief that Marcus had been idealized in the lost work known as Enmann's Kaisergeschichte, cannot really be proved or disproved. Though in our opinion the correction of our image of Marcus Aurelius has gone too far,[37] the reaction against policies of Lucius Verus cannot be denied. Only we need not, we ought not, to visualize Marcus as an opportunist in his treatment of Herodes.

The chronology [38] at which we arrive may be summarized as follows:

dotus to the period 173-175. Theodotus was probably appointed " eo tempore . . . quo et Athenienses et Marcus imperator Herodi suscensuerunt," and he connects the biennium of Theodotus with the period until " Marcus Herodem in amicitiam revocavit."

[36] S. Mazzarino, " Prima cathedra," *Mélanges André Piganiol*, Paris, 1966, pp. 1653-1665, especially pp. 1660 ff.

[37] The ability of Marcus as an emperor appears in a poor light in the careful study of Franco Carrata Thomes, *Il regno di Marco Aurelio*. See also S. Mazzarino's address, " La Historia Augusta e la EKG," *Atti del Colloquio Patavino sulla Historia Augusta*, Rome, 1963, pp. 29-40. At least the finances of Marcus Aurelius now appear somewhat better than we expected as a result of the investigation by Thomas Pekáry, " Studien zur römischen Währungs- und Finanzgeschichte von 161 bis 235 n. Chr.," *Historia*, VIII, 1959, pp. 443-489.

[38] The writer, having drawn on his predecessors, takes this occasion to mention the following studies: W. Zwikker, *Studien zur Markussäule*, I, Amsterdam, 1941, pp. 166-173, who dates the raid of the Costoboci early in 170 rather than 171; Josef Dobiáš, " La seconda spedizione germanica degli imperatori Marco e Commodo alla luce delle iscrizioni," *Atti del III Congresso Internazionale di Epigrafia Greca e Latina*, Rome, 1959, pp. 1-14; Franz Hampl, " Kaiser Marc Aurel und die Völker jenseits der Donaugrenze," *Festschrift zu Ehren Richard Heubergers*, Innsbruck, 1960, pp. 33-40, who denies that Marcus ever intended to annex Marcomannia and Sarmatia (very important article); K. H. Ziegler, *Die Beziehungen zwischen Rom und dem Partherreich*, Wiesbaden, 1964, pp. 113-116; Erich Swoboda, *Carnuntum*, fourth ed. (*Römische Forschungen in Niederösterreich*, I), 1964, pp. 249-254; Josef Dobiáš, " Rom und die Völker jenseits der mittleren Donau," *Corolla memoriae Erich Swoboda dedicata* (*Röm. Forschungen in Niederöst.*, V), 1966, pp. 115-125, who argues against Hampl that Marcus after 179 did intend to annex two new provinces; Anthony Birley, *Marcus Aurelius*, Boston and Toronto, 1966, who does not mention the professorships at Athens but who on p. 224 places the siege of Aquileia in A.D. 170; Jenö Fitz, " Der markomannisch-quadische Angriff gegen Aquileia," *Historia*, XV, 1966, pp. 336-367, who dates the attack on Aquileia and the destruction of Opitergium to May, June and July of 169, and the reply of A. Birley, " The Invasion of Italy in the Reign of Marcus Aurelius," *Provincialia, Festschrift für Rudolf Laur-Belart*, Basel, 1968, pp. 214-225. In addition to these works by other

A.D. 161   Accession of Marcus Aurelius on March 7
           Lucius Verus elevated to partnership as co-emperor
           Parthian invasion
     162   late: Lucius Verus initiated into the Eleusinian Mysteries
     162-166   Lucius Verus in the East
     166   Oct. 2: Marcus Aurelius and Lucius Verus at Rome celebrate victory
     167   June: Beginning of serious trouble with Germans
           Aelius Aristides delivers an address at the Panathenaea in Athens
     168   Avidius Cassius placed in charge of provinces in Asia
           Marcus Aurelius and Lucius Verus depart for war against the Marco-
               manni but return to Aquileia for Winter of 168/9
     169   Death of Lucius Verus in January or February
           Financial crisis and auction of imperial property
     169 or 170   Marcomanni and Quadi in Italy
     168-172   Reforms at Sparta
     169-174   Earlier letter of Marcus to the Athenians concerning descendants of
                   freedmen (not extant)
     170   Raid of Costoboci on Eleusis
           The Quintilii in Greece *vice principis*
     171   Emperor's headquarters moved to Carnuntum
     170-174   Quarrel of the Athenians with Herodes Atticus
     174   Case of Herodes Atticus vs. the Athenian leaders is heard at Sirmium
           Establishment of state-supported chair of rhetoric at Athens and appoint-
               ment of Julius Theodotus
     174/5   Long letter of Marcus in edict form concerning appeals from Athens
     175   Return of Herodes Atticus to Athens
           Revolt of Avidius Cassius: peace hastily concluded with the Iazyges
     175/6   The Quintilii accompany Marcus to Asia
     176   Aug.-Sept.: Marcus visits Athens and is initiated into the Mysteries
           Establishment of professorships of philosophy at Athens to be financed
               by the fiscus
     177   War with Iazyges and Germans breaks out again
           Quintilii in Illyricum *vice principis*
           Victory and death of M. Bassaeus Rufus
           First epistle of Marcus concerning Gerusia of the Athenians

scholars the reader may wish to consult J. H. Oliver, *The Civilizing Power* (Transactions of the
American Philosophical Society, 58, Part I, 1968), pp. 33-35, where it is argued that the extant
Panathenaic of Aelius Aristides was composed for the Panathenaea of 167 and submitted to
Herodes Atticus for his approval but was not actually delivered, being replaced by a short address
no longer extant.

Commodus raised to position as co-emperor on November 27

ca. 177   Death of Herodes Atticus

178   Quintilii have assumed military command in Illyricum (Occidentale)

Marcus and Commodus stop using titles Germanicus and Sarmaticus

Marcus and Commodus leave Rome on August 3

179   Victory of Tarrutenius Paternus

180   Death of Marcus at Vindobona or Sirmium on March 17

Peace treaty made by Commodus

PROFESSORS AND GERUSIA

What particularly moves Marcus Aurelius, No. **1**, line 89, about Herodes Atticus is the man's glorious enthusiasm for education.

Since Marcus Aurelius was establishing the Sacred Gerusia and the state-supported chairs of philosophy at the same time in the same place, is it not likely that in addition to its responsibility for the proper maintenance of the Panathenaea, the Sacred Gerusia of the Athenians was responsible for the proper maintenance of the institutions of higher education at Athens? The latter, in this interpretation, were treated as belonging to the service of Athena. Does not the name of the similar institution of Greek higher education at Rome, the Athenaeum,[39] suggest a natural connection between Athena and the higher education? If so, the establishment of the Sacred Gerusia at Athens may be regarded as a result of the quarrel of Herodes Atticus and the Athenians. The difficulty of financing the national festival of the Athenians for their goddess and the difficulty of maintaining the cultural preeminence of Athens both became acute during this quarrel and were both relieved by the emperor's personal attention and his old-fashioned piety.

Though the Sacred Gerusia is not specifically mentioned in the literary sources, it may well be the corporation which sat in judgment over the candidates for a chair of philosophy according to Lucian, *Eunuch*, 2: " Nevertheless, a trial had been arranged, and the judges, endowed with the deciding vote, were the most prominent and oldest and wisest men in the city, in whose presence one would have been ashamed to strike a false note, let alone resorting to such shamelessness " (A. M. Harmon's Loeb translation). Is Lucian not reflecting, say, the style of Plutarch, *Lysander*, 17, 1, οἱ φρονιμώτατοι τῶν Σπαρτιατῶν, by which Plutarch meant the *gerontes*?

The theory that the Sacred Gerusia had a general supervision over the whole cultural life of Athens derives some support from the presence of the Athenian sophist Apollonius in the emperor's *consilium*.

---

[39] Hans Braunert, " Das Athenaeum zu Rom bei den Scriptores Historiae Augustae," *Historia-Augusta-Colloquium Bonn 1963* (= *Antiquitas*, Reihe 4, 2), 1964, pp. 9-41. See the lead tessera with the figure of Athena and the legend Γερ[ου]σίας discovered in Greek excavations at Athens near the Theatre of Herodes Atticus (*B.C.H.*, LXXXI, 1957, p. 498).

Those interested in the new inscription, No. **1**, of Marcus Aurelius at Athens, may wish to have the series of letters concerning the Sacred Gerusia of the Athenians available for reference. We here reproduce as No. **4** the text originally published by J. H. Oliver, *The Sacred Gerusia* (*Hesperia*, Suppl. VI), 1941, No. 26, with the additions and corrections made by A. E. Raubitschek, " Commodus and Athens," *Commemorative Studies in Honor of Theodore Leslie Shear* (*Hesperia*, Suppl. VIII), 1949, p. 286, B. D. Meritt, *Hesperia*, XXIX, 1960, p. 22, No. 29, D. J. Geagan, *The Athenian Constitution after Sulla* (*Hesperia*, Suppl. XII), 1967, pp. 187-193. See also J. H. Oliver, " The Sacred Gerusia and the Emperor's Consilium," *Hesperia*, XXXVI, 1967, pp. 329-335.

4.

Ἐ π ώ ν ν μ ο ς
Κλ Δ ᾳ δ ο ῦ χ ο ς
Κλ Λ ε ω ν ί δ ο υ
[– – – – – – – –]

I

[– – – – ca. 14 – – – –] ο [– –]
[– – – – ca. 13 – – – –] τὴν πρ [– – – – – – – – – – – – – – – – – – –]
[– – – – ca. 13 – – – –]ι δὴ χωρία [– – – – – – – – – – – – – – – – – – –]
[– – – – ca. 13 – – – –] οἱ τετρακόσ[ιοι – – – – – – – – – – – – – – – – –]
5 [– – – ca. 9 – – – κατ]ὰ τὸν ἐπιβάλλ[οντα λόγον (?) – – – – – – – – – – –]
[– – – – ca. 12 – – –]τες κατὰ τὰ νο[μιζόμενα – – – – – – – – – – – – –]
[– – ca. 6 – – τὰ γενέ]θλια τὰ ἐμὰ κα[– – – – – – – – – – – – – – – –]
[– – – – ca. 12 – – – –] ὑμεῖν τοῦ κατὰ [– – – – – – – – – – – – – – – –]

II [Αὐτοκράτωρ Καῖσ]αρ θεοῦ Ἀντωνίνο[υ Εὐσεβοῦς υἱός, θεοῦ Οὐήρου Παρθικοῦ
  Μεγίστου ἀδελφός, θεοῦ Τραϊανοῦ Παρθικοῦ ἔγ]
10 [γονος, θεοῦ Νέρο]υα ἀπόγονος, Μᾶρκ[ος Αὐρήλιος Ἀντωνῖνος Σεβαστὸς Γερμανικὸς Σαρματικός, ἀρχιερεὺς μέγιστος, δημαρ]
  [χικῆς ἐξουσίας τ]ὸ ᾽ΛΒ᾽ αὐτοκράτωρ τὸ [᾽Θ᾽ ὕπατος τὸ ᾽Γ᾽, πατὴρ πατρίδος,
  καὶ Αὐτοκράτωρ Καῖσαρ Λούκιος Αὐρήλιος Κόμμοδος]
  [Σεβαστός, Αὐτοκρ]άτορος Ἀντωνίνο[υ Σεβα]στο[ῦ υἱός, θεοῦ Εὐσεβοῦς υἱωνός, θεοῦ Ἀδριανοῦ ἔγγονος, θεοῦ Τραϊανοῦ Παρθικοῦ]
  [καὶ θεοῦ Νέρουα ἀ]πόγονος Γερμανικ[ὸς Σα]ρμα[τικός, δημαρχικῆς ἐξουσίας
  τό ᾽Γ᾽, αὐτοκράτωρ τὸ ᾽Β᾽, ὕπατος, πατὴρ πατρίδος,]
  [τῆι ἐξ᾽ Ἀρείου πάγ]ου βουλῆι καὶ τῆι βο[υλῆι] τῶν Πεν[τα]κο[σίων καὶ
  τῶι δήμωι τῶι Ἀθηναίων   vacat]
15 [vacat   ]   χαί[ρειν   vacat   ]
  [τὰ μὲν γράμματα ἃ] ἐπεστείλατε περὶ [τῶ]ν κατὰ τὴν γερ[ουσίαν – – – –]
  [– – – ca. 14 – – –]χθῆναι τὸν ἀριθμ[ὸ]ν τοῦτον μνημ[– – – – – – – – – – –]
  [– – – – ca. 14 – – –] τῶν ἐκκλησιαζόν[τω]ν κατὰ τὰ νομ[ιζόμενα – – – – – – –]

       [-- *ca. 14* --] διωρισμένον ὥστ[ε μ]έντοι μήτε [--------------]

20 [-- *ca. 15* --] πλείστων προσδ[έχε]σθε εἰς ἀξ[--------------]

     [-- *ca. 13* --]ένων τὴν ἡλικίαν [καὶ] τούτων μο[-----------]

     [-- *ca. 13* ---] τὴν χώραν τοῦ ἐγλι[πό]ντος μέχρι [----------]

     [-- *ca. 13* ---] ἐκ τῶν ἀστῶν εἰσάγ[ειν] δεήσει ἀεὶ με[-------]

     [-- *ca. 10* --- δημ]οποιήτων εἰσιόντ[ων] καὶ ἐπιτείμου[ς --------]

25 [-- *ca. 12* ---] γὰρ μετέχειν τῆς Ἀθ[ήν]ησιν [πολιτεί]ας [--------]

     [-- *ca. 12* --]ες ἐπέστειλαν βου[λό]μενοι μαθεῖν ὑφ' [--------]

     [-- *ca. 6* --γερουσ]ίαν εἰσιόντων ὁπό[ταν] ἀναπληρωθῆν[αι --------]

     [-- *ca. 12* ---] γερόντων τινὰς αἱρ[εῖσ]θαι τη[-----------]

     [-- *ca. 12* ---]σει τὸν πρεσβύτατον [---]γ[. [-----------]

30 [-- *ca. 11* -- ψ]ήφῳ δηλοῦν τὴν αὐτ[--------------]

     [-- *ca. 12* ---]σῆς ἂν αἱρεθῶσι νῦν[--------------]

     ε[--]ο[--------] *vacat* [--------------]

III   Αὐτοκράτωρ Κα[ῖσαρ θεοῦ Ἀντωνίν]ου υ[ός, θεοῦ Οὐήρου Παρθικοῦ Μεγίστου
       ἀδελφός, θεοῦ Ἁδριανοῦ υἱωνός, θεοῦ Τραιανοῦ]

       Παρθικοῦ ἔγγο[νος, θεοῦ Νέρουα ἀ]π[όγονος, Μᾶρκος Αὐρήλιος Ἀντωνῖνος
       Σεβαστὸς Γερμανικὸς Σαρματικός, ἀρχιερεὺς]

       μέγιστος, δημαρχι[κῆς ἐξ]ο[υσίας τὸ —, αὐτοκράτωρ τὸ —, ὕπατος τὸ ˀΓˁ, πατὴρ
       πατρίδος· καὶ Αὐτοκράτωρ Καῖσαρ Λούκιος Αὐρήλιος]

35 Κόμμοδος Σεβαστὸς Αὐτοκράτορος Ἀ[ντωνίνου Σεβαστοῦ υός, θεοῦ Εὐσεβοῦς
       υἱωνός, θεοῦ Ἁδριανοῦ ἔγγονος, θεοῦ Τραιανοῦ Παρθι]

       κοῦ καὶ θεοῦ Νέρουα ἀπόγονος, Γερμανικὸ[ς Σαρματικός, δημαρχικῆς ἐξουσίας
       τὸ —, αὐτοκράτωρ τὸ —, ὕπατος τὸ —, πατὴρ πατρίδος,]

       ἀνθύπατος, Ἀθηναίων γερουσίᾳ *vacat* [χαίρειν *vacat*]

       Περὶ μὲν τῶν τὴν ὕλην ἐκκο[π]τόντων ἐκ τῶν χωρ[ίων -----------πε]

       ρὶ αὐτὰ τὸν ἐπίτροπον Καίλ[ι]ον Κουαδρᾶτον διδάσκ[-----------ἐ]

40 πιμελουμένους τῶν χωρίων ἄνδρας ἀξιολόγους οἷς τ[-----------]

       ξειν ὑμεῖν· παρέξεσθε δὲ τῷ Κουαδράτῳ ταῦθ' ἡμῶν τὰ [-----------]

       των φανερὸν καὶ ἡμῖν ἐπιστείλας ποιήσει, φροντίσας κα[-----------]

       σθαι περὶ αὐτῶν καταστῆτε· ὀρθῶς δὲ ἐποιήσατε καὶ ἐπιστε[ίλαντες ἡμῖν --
       ---- ἐξου]

       σίαν ταύτην καὶ τὸ δίκαιον ὑμῖν ἐδίδομεν τοῦ γράφειν ᾧ δὴ [-------]

45 ταῖς γερουσίαις· περὶ μέντοι τῆς τοῦ ἄρχοντος καταστάσεως [-------]

       οὕστινας ἐκθέμενοι τρόπους ἐξ ὧν ἐπιλεξόμεθα τὸν ἐπίτρ[οπον ----- εἰ δὲ]

       βούλεσθε πορισθῆναι τοιοῦτον, ἐπιστελεῖτε τὰ γράμματα ἐκ[είνῳ *vacat*
       εὐτυχεῖτε *vacat*]

IV   Αὐτοκράτωρ Καῖσαρ θε[ο]ῦ Ἀντωνίνου υός, θεοῦ Οὐήρου Παρθικοῦ [Μεγίστου
       ἀδελφ]ός, θ[εοῦ Τραιανοῦ Παρθικοῦ ἔγγονος, θεοῦ Νέρουα]

       ἀπόγονος, Μᾶρκος Α[ὐ]ρήλιος Ἀντωνῖνος Σεβαστὸς Γερμανικ[ὸς Σαρματικός,
       ἀ]ρχιερ[εὺς μέγιστος, δημαρχικῆς ἐξουσίας τὸ ˀΛΓˁ]

50 αὐτοκράτωρ τὸ ⟩ΑΙ⟩, ὕ[πα]τος τὸ ⟩Γ⟩, πατὴρ πατρίδος, ἀνθύπατος· [καὶ Αὐτοκράτωρ Καῖ]σαρ Λούκιος [Αὐρήλιος Κόμμοδος Σεβαστός, Αὐτο]
κράτορος Ἀντωνί[νο]υ Σεβαστοῦ ὑός, θεοῦ Εὐσεβοῦ[ς υἱωνός, θεοῦ Ἀδριανοῦ
ἔγγον]ος, θεοῦ Τραια[νοῦ Παρθικοῦ καὶ θεοῦ Νέρονα ἀπό]
γονος, Γερμανικ[ὸ]ς Σα[ρμ]ατικός, δημα[ρχικῆς ἐξουσία]ς τὸ [⟩Δ⟩, αὐτοκράτωρ τὸ ⟩Β⟩, ὕ]πατος τὸ ⟩Β⟩, πατὴ[ρ πατρίδος, ἀνθύπατος, Ἀθη]
ναίων γερουσίᾳ vacat χαίρειν vacat
Ἥσθημεν τοῖς γ[ρ]άμμα[σ]ιν ὑμῶν ἐντυχόντες, ἐπεὶ καὶ τοῖς ἀ[------]
ἀνδράσιν ἐπὶ τὴν τῶν [-------]
55 περ ἐωνήμεθα τῷ συ[ν]εδρίῳ πρὸς τὴν χορηγίαν τῶν διανο[μῶν, ------]ᾳ
διατάξαντες ἐπεστείλαμ[εν ----- ἐ]
χρῆν προσεῖσθε ⱽ τὰς μὲν οὖν εἰκόνας ἃς ἡμῶν τ’ αὐτῶν καὶ [τῶν ἡμῶν γυναι-
κῶ]ν ποιήσασθαι βεβούλησθε χ[ρυσᾶς ἢ ἀργυρᾶς, ἢ]
τε μάλιστ’ ἐ[π]ὶ τῆς ἡμε[τ]έρας γνώμης συνιέντες βούλεσθε χα[λκαῖς εἰκόσιν
ἀρκεῖ]σθαι, δῆλον δ’ ὡς ποιήσεσθε ἀ[νδριάντας οἵους]
κοινότε[ρο]ν οἱ πολλο[ὶ] προτομὰς καλοῦσιν, καὶ συνμέτρους [αὐτὰς ἐκτελέ-
σετε τὰ]ς τέτταρας ἴσας ὡς ῥᾴδιον ε[ἶναι ἐν ταῖς ἑορταῖς]
ὑμῶν κ[αθ’ ἑκ]άστην τ[ῶ]ν συνόδων εἰσκομίζειν ἔνθα ἂν βο[ύλησθε αὐτὰς
ἑκάστο]τε ὥσπερ δὴ καὶ εἰς τὰς ἐκκλ[ησίας· καταλλήλοις]
60 δὲ ἐπ[ὶ βάσεσιν] εἶναι τὸ [ἐπί]στημα τῶν ἡμετέρων ὀνομάτων [τῆς εἰς ἡμᾶς
εὐνοίας ἕ]νεκα προσείμεθα, ἡδέω[ς ἀποδεχόμενοι τοι]
αὐτ’ [ἀλλὰ τὰ θεῖα] καὶ τὰ δο[κ]οῦντα ἐπίφθονα ὀκνοῦντες ἐν ἅπ[ασι καιροῖς·
διὸ καὶ νῦ]ν ὑμεῖν εὐγνωμόνως ἐμ[φανίζομεν ποιήσα]
σ[θαι μόνον χαλκ]ᾶς ὡς [το]ῦτ’ ἂν εἴη μᾶλλον ἡμε[ῖ]ν κεχαρισμέ[νον· τοὺς
δὲ ἄλλους] τὴν αὐτῶν γνώμην ὑπ’ [αὐτῶν διδασκόμενος]
[δηλώσει ὑμεῖν Κ]αίλι[ος] Κουαδρᾶτος ὁ ἐπίτροπος ἡμῶν vacat [εὐτυ]-
χεῖτε vacat

V [Αὐτοκράτωρ Καῖσαρ], θε[οῦ Ἀ]ντωνίνου ὑός, θεοῦ Οὐήρου Παρθικο[ῦ Μεγίστου ἀδελφό]ς, θεοῦ Τραιανοῦ Π[αρθικοῦ ἔγγονος, θεοῦ Νέρονα]
65 [ἀπόγονος, Μᾶρκος] Αὐ[ρήλιο]ς Ἀντωνῖνος Σεβαστὸς Γερμανικ[ὸς Σαρματικός, ἀρχι]ερεὺς μέγιστο[ς, δημαρχικῆς ἐξουσίας τὸ]
[–, αὐτοκράτωρ τὸ] δέ[κατον], ὕπατος τὸ ⟩Γ⟩, πατὴρ πατρίδος, [ἀνθύπατος·
καὶ Αὐτοκ]ράτωρ Καῖσ[αρ Λούκιος Αὐρήλιος Κόμμοδος]
[Σεβαστός, Αὐτοκράτορος Ἀν]τωνίνου Σεβαστοῦ ὑός, θεο[ῦ Εὐσεβοῦς υἱωνός,
θεοῦ Ἀ]δριανοῦ [ἔγγονος, θεοῦ Τραιανοῦ Παρθικοῦ καὶ]
[θεοῦ Νέρουα ἀπόγονος, Γερμαν]ικὸς Σαρματι[κός, δημ]αρχικ[ῆς ἐξουσίας
τὸ ⟩–⟩, αὐτο]κράτω[ρ τὸ ⟩Γ⟩, ὕπατος τὸ ⟩Β⟩, πατὴρ πατρίδος, ἀνθύ]
[πατος, -------] vacat χαίρειν vacat
70 [-------]υτο, προσέστω δὲ ὁ τῆς γερουσ[ίας ------------]
[-------]ν δεῖ παράδειγμα τῶν Ἀθηνα[ίων ------------]

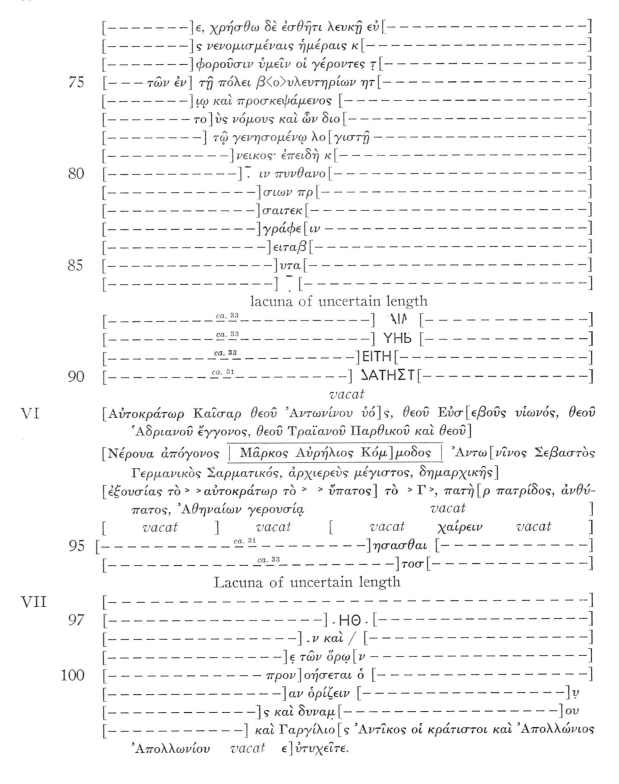

[– – – – – – –]ε, χρήσθω δὲ ἐσθῆτι λευκῇ εὐ[– – – – – – – – – – – – – –]

[– – – – – –]ς νενομισμέναις ἡμέραις κ[– – – – – – – – – – – – – – – –]

[– – – – – – –]φοροῦσιν ὑμεῖν οἱ γέροντες τ[– – – – – – – – – – – – –]

75 [– – – τῶν ἐν] τῇ πόλει β⟨ο⟩υλευτηρίων ητ[– – – – – – – – – – – – –]

[– – – – – – –]ιῳ καὶ προσκεψάμενος [– – – – – – – – – – – – – – – –]

[– – – – – – το]ὺς νόμους καὶ ὧν διο[– – – – – – – – – – – – – – – –]

[– – – – – – –] τῷ γενησομένῳ λο[γιστῇ – – – – – – – – – – – – – – –]

[– – – – – – –]νεικος· ἐπειδὴ κ[– – – – – – – – – – – – – – – – – –]

80 [– – – – – – – – –]⁻ ιν πυνθανο[– – – – – – – – – – – – – – – – –]

[– – – – – – –]σιων πρ[– –]

[– – – – – – –]σαιτεκ[– –]

[– – – – – – –]γράφε[ιν –]

[– – – – – – –]ειταβ[– –]

85 [– – – – – – –]ντα[– –]

[– – – – – – –]⁻ .[– –]

lacuna of uncertain length

[– – – – – – – ca. 33 – – – – – – – –] ΛΙΛ [– – – – – – – – – – –]

[– – – – – – – ca. 33 – – – – – – – –] ΥΗЬ [– – – – – – – – – – –]

[– – – – – – ca. 33 – – – – – –]ΕΙΤΗ[– – – – – – – – – – – – –]

90 [– – – – – – ca. 31 – – – – – –] ΔΑΤΗΣΤ[– – – – – – – – – – –]

vacat

VI [Αὐτοκράτωρ Καῖσαρ θεοῦ Ἀντωνίνου υό]ς, θεοῦ Εὐσ[εβοῦς υἱωνός, θεοῦ

Ἀδριανοῦ ἔγγονος, θεοῦ Τραϊανοῦ Παρθικοῦ καὶ θεοῦ]

[Νέρουα ἀπόγονος | Μᾶρκος Αὐρήλιος Κόμ]μοδος | Ἀντω[νῖνος Σεβαστὸς

Γερμανικὸς Σαρματικός, ἀρχιερεὺς μέγιστος, δημαρχικῆς]

[ἐξουσίας τὸ ⟩ ⟩ αὐτοκράτωρ τὸ ⟩ ⟩ ὕπατος] τὸ ⟩ Γ⟩, πατὴ[ρ πατρίδος, ἀνθύ-

πατος, Ἀθηναίων γερουσίᾳ   vacat   ]

[vacat   ]   vacat   [vacat   χαίρειν   vacat   ]

95 [– – – – – – – – – – ca. 31 – – – – – – – –]ησασθαι [– – – – – – – –]

[– – – – – – – – – – – ca. 33 – – – – – – – – –]τοσ[– – – – – – – –]

Lacuna of uncertain length

VII [– –]

97 [– – – – – – – – – – – –]· ΗΘ ·[– – – – – – – – – – – – – – –]

[– – – – – – – – – –]·ν καὶ / [– – – – – – – – – – – – – – – – –]

[– – – – – – – – –]ε τῶν ὅρω[ν – – – – – – – – – – – – – – – –]

100 [– – – – – – – προν]οήσεται ὁ [– – – – – – – – – – – – – – –]

[– – – – – – – – –]αν ὁρίζειν [– – – – – – – – – – – – – – –]ν

[– – – – – – – – –]ς καὶ δυναμ[– – – – – – – – – – – – – –]ου

[– – – – – – – – –] καὶ Γαργίλιο[ς Ἀντῖκος οἱ κράτιστοι καὶ Ἀπολλώνιος

Ἀπολλωνίου   vacat   ε]ὐτυχεῖτε.

VIII   [Αὐτοκράτωρ Καῖσαρ Θεοῦ Μάρ Αὐρ Ἀντω]νίνου Εὐσεβο[ῦς Γερμανικοῦ Σαρ-
         ματικοῦ υἱὸς Θεοῦ Εὐσεβοῦς υἱω]νὸς Θε-

105   [οῦ Ἁδριανοῦ ἔκγονος Θεοῦ Τραιανοῦ] Παρθικοῦ καὶ [Θεοῦ Νέρουα ἀπόγονος
         |Μᾶρ Αὐρήλιος Κόμμοδος| Ἀν]τωνῖνος

         [Σεβαστὸς Σαρματικὸς Γερμανικὸς] Μέγιστος ἀρχιερ[εὺς μέγιστος δημαρ-
         χικῆς ἐξουσίας τὸ ꞌ⎯ꞌ αὐτοκρ]άτωρ τὸ ꞌΕꞌ

         [ὕπατος τὸ ꞌ⎯ꞌ πατὴρ πατρίδος Ἀθη]ν[αί]ων γερουσίᾳ   vac[at χαίρειν
         vacat   ]   vacat

         [Τὰ μὲν γράμματα ἃ ἐπεστείλατε π]ερὶ τὴν τοῦ ἐλαίου [θέσιν — — — — — —
         — — — — — — — — — — — — — —]ιδου τοῦτο καὶ

         [— — — — — — — — — — ὑπὲ]ρ τῶν προϋπαρξά[ντων — — — — — — — — — —
         — — — — — — — — —μὴ] καινοτομεῖν πε-

110   [ρὶ — — — — — — — — — — τὴ]ν ἡλικίαν [. . .] ⌐[— — — — — — — — — — —
         — — — — καὶ Γαρ]γίλιος Ἀντῖκος οἱ

         [κράτιστοι καὶ Ἀπολλώνιος Ἀπολλ]ωνίου   va[cat εὐτυχεῖτε   v]acat

IX   [Αὐτοκράτωρ Καῖσαρ Θεοῦ Μάρ Αὐρ Ἀ]ντωνίνου Εὐσ[εβοῦς Γερμανικοῦ Σαρ-
         ματικοῦ υἱὸς Θ]εοῦ Εὐσεβοῦς υἱωνὸς

         [Θεοῦ Ἁδριανοῦ ἔκγου]ος [Θεοῦ Τρα]ιανοῦ Παρθικο[ῦ καὶ Θεοῦ Νέρουα ἀπό-
         γονος |Μᾶρ Αὐ]ρήλιος Κόμμοδος| Ἀντωνῖ-

         [νος Σεβαστὸς Σαρμ]ατικὸς [Γερμ]ανικὸς Μέγιστ[ος ἀρχιερεὺς μέγιστος
         δημαρχικ]ῆς ἐξουσίας τὸ ꞌΗꞌ αὐτοκράτωρ

115   [τὸ ꞌ⎯ꞌ ὕπατος τὸ ꞌ⎯ꞌ] πατὴρ πα[τρίδ]ος Ἀθηναίων γ[ερουσίᾳ. vacat
         χαίρειν   v]acat

         [— — — — — — — — —]σθαι τὰ πά[τρι]α τῆς πόλεως τ[— — — — — — — — —
         — — — — —]ες καὶ ὑμεῖς οἱ ταύτην γεγονότες

         [— — — — — — — — —]ηκην ἔχει[ν τ]οῦ τοιούτου πεφ[— — — — — — — — — —
         — — —]ιει δὲ ἐπιστέλλοντες νῦν ἠξιώσατε τὸν

         [— — — — — — — — ἀ]γωνιζομέν[ω]ν ἐνκωιμίωι τ[— — — — — — — — — —]ν
         γραφομένωι τοῦτον εὐθέως τῆς πολει-

         [τείας μετέχειν] παρ᾽ ὑμῶν κα[ὶ τ]ὸ προκείμεν[ον — — — — — — — — — — τοῦ
         στ]εφάνου λαμβάνειν εἰς τοῦτό τε παράδειγμα

120   [— — — — — — — ἐπι]θύμ[ω]ς τότ[ε . .] οἱ ἐπὶ τοῖς ηρ[— — — — — — — — — —]
         λόγωι μετὰ τὸ κριθῆναι ἀξιόνικοι εἶναι εὐ-

         [— — — — — — — —]ΓΜ[. . . . .]υσιν συνκεχ[ώρηκα — — — — — — — ε]ν τῶι
         κριθέντι τῆς νίκης ἀξίωι εὐθέως καὶ πολει-

         [τείας — — — — — — — — — Ἀντ]ίπατρος κ]αὶ Γαργίλιος Ἀντῖκος] οἱ κράτιστοι
         καὶ Ἀπολλώνιος Ἀπολλωνίου. εὐτυχεῖτε.

X   [Αὐτοκράτωρ Καῖσαρ Θεο]ῦ Μάρ [Α]ὐ[ρ Ἀντω]ν[ίν]ου Ε[ὐσεβοῦς Γερμανικοῦ
         Σ]αρματικοῦ υ[ἱὸς Θεο]ῦ Εὐσεβοῦς υἱωνὸς Θεοῦ

['Αδριανοῦ ἔκγονος Θ]εοῦ Τρ[αι]α[ν]οῦ [Παρθικοῦ καὶ Θεοῦ Νέρουα ἀπό-
γονος |Μᾶρ Αὐρήλιος Κόμμοδος| 'Αντωνῖνος]

125 [Σεβαστὸς Σαρματικ]ὸς Γερ[μαν]ικὸς Μ[έγιστος ἀρχιερεὺς μέγιστος δημαρχικῆς ἐξουσίας τὸ ᐟ ᐟ αὐτοκράτωρ τὸ ᐟ ᐟ]

[ὕπατος τὸ ᐟ ᐟ πα]τρὶδος 'Αθηναί[ων γερουσίᾳ vacat χαίρειν vacat]

[– – – – – – – – – –]ΑΣ̣ [– – – – – –]ΟΥΜΕ[– – – – – – – – – – – –]

[– – – – – – – – – – – – – –]Ι̣Ṇ̣ΑṬΑᐱᐸ [– – – – – – – – – – – –]

traces

130 [– –]

[– –]

Lacuna of uncertain length.

[– –]

[– va]cat

XI [Αὐτοκράτωρ Καῖσαρ Θεοῦ Μᾶρ Αὐρ 'Αντωνίνου Εὐσεβοῦς Γερμανικοῦ Σαρ-
ματικοῦ υἱὸς Θεοῦ Εὐσεβοῦς υἱ]ωνὸς

135 [Θεοῦ 'Αδριανοῦ ἔκγονος Θεοῦ Τραιανοῦ Παρθικοῦ καὶ Θεοῦ Νέρουα ἀπόγονος
|Μᾶρ Αὐρήλιος Κόμμοδος|] 'Αντωνῖνος

[Σεβαστὸς Σαρματικὸς Γερμανικὸς Μέγιστος ἀρχιερεὺς μέγιστος δημαρχικῆς
ἐξουσίας τὸ ᐟ.ᐟ αὐτοκρ]άτωρ τὸ ᐟΖᐟ (sic)

[ὕπατος τὸ ᐟ.ᐟ πατὴρ πατρίδος 'Αθηναίων γερουσίᾳ vacat χαίρειν vacat]
vacat

[– – – – – – – – – – –]– – – – – – – – – – – –]ρηται καὶ αἱ ἐξ

[– –]ρας καὶ φιλαν-

140 [θρωπ –]ρεθειεν καὶ

[– –]. μεν

[– –]

Restorations: Epistle I Meritt (*Hesperia*, XXX, 1961, pp. 232 f.).   Epistle II Meritt
except for line 25 πολιτεί]ας Oliver (γερουσί]ας Meritt).   Epistle III, lines 1-5, ᾠδὴ[ν in 14, ἐπίτρ[οπον
in 15, and ἐκ[εῖ in 16 Meritt (*Hesp.*, II, 1933, p. 167) ; cetera Oliver.   Epistle IV Oliver.   Epistle V
Oliver.   Epistle VI Meritt.   Epistle VII Geagan.   Epistles VIII and IX the imperial titles by A. E.
Raubitschek (*Hesp.* Suppl. VIII, 1949, p. 286, though the restoration T. Αἰλίου 'Αντωνίνου Εὐσεβοῦς
Σεβαστοῦ, *pace* Meritt, *Hesp.*, XXIX, 1960, p. 22, is not confirmed and has been improved by Geagan),
πά[τρι]α and συνκεχ[ώρηκα Meritt, *cetera* Geagan.   Epistle X Geagan.   Epistle XI Geagan, who
restored numerals to indicate the ninth tribunician power and the fourth consulship because of
the seventh imperial acclamation (but the absence of the epithets Pius and Britannicus suggests
that the numeral Z (= VII) for the imperial acclamation is an error).

" The most prominent, oldest and wisest men in the city " (Lucian, *Eunuch* 2)
would have been a philosopher's dream of a true aristocracy chosen without regard
for wealth or social position or even citizenship.   The reference in Epistle II to the
entry of naturalized Athenians does not suggest that ex-slaves could be accepted, upon
a grant of Athenian citizenship, in the Gerusia of the Athenians created by Marcus

Aurelius, but does not exclude it either. The emperors seem to give preference to *astoi* and they say *astoi*, not *eugeneis*.

Marcus Aurelius shares the educated man's usual admiration for a slave like Epictetus and the citizen's prejudice against the intriguing slave who becomes a successful freedman operator and against the offspring who resemble him. The prejudice was discriminating and defensible. The fig tree brings forth figs. Marcus did not oppose all change. His reign brought many admirable reforms in Roman Law, some of which aided the slaves; but he checked the manumission of those unworthy to be citizens, *prohibuit ex acclamatione populi manumittere*.[40]

The basic issue between Marcus Aurelius and Lucius Verus was the allocation of resources. The peasantry and the propertyless were not here concerned. The question was rather to what extent the urban middle class of citizen background could be relieved of economic burdens and oppressive calls upon their time. The admission of the eager middle class of non-citizen background into the service of the city state (the local city primarily but also Rome, of which men still thought in an inherited pattern of political or city-government theory) could provide this relief. Should any respect for tradition be allowed to interfere? The Athenians have asked the emperor not to insist on the ancient standards, which he tried to restore, and in No. **1**, the " edict " from the Roman Market Place, he meets the Athenians halfway by reducing the requirement for the present. Probably some of the old bourgeoisie had intermarried with the new bourgeoisie for economic reasons. Lucius Verus had gone to unnecessary lengths, so Marcus thought, in showing contempt for ancient traditions. One has to visualize these attitudes and reactions within the context of a cultural conflict between the *paideia* of the Hellenes and the *dogmata* of the non-Hellenes, the standards of ancient Greek manliness and the crudity of the new rich.

Access to the highest political offices and to the Areopagus attracted one type descended from freedmen; access to the Sacred Gerusia was opened to a very different type. Those who aspired to the highest political offices were often rich men of mercenary antecedents, whose influence the emperor wished to check; those who were welcomed in the Sacred Gerusia were men with a place in the cultural life of the community, outstanding among citizens for their moral and intellectual worth alone, the true aristocracy of Athens. Marcus preserved the old community with its great traditions but he founded also a new community to supplement it and to foster education. In regard to the Areopagus he took negative action where it was probably needed, and in the Sacred Gerusia he took positive action.

The unity of the city was preserved; the best non-political elements were allowed to play their part, and the Areopagus avoided the semblance of dissolution. The founding of a Sacred Gerusia follows upon the purging of the Areopagus. New avenues are opened. New standards are recognized, but old standards are not demolished where they really belong.

[40] Digest, XL, 9, 17.

CHAPTER IV

THE ATTIC PANHELLENION

THE *PROSTATES* [1]

Three cases, contained in No. **1**, lines 15-30, concern membership in the Panhellenion, ἡ τοῦ Πανελληνίου κοινωνία (line 21) and ἡ κοινωνία τοῦ συνεδρίου τῶν Πανελλήνων (line 29). The information that the Panhellenes were elected is new but not surprising, likewise the information that the term of the archon was four years and coincided with the quadrennium that ran from one festival to another. Of greater interest are the implications that Hadrian had set a minimum age and a preliminary requirement of experience in public office, and that within a certain period after election the Panhellene's qualifications could be challenged.

The implication of the new inscription, E, lines 76-79 is that at Athens only those qualified to be or become Areopagites were eligible for election to the Panhellenion. The Areopagites were nominally men who had served satisfactorily as archon or king archon or polemarch, perhaps even as thesmothete, but among the Areopagites were some who had never held an archonship but had performed such a liturgy or benefaction that they were classed as ex-archons by adlection. One may infer by analogy that in other cities too the Panhellenes were drawn exclusively from those who had served in one of the two or three highest posts or were locally classed as having so served. At Canusium the names in the album (*I.L.S.* 6121) are divided into groups, *quinquennalicii, allecti inter quinq., IIviralicii, aedilicii, quaestoricii* and *pedani*. At Athens the divisions may not have been so precise, but a list existed.

The case of the otherwise unknown Ladicus son of Polyaenus in E, lines 15-20, who succeeded in getting himself elected Panhellene below the legal age, shows that the elections were not held in the Areopagus. Only a popular movement could have raised a young man who had never held office. He was soon disqualified, but his election reflected discontent and probably shows that the public looked to the Panhellenion for leadership in social reforms. We do not have sufficient information to say what the Panhellenion could have done; perhaps the rebels hoped for a recommendation of their program to the emperor by the Panhellenion.

It is very interesting that the elected Panhellenes who were disqualified had sufficient confidence in the emperor or the Quintilii to appeal their cases. Some expense was involved. Some intimation of concern in high places encouraged them, and one

---

[1] The emperor's *prostasia* has of course many other aspects, as readers of Jean Béranger, *Recherches sur l'aspect idéologique du principat*, pp. 252-278, are well aware.

thinks of both Lucius Verus and Marcus himself at Athens, as well as the memorable period in which the Quintilii " ruled Greece."

It is altogether likely that the emperor, who felt an obligation to help the Greek cities, and even to conform to public opinion among respectable people there, was steeped in the literature of the fourth century B.C., and among the most important influences was the *Philippus*, in which Isocrates, despairing of the ability of any one Greek city to rise above a selfish imperialism, turned to Philip of Macedon and portrayed the advantages of a policy worthy of a Heraclid. There were two aspects of the role which Isocrates so vaguely but attractively dangled before Philip [2] that Philip eventually founded the League of Corinth. One aspect was a general reconciliation and strengthening of Greek cities and the other was a military expedition against Persia. The Panhellenic role which Philip recognized as advantageous was taken over by Alexander but later neglected under the pressure of military business; it interested Antigonus and Demetrius but they were never so clearly *prostatai*. This role devolved upon the Roman emperors [3] in three outstanding and rather different incarnations, Augustus, Hadrian and Marcus Aurelius.

Augustus encouraged the union of Greek cities into local *concilia*, and in European Greece he reorganized not the League of Corinth but the Delphic Amphictyony with strong participation of his own favorite Nicopolis. One might say that the *prostates* of the Hellenes was feeling his way cautiously. The Delphic Amphictyony, however, did not have the necessary Panhellenic character either geographically or otherwise to fill completely a purpose beyond the rather narrowly oriented aims of a provincial assembly.

Another Persian War in the time of Trajan turned everyone's attention to memories of the *imperium Macedonicum,* and the Jewish Disturbances in the reign of Hadrian offered an exasperating lesson in the blessings of concord. Another exasperation came to Hadrian from the absurd rivalry between Smyrna and Ephesus; the sophist Favorinus, spokesman for Ephesus, was relegated to Chios, as we learn from P. Vat. 11. It was highly desirable for the Roman emperor to have the co-operation and peaceful support of the Greek cities. On the other hand, the League of Corinth had obviously not been founded in the right place and had not produced the kind of trust which Isocrates had adumbrated. Who continued to be read. The same kind of league could not be considered, but a league which would foster Panhellenic interests provided a means of uniting and strengthening the forces of Hellenic city life, equivalent to Hellenic civilization. The new league had to be based on Athens and on the *koinotes* or Panhellenism of which Athens had been the leading exponent at least in literature.

[2] G. Dobesch, *Untersuchungen zum Korinthischen Bund*, I, Vienna, 1968.
[3] E. Skard, *Zwei religiös-politische Begriffe: Euergetes-Concordia* (Avhandlinger utgitt av det Norske Videnskaps-Akademi i Oslo, II, Hist.-Filos. Kl. 1931, 2).

Plutarch, who praises the great spirit of Pericles for trying to establish after victories over the Persians a Panhellenic League based on Athens and Eleusis, shows the attitude of an important element in Old Greece. Influential Greeks in the time of Hadrian desired a union of this type, and Hadrian in the role of the *prostates*, which Isocrates outlined for Philip, had this and other reasons.[4] Now the " edict " of Marcus Aurelius reveals how seriously another Roman emperor, who viewed the *prostateia* of the Hellenes as an obligation, treated the Panhellenion.

The new information, which includes the names of two previously unknown archons of the Panhellenion, Julius Damostratus (lines 16 and 20) and Papius Rufus (lines 23-24), amounts to so much that the time has come to lay before the reader all the evidence now available concerning the Panhellenion.

THE OTHER INSCRIPTIONS

5. Decree of the Panhellenes about Magnesia ad Maeandrum

Athens, now at Paris. A. Boeckh, *C.I.G.*, II (1843), 2910 from copies by Fourmont, Fauvel and Pittakys; W. Froehner, *Les Inscriptions grecques*, Paris, Musée Nationale du Louvre, 1865, No. 66; W. Dittenberger, *I.G.*, III (1878), 16; O. Kern, *Die Inschriften von Magnesia am Maeander*, Berlin, 1900, p. xvii, No. LXVI; [*O.G.I.* 503]; J. Kirchner, *I.G.*, II², 1091, with notes by A. von Premerstein. For the two extant fragments see the photograph which we reproduce on Plate 7, a through the courtesy of the Musée du Louvre. A third fragment recorded by Boeckh is now lost.

[– deity –   ]ᵛ Ἀγαθῆι· Τύχηι Λεύκιππος
[– – – – – – ψήφισ]μα τὸ γενόμενον ὑπὸ τῶν Πανελλήνων·
[ἐπειδὴ Μάγνητες οἱ] πρὸς τῷ Μαιάνδρῳ ποταμῷ ἄποικοι ᵛ
[μὲν ὄντες Μαγνήτων] τῶν ἐν Θεσσαλίᾳ, πρῶτοι Ἑλλήνων
5   [δὲ καὶ διαβάντες εἰ]ς τὴν Ἀσίαν καὶ κατοικήσαντες, συνα
[γωνισάμενοι ἐκτενῶς] πολλάκις Ἴωσι καὶ Δωριεῦσι καὶ τοῖς ἐ
[πὶ τῆς Ἀσίας ταυτοῦ γ]ένους Αἰολεῦσι, τιμηθέντες καὶ ὑπὸ
[τῆς συγκλήτου τῆς Ρω]μαίων δι' ἃς ἐποιήσαντο συμμα
[χίας πρὸς αὐτοὺς καὶ δ]ωρεῶν ἐξαιρέτων τυχόντες ὑ

---

[4] The Spaniard Hadrian may have drawn ideas also from the tradition of the Spaniards behind Galba, whose program followed that publicized by Octavian, later Augustus. As soon as Galba received the imperial salutation in Spain and proclaimed himself legate of the Senate and Roman People, he collected a *consilium* of provincials according to Suetonius, *Galba*, 10, 2: *e primoribus prudentia atque aetate praestantibus velut instar senatus, ad quos de maiore re quotiens opus esset referretur, instituit*. See R. Syme, *Tacitus*, Oxford, 1958, p. 592 on who they were.

10   [. . . . . . . παρὰ θεοῦ ʼΑδ]ριανοῦ, πατρὸς T̄. Αἰλίου Καίσαρος
       [Σεβαστοῦ Αὐτοκράτο]ρος ʼΑδριανοῦ ʼΑντωνίνου, τὰς
       [— — — — — — — — — — — — — — — — —]ντ[. .]εκ[. .]α

2-3 Boeckh. 4 ὄντες Μαγνήτων Boeckh, μὲν Oliver. 5 διαβάντες εἰ]ς Boeckh, δὲ καὶ Oliver. 6 συνα|
[γωνισάμενοι δὲ Kern, σὺν ἄ|[λλοις Ἕλλησι Boeckh, ἐκτενῶς Oliver. 7 πὶ τῆς ʼΑσίας ταυτοῦ Oliver, ἐ|[κ
τοῦ αὐτοῦ γ]ένους Boeckh. 8 τῆς συγκλήτου τῆς Oliver, τοῦ δήμου τοῦ ʽΡω Boeckh. 9 χίας πρὸς αὐτὸν
καὶ δ Boeckh, αὐτοὺς Oliver. 10 ὑ|[πὸ Τραιανοῦ ʼΑδ]ριανοῦ Boeckh, ὑ|[πὸ θεοῦ Dittenberger, θεοῦ
Πανελληνίου? Premerstein, παρὰ Oliver. 11 Σεβαστοῦ Premerstein, [Αὐτοκράτο]ρος Boeckh.

The inscription has been presented according to Boeckh's reconstruction as adapted by later scholars to spatial and formulaic requirements. The adverbs in lines 6 and 10 are less certain than the other restorations. The name Leucippus in line 1 is that of the founder of Magnesia, hence is not thought to be connected with the pre-script of the decree. If Leucippus was not the archon of the Panhellenion or proposer of the decree or both, the word ἀρχηγέτης may have stood at the beginning of line 2 and been part of the city's record.

The Magnesians receive recognition from the Panhellenion for their ancient Hellenic origin, their services to other Hellenes, and their good reputation at Rome. They are presumably being admitted.

It is worth noticing perhaps that ancient origins and services to Rome (*vetustate generis, studio in populum Romanum*) were the arguments used by cities in the time of Tiberius according to Tacitus, *Ann.*, IV, 55, 2, in order to obtain the honor of erecting the emperor's temple.

6. Decree of the Panhellenion concerning Cibyra

G. Castaldi, *Memorie della R. Accademia Ercolanese di Archeologia*, I, 1822, pp. 193-205; J. Franz, *C.I.G.*, III (1853), 5852; G. Kaibel, *I.G.*, XIV (1890), 829. The inscription was found at Puteoli, but how it got to Italy is unknown.

        [ʼΑ]γαθῆι Τύ[χ]ηι Ζεὺς Σω[τήρ]
        Ἡ Κιβυρατῶν πόλις ἄποικος Λ[υδῶν οὖσα καὶ]
        συγγενὶς ʼΑθηναίων καὶ φι[λ . . . . καὶ]
        αὐτὴ τοῦ κοινοῦ τῆς Ἑλλάδος [ἐν ταῖς μάλιστα]
5   ἐνδόξοις οὖσα καὶ μεγάλαις [τῆς ʼΑσίας πόλε]
        σιν διά τε τὸ γένος Ἑλληνι[κὸν καὶ διὰ τὴν]
        πρὸς ʽΡωμαίους ἐκ παλαιοῦ φι[λίαν καὶ εὔνοι]
        αν καὶ διὰ τὸ εὐξῆσθαι τειμαῖ[ς μεγάλαις ὑπὸ]
        θεοῦ ʼΑδριανοῦ ἀνέθηκε τῆι [. . . . . δό]
10   γμα τ[ο]ῦ Πανελληνίου ἐνγρα[. . . . .]
        [— — — — — — — — — — — — — — — — — — —]

Restorations: 1 Castaldi. 2 Λ[υδῶν C., cetera Franz. 3 φί[λη C., καὶ ἡ Franz. 4 ἐν C., cetera Franz. 5 πόλε C., cetera Franz. 6 Ἑλληνι[κόν C., cetera Franz. 7 φι[λί C., cetera Franz. 8 Franz. 9 δό C., πόλει Franz. 10 ἐν γρ[άμμασι C.

With the infinitive εὐξῆσθαι (from αὐξάνω) in line 8 compare the aorist εὔξησα on the Monumentum Ancyranum, IV, 8.

7. Epistle of Hadrian and other documents of inscription at Cyrene

Cyrene. P. M. Fraser, " Hadrian and Cyrene," *J.R.S.*, XL, 1950, pp. 77-87, with a good photograph; J. H. Oliver, " New Evidence on the Attic Panhellenion," *Hesperia*, XX, 1951, a report on evidence which had come to light since 1922, with discussion of the inscription from Cyrene on pp. 32 f.; J. A. O. Larsen, " Cyrene and the Panhellenion," *Cl. Phil.*, XLVII, 1952, pp. 7-16; C. B. Welles, *A.J.A.*, LVI, 1952, pp. 76 f.

θεός ^{vv} Τύχ[ᾳ Ἀγαθᾷ]

Αὐτοκράτωρ Καῖσαρ θεοῦ Τρα[ιανοῦ Δακικοῦ Παρθικοῦ υἱός, θεοῦ]
Νέρουα υἱωνός, Τραιανὸς Ἀδριαν[ὸς Σεβαστός, ἀρχιερεὺς μέγιστος,]
δημαρχικῆς ἐξουσίας τὸ ῑθ, ὕπατ[ος τὸ γ̄, πατὴρ πατρίδος,]

5   Κυρηναίοις   [χαίρειν.]

Ὁ ἄρχων τοῦ Πανελληνίου ἐφολκεῖ, ἐπιστεῖλαί μοι π[ροτιμῶν, περὶ — — — — — — —]·
τὰ δόξαντά μοι ἀντέγ[ρ]αψα καὶ ὑμεῖν ἔπεμψα τὴν προ[— — — — — — — — — ἣν
ἔγραψε Σαλούιος]
Κᾶρος ὁ κράτιστος ἀνθύπατος *vacat* εὐτυχεῖ[τε *vacat* Λέγουσιν ὅτι σύνεδρον καὶ
ἐξ αὐτῶν]
δέχεσθαι δεῖ· οὐ μέντοι δίκαια ἀξιοῦσιν· τῶν αὐτ[οφυῶν Κυρηναίων ἦν ἐκ παλαιοῦ
τὸ γέ]
10   νος Ἀχαιὸν καὶ ἀκρειβῶς Δώρ[ι]ον, αὐτοὶ δὲ ἰθαγεν[εῖς μᾶλλον ἢ Ἕλληνες τὰ
ἄνωθεν ὄντες]
προσεκτήσαντο τὴν προσηγορίαν ἀπὸ τοῦ ἐπικρυ[— — — — — — — — — — — — — —πό]
λιν· Κυρηναίων δὴ δύο συνέδρους πεμπόντω[ν — — — — — — — — — — — — — — — —]
κεφάλαια ἐξ ἐπιστολ[ῆς Σαλουίου Κάρου]
Προσκειμένου δὲ ἐπὶ τέλους ἑνί, ὅτι ἄρα ἐπέθεσ[αν — — — — — — — — — — — — — —]
15   συμ[φ]έρειν τῇ πόλει προϋποσυλλέγειν αὐτὸν ἐπι[— — — — — — — — — — — — — —]
ἀνάμνησιν τῆς παλαιᾶς ὑμῶν εὐγενείας διε[— — — — — — — — — — — — — — — — —]
θω θήσεσθαι δοκεῖ ἐπέδωκέ μοι ^{vv} ϛ ^{vv} νῦν [— — — — — — — — — — — — — — — —]
πολυανθρωποτάτην καὶ καλλίστην πόλιν, γένος[— — — — — — — — — — — — — — — —]
μητρόπολις [ἄ]ρα πλείστους Ἕλληνας ΕΡΓΛΑ[— — — — — — — — — — — — — — — —]
20   γραφα ὅτι καλὰ καὶ πρέποντα αὐτοῖς ἐστιν[— — — — — — — — — — — — — — — — —]
εἶναι δίκαιον τὸ πρὸς τὴν μητρόπολιν[— — — — — — — — — — — — — — — — — — —]
θεστῶτας, τὴν ἐπ[ικ]ουρίαν παρὰ τῶν θ[— — — — — — — — — — — — — — — — — —]
ὡς μὲν βούλοιμι, [π]λῆθος ἀνδρῶν παρ[— — — — — — — — — — — — — — — — — — —]
πᾶν [γ]ένος καὶ πολυδύναμον τὴν Κυρ[ήνην — — — — — — — — — — — — — — — — —]
25   κεφάλαιον ἐκ [— — — — — Ἀδριανοῦ]

Βουλοίμην δ' ἂν πα[?σ]ῶ[ν] τῷ φόβῳ τῶν ε[– – – – – – – – – – – – – – – – – –]
τας καὶ ἀναμνησθέντας ὅτι αἰσχρόν ἐστι[– – – – – – – – – – – – – – – – – – –]
᾽Απόλλωνος ᾠκισμένην ἀναξίως και[–]
κειμένην συνελθεῖν καὶ συναυξῆσαι τ[ὴν ὑμετέραν πόλιν? – – – – – – – – – – – –]
30   καὶ οἰκιστὰς γενέσθαι τῆς πατρίδος ᵛ [– – – – – – – – – – – – – – – – – – –]
Πυνθάνομαι τὸ γυμνάσιον ὑμῶν κα[–]
λοὺς ἤδη παῖδας τρεφομένους καὶ αὐ[–]
νῷ γυμνασίῳ συναναφύρωνται τοῖς α[–]
εἰς ἣν φοιτῶντες καὶ τὰς διατριβὰς ποι[ούμενοι ? – – – – – – – – – δωρεὰς τὰς]
35   παρ᾽ ἐμοῦ διδομένας   vacat
῾Ο μάλιστα ἀνανκαῖον ἦν ὡς ἠξιώσατ[ε – – – – – – – – – – – – – – – – – – –]
.ην ἐστὶν δὲ οὐδὲν νόμῳ πρου[–]
κατοικιζομένην· ᵛ τινὲς δ᾽ ἂν νο[–]
καὶ τύχῃ τινὶ ἀγαθῇ τῆς Κυρήνη[ς –]
40   [μ]ονίοις ἐπηνωρθωκὼς τοὺς[–]
[– – –]ηο[– – – – – – – – –]ν[–]
Δωριέων γαρ ἀνθρώπω[ν –]
σωφροσύνη καὶ ἄσκη[σις –]
45   ὁ[ρ]ῶ γὰρ καὶ διὰ τὸ γρ[–]
ατω τῶν[   ]ου[–]
μην τ[–]
καὶ τη[–]
]ο[–]

The text here presented retains Fraser's formulaic restorations of lines 1-5 and offers new restorations by Oliver at the ends of lines 6-10.

Line 6: Punctuation here introduced after ἐφολκεῖ (so rather than ἐφέλκει) implies that the infinitive ἐπιστεῖλαι is not governed by this verb. The infinitive could depend upon a participle lost in the lacuna. The verb ἐφολκεῖ, found on the Archilochus monument as Fraser reports, means " is hesitant."

Lines 9-11: The antithesis εἶναι-καλεῖσθαι seems to appear in this passage and gives us a basis for restoration. For the Achaean element in the Dorian population of Thera, whence Cyrene was colonized, see Franz Kiechle, *Lakonien und Sparta* (*Vestigia*, V), 1963, pp. 81-95. These were old traditions; in a real sense (ἀκρειβῶς)[5]

---

[5] The word ἀκριβῶς means that in the truest sense they were Dorians whatever they might seem to be superficially. Compare Cassius Dio, LII, 1, who says that in 27 B.C. the Romans *really* (ἀκριβῶς) began to be ruled monarchically, although Octavian *talked* about laying down arms and restoring the republic: ἐκ δὲ τούτου μοναρχεῖσθαι αὖθις ἀκριβῶς ἤρξαντο, καίτοι τοῦ Καίσαρος βουλευσαμένου τά τε ὅπλα καταθέσθαι καὶ τὰ πράγματα τῇ τε γερουσίᾳ καὶ τῷ δήμῳ ἐπιτρέψαι. Compare also the use of the noun ἀκρίβεια by Arrian, *Anabasis*, I, 9, 4, who says that the attack of Boeotians and Arcadians under Epaminondas against Sparta frightened the Lacedaemonians and their friends by

the Theran settlers were Dorian. Fraser read Δῶρον, but Δώρ[ι]ον seems possible.

Line 11: Some form or derivative of the verb ἐπικρύπτεσθαι must be assumed here, and a reference to irregular infiltration in a period of confusion seems likely.

Lines 16-17: Perhaps ἐπ᾽ ἀγα]θῷ.

The inscription begins with an epistle from the emperor to the Cyrenaeans concerning a matter referred to him by the archon of the Panhellenion. The emperor tells the Cyrenaeans that he has sent the archon of the Panhellenion a rescript on the subject. The rescript procedure was used to clarify a legal point, and our chief clue to the nature of this one lies in the word συνέδρους of line 12. The epistle ends in line 8 with the word εὐτυχεῖ[τε. The rescript or rather a paraphrase of the rescript which the emperor sent to the archon of the Panhellenes follows in lines 8-12, because the Cyrenaeans would have to be informed of the imperial ruling. For the kind of document we have in the rescript the reader may consult P. Col. 123 in the edition of H. C. Youtie and A. A. Schiller, " Second Thoughts on the Columbia *Apokrimata* (P. Col. 123)," *Chronique d'Égypte*, XXX, 1965, pp. 327-345.

In the writer's opinion the situation was one in which an excluded group connected with Cyrene demanded representation in the Panhellenion. The group cannot have been mere Libyans because they could not then have called themselves Hellenes, but they were partly Libyans (ἰθαγεν[εῖς) and could not claim the kind of credentials we find attested for the Magnesians (No. **5**) and the Cibyriates (No. **6**). Unlike the real Cyrenaeans they do not have the ancient traditions of free Hellenes, the *logoi* which educate.

Welles, who recognized that lines 8-12 did contain the decision of the emperor, thought that the city of Cyrene had sent a request " that they be admitted to the Panhellenion," but as Larsen notes, Cyrene had clearly been admitted previously. In discussing the problem the emperor treats the claim as unjustified. If the humiliation were their own, the Cyrenaeans would not have publicized it.

Fraser identified lines 14-24 as from another epistle of the emperor, Oliver as from an epistle of the governor. Welles argues that if κεφάλαια in line 13 means " Extracts," it proves that the document of lines 13-24 was an epistle of the Cyrenaeans themselves, " for they would not have abbreviated a letter from the proconsul,

the unfamiliarity of the sight rather than by the *reality* of the perils (τῷ ἀήθει τῆς ὄψεως μᾶλλον ἢ τῇ ἀκριβείᾳ τῶν κινδύνων). When Nicias (in Thucydides, VII, 13, 2) writes that the allied sailors were going off to trade and persuading the trierarchs to embark Hyccarian slaves in their place, he says that thereby they have removed the perfection which really made it the fleet, τὴν ἀκρίβειαν τοῦ ναυτικοῦ ἀφήρηνται. Compare Thucyd., VIII, 46, 5, τὴν ἀκμὴν τοῦ ναυτικοῦ αὐτῶν ἀφείλετο, and Arrian, *Anabasis*, I, 2, 7, τὴν ἀκρίβειαν τῆς διώξεως ἀφείλοντο. There is also the ἀκρίβεια (perfection) of a τέχνη and in Thucydides it is hard to tell which meaning predominates, perfection or reality. For further discussion of the words ἀκρίβεια, ἀκριβής and ἀκριβῶς in reference to the deeper truth or reality consult J. H. Oliver, *The Civilizing Power*, pp. 25-32.

whose every word partook of the sanctity which hedged the imperial service." This pronouncement does not convince us. The Cyrenaeans could have selected the pertinent parts of two documents and engraved them below the main one. That the document of lines 13-24 did not emanate from the Cyrenaeans is certain because of the first person singular. It is possible that the emperor sent them only paraphrased extracts, because the phrase in line 16, ἀνάμνησιν τῆς παλαιᾶς ὑμῶν εὐγενείας, must refer to the good ancestry of the Cyrenaeans, even if the proconsul's letter was addressed to the group with the unacceptable pretensions. With this interpretation we should connect the first person with the emperor and the third person singular with the governor Salvius Carus. Perhaps the group—the honor of an epistle suggests an independent city—claimed admission to the Panhellenion as Cyrenaeans themselves.

Lines 25 ff. may well have contained extracts from an edict of the emperor, as Fraser thought. The connection escapes us, but the subjects are clearly Cyrenaean.

Compare No. **8**.

8. M. Julius Praxis, Panhellene from Cyrene

Eleusis. A. Boeckh, *C.I.G.*, I, 351 from copies by Spon and Fourmont; W. Dittenberger, *I.G.*, III (1878), 534; J Kirchner, *I.G.*, II² (1935), 3407 from autopsy and squeeze.

A.D. 172-175

Αὐτοκράτορα Καίσ
αρα Μ· Αὐρήλιον Ἀντωνῖν
ον Γερμανικὸν Παρθικὸν
Μηδικὸν ﬦ Ἀπολλωνιᾶται
5 οἱ κατὰ Κυρήνην διὰ Μ·
Ἰουλίου Πράξιδος
Πανέλληνος

An inscription of 67 B.C. (so dated by J. Reynolds, *J.R.S.*, LII, 1962, p. 99) attests a dispute involving Cyrene and Apollonia.

Strabo, XVII, 837 describes Apollonia as a harbor of Cyrene. It presumably came at that time within the territory of Cyrene, but even if it went back to Ecdemus and Demophanes, its independence was not very ancient. The Apolloniates could have been the group which tried to obtain representation in the Panhellenion and caused the archon of the Panhellenes to consult with Hadrian, who notified the Cyrenaeans and sent a copy of his adverse ruling, which the Cyrenaeans publicized in the preceding inscription. This is far from certain, but if it were true, we should then ask whether they obtained representation at some later date. Is M. Julius Praxis a Panhellene from the Apolloniates or one of the two *synedroi* of the Cyrenaeans?

In the Olympieum at Athens these same Apolloniates had erected a statue of

Hadrian, *I.G.*, II², 3306, through a certain L. Novius Rufus,[6] who is not identified as a Panhellene. This could have been erected at the time they were seeking admission, if they really were the group. They honored Hadrian as their founder and benefactor, and this shows that they were an independent city from the Hadrianic period on, but not that they were eligible for the Panhellenion. In fact they would seem to have been without the qualification from antiquity.

9. The Archon T. Flavius Cyllus of Hypata

Athens. Anna S. Benjamin, *Hesperia*, XXXVII, 1968, pp. 340-344, No. 48.

A.D. 157

τὸ κοινὸν τῶν Θεσσα
λῶν Τίτον Φλάουιον
Κύλλον ἄρξαντα Πα
νελλήνων καὶ ἀγω
5   νοθετήσαντα τῶν
μεγάλων Πανελλη
νίων ἀρετῆς ἕνεκεν
καὶ εὐνοίας τῆς τε
εἰς τὸ Πανελλήνι
10   ον καὶ τὴν Ἀθηναί
ων πόλιν

Compare **28**. Miss Benjamin points out that as Larsen had suspected, " Thessaly was a member of the Panhellenion as a league and the Panhellenes were sent from the Thessalian League."

This archon of the Panhellenes belongs to a famous family of Hypata studied by J. A. O. Larsen, " A Thessalian Family under the Principate," *Cl. Phil.*, XLVIII, 1953, pp. 86-95, whether or not he is the Cyllus of an epigram by Ammianus, *Anth. Pal.*, XI, 16:

Κύλλος καὶ Λεῦρος δύο Θεσσαλοὶ ἐγχεσίμωροι,
Κύλλος δ' ἐκ τούτων ἐγχεσιμωρότερος.[7]

[6] An L. Novius Rufus shortly after Hadrian's death appears in *Supplemento Epigrafico Cirenaico*, No. 68 at Cyrene (G. Oliverio, *Annuario*, XXXIX-XL, 1961-1962, p. 257).

[7] The poetical word ἐγχεσίμωρος occurs in Iliad, II, 692 and 840 and VII, 134, also Odyssey, III, 188. Three of these passages concern Thessalians, and one of them couples two names, Iliad, II, 692, where it is said of Achilles:

κὰδ δὲ Μύνητ' ἔβαλεν καὶ Ἐπίστροφον ἐγχεσιμώρους
υἱέας Εὐηνοῖο Σεληπιάδαο ἄνακτος.

We do not know what kind of defeat Flavius Cyllus suffered, but we do know that Ulpius Leurus married Flavia Habroea and so into the family of Flavius Cyllus. The epigram implies that they were allied or opposed and declares that Cyllus showed himself more stupid than Leurus. While

10. The Archon Claudius Jason Magnus

Athens. Anna S. Benjamin, *Hesperia*, XXXVII, 1968, pp. 338-340, No. 47.

A.D. 161

καθ' ὑπομνηματισμὸν
τῆς ἐξ Ἀρείου πάγου βουλῆς
Τιβ. Κλ. Ἰάσονα Μάγνον ἄρξαν
τα Πανελληνίου Τιβ. Κλ.
5   Ἰάσων Μάγνος τὸν πατέρα

For the archon Claudius Jason (*PIR*² C 890) see No. **30**, which gave him the predicate of a knight according to A. Stein.

Claudius Jason Magnus is known from three inscriptions at Cyrene, which was undoubtedly his city of origin:

a) *S.E.G.*, IX, 172, first published by G. Oliverio, *Africa Italiana*, I, 1927, p. 335, No. 17: [Αὐτοκρα]τόρων Καισάρων Μ. Αὐρηλίω{ι} Ἀντ[ω]νεί[νω καὶ Λ. Αὐρη-λί]ω{ι} Κομόδω{ι} | [Σεβαστῶν] Τι. Κλαύδιος Ἰάσων Μᾶγνος ἱαρεὺς ἐπώνυμος τῶ κτίστα Ἀπόλλωνο[ς τ]ὸν ναὸν ἐκ | [τῶν ἀρχιδίων ἐκ τᾶν τῶ Ἀπόλλωνος προσόδ]ων κατεσκεύασεν vac ἀφιερώσαντος | [τῶ ἱαρεῦς τε καλλιέτευς Τι. Κλαυδί]ω Θευ[φράσ]τω{ι} καὶ πρεσ-β[ευτᾶ] ἐπ' ἀγαθῷ.

b) a mosaic inscription published by G. Pugliese Carratelli, *Supplemento epigrafico cirenaico*, No. 111 (*Annuario della Scuola Archeologica di Atene*, XXXIX-XL, 1963, p. 285): θεῷ μεγάλῳ Ἑρμῖ | Ἰανουάριος δοῦλ(ος) | εὐχὴν ἣν εὐξάμην | ὑπέρ τε σωτ[ηρί]ας | καὶ νείκης Τι. Κλ. | Ἰάσονος Μάγνω | ἐκ τῶν ἰδίων | ἐψηφοθέτη[σα]. P. Mingazzini, *L'insula di Giasone Magno a Cirene* (Monografie di Archeologia Libica, VIII), Rome, 1966, p. 14 dated the victory either in 177 or in the time of Septimius Severus if the Jason Magnus was the homonymous son; but a narrow escape and victory under his own auspices by a man known to be a knight point, I think, to the surprise raids of barbarians in 170. He may have raised a fleet or a force of police like the *diogmitae* of the *Vita Marci*, 21, 7.

c) *S.E.G.*, IX, 161, first published in *Africa Italiana*, I, 1927, pp. 335 f., No. 18/19: Τι. Κλ. Ἰάσων Μᾶγνος ἱερώμενος ἐκ τῶν ἰδίων.

11. Flavius Sulpicianus Dorion of Hierapytna

Athens, from the Agora. Six fragments published by A. Raubitschek, *Hesperia*, XII, 1943, pp. 73-76, No. 22, including two previously published by J. Kirchner as *I.G.*, II², 4076.

the family of Cyllus had been prominent for generations, Ulpius Leurus is for us the first known member of his family. Outside of this family the name Leurus never occurs in extant inscriptions from Greece. It is a Celtic name, which occurs in Lusitania in an inscription published by F. de Almeida, *Egitânia: história e arqueologia*, Lisbon, 1956, No. 131.

['Ἀππίαν 'Αννίαν 'Ρή]γιλλ[αν 'Ατι]
λία[ν Καυκιδίαν Τερτύλλα]ν
'Απ[πίου ὑπάτου ποντίφ]ικος
θυγ[ατέρα 'Ηρώιδου Μα]ραθω
5 νίου [ὑπάτο]υ ἐξηγητο[ῦ] γυναῖκα
Φλ⟩ Σο[υλπι]κιανὸς Δωρ[ίω]ν ἄρχων
τοῦ Π[ανελ]ληνίου εἰς [πα]ρηγορίαν
φ[ιλ]ου

Raubitschek dated the inscription shortly after 160/1. For the Roman (not Athenian) priesthood of line 5 see J. H. Oliver, *The Athenian Expounders*, pp. 110-116.

L. Flavius Sulpicianus Dorion appears (usually with the differentiating praenomen) in *I. Cret.*, III, pp. 60-63, Nos. 16, 17, 18, 20 and 21 at Hierapytna, where he honored Lucius Verus and Marcus with statues representing each as τὸν κύριον τῆς οἰκουμένης. In *I. Cret.*, III, p. 62, No. 22 he honors his son L. Flavius Sulpicianus Dorion Polymnis as praetor designate. His father, T. Flavius Sulpicianus Dorion, had been high priest in the Cretan *koinon* in A.D. 129 (*I. Cret.*, IV, 275). Marini and Groag suspected that the very rich Arval Brother and would-be emperor T. Flavius Sulpicianus Flaccus (*PIR²*, F, 373) came from the same family, not so G. Alföldi, *Bonner Jahrbücher*, CLXVIII, 1968, pp. 121 and 142.

12. Flavius Xenion of Gortyn

Eleusis. *I.G.*, II², 3627 plus two new fragments added by Kevin Clinton, who will publish it in the 'Αρχαιολογικὸν Δελτίον.

['Ἀγ]αθῆι Τύ[χη]ι
τὸν κράτιστο[ν Ξ]ενί
ωνα τὸν ἄρξα[ντα] τῶν
Πανελλήνω[ν τὸ]ν ἄρι
5 στον πολειτ[ευτ]ὴν
οἱ Πανέλλη[νες] *vac*

Restorations in lines 1, 3 and 6 are by Kirchner, those in lines 2, 4 and 5 are by Clinton.

Clinton restored the name in line 2 from *Hesperia*, XXI, 1952, pp. 396 f., where it is argued that Flavius Xenion was a friend of Lucius Verus.

13. Unknown Archon, Priest and Agonothete

Athens, " in gradibus Parthenonis." W. Dittenberger, *I.G.*, III, 681; [J. Kirchner, *I.G.*, II², 3626].

Ἀγαθῇ [Τύχῃ]
τὸν ἄρχο[ντα τῶν]
σεμνο[τάτων Παν]
ελλήνω[ν καὶ ἱερέα]
θεοῦ Ἀδ[ριανοῦ Παν]
5 [ελ]ληνί[ου καὶ ἀγω]
νοθ[έ]τ[ην τῶν Παν]
[ελλη[ν[ίων – – –]
[– – – – – – – –]

Dittenberger's restorations.

14. Unknown Archon, Priest and Agonothete

Athens, "in gradibus Parthenonis." W. Dittenberger, *I.G.*, III (1878), 17, from Koehler's copy; [J. Kirchner, *I.G.*, II², 1093].

[– – – – – – – – – – – – – – – – – – – –]
[τὸν τῶν Πανελλήν]ων ἄρχ[οντα καὶ ἱερέα]
[θεοῦ Ἀδριανοῦ Πα]νελληνίο[υ καὶ ἀγωνο]
[θετοῦντα τῶν μεγ]άλων Πανελλ[ηνίων – –]
[– – – – – – – – –]οι Αὐρ Ρουφ[ο – – –]
5 [– – – – – – – – – – – –]ν καὶ το[– – –]
[– – – – – – – – – – – – – – – – – –]

Restorations: 1 Oliver. 2 Πα]νελλήνιο[ν Dittenberger, cetera Oliver. 3 θετοῦντα Oliver, cetera D. 4 Ρούφ[ου D.

Dittenberger identified Aurelius Rufus as the sophist from Perinthus, whose biographer, Philostratus, *V.S.*, p. 100 Kayser, p. 248 Wright, reported τὴν τῶν Πανελ-λήνιων Ἀθήνησιν εὐκλεῶς ἦρξεν.

15. Archon Flavius Amphicles

Eleusis. A. N. Skias, Ἐφ. Ἀρχ., 1894, col. 184; J. Kirchner, *I.G.*, II² (1935), 2957.

Οἱ ἐπὶ Φλαουί
ου Ἀμφικλέ
ους ἄρχοντος
Πανέλληνες
5 ἐκ τῆς τοῦ Δη
μητρίου καρ
ποῦ ἀπαρχῆς

As M. N. Tod, *J.H.S.*, XLII, 1922, p. 117, note 30 pointed out, Flavius Amphicles was archon of the Panhellenes. Graindor, *Chronologie*, p. 132, note 1 and *Athènes sous Hadrien,* p. 104, note 3 identified him with Amphicles of Chalcis, attested as a student of Herodes Atticus by Philostratus, *V.S.*, II, 8, 1-2, p. 84 Kayser, and II, 10, 1-2, p. 90 Kayser.

For the first fruits see Meiggs-Lewis, *G.H.S.*, No. 73 with commentary.

16. Archon Aristaeus

Eleusis. J. Spon and G. Wheler, *Voyage d'Italie, de Dalmatie, de Grece, et du Levant fait aux années 1675 et 1676*, Amsterdam, 1679, II p. 408; A. Boeckh, *C.I.G.*, I (1828), 484; W. Dittenberger, *I.G.*, III (1878), 85; A. N. Skias, Ἐφ. Ἀρχ., 1894, cols. 184 f.; J. Kirchner, *I.G.*, II² (1935), 2956; P. Graindor, *Athènes sous Hadrien,* p. 126.

> οἱ Πανέλληνες [ἐπὶ . . .]
> Ἀρισταίο[υ ἄρχοντος]
> ἐκ [τῆς τοῦ Δημητρίου]
> καρποῦ ἀπαρχῆς

M. N. Tod, *J.H.S.*, XLII, 1922, p. 117, note 30 suggested that the name of an archon stood in line 2. This is our opinion too, and probably only one name is short enough. After the second alpha of line 2 Skias saw a vertical hasta, and then trace of a circular letter, then a horizontal stroke as of a gamma (we read upsilon with a horizontal tip) and then an uncertain eta (which we interpret as alpha).

The restorations ἐπί . . . and Ἀρισταίου are by Oliver, the former filling out the line to agree with the length of line 3 as restored uncertainly but correctly by Skias.

17. Iobacchi Inscription

Athens. *S.I.G.*³, 1109 = *I.G.*, II², 1368, translated by M. N. Tod, *Sidelights on Greek History*, Oxford, 1932, pp. 85-96. For the date, around A.D. 162/3, see P. Graindor, *Un milliardaire antique: Hérode Atticus et sa famille*, p. 70, and compare *Hesperia*, XXIV, 1955, p. 323. For complete text and commentary see now F. Sokolowski, *Lois sacrées des cités grecques*, Paris, 1969, No. 51.

> ὃς δ' ἂν τῶν ἰοβάκχων λάχῃ κλῆ
> ρον ἢ τειμὴν ἢ τάξιν, τιθέτω τοῖς ἰο
> βάκχοις σπονδὴν ἀξίαν τῆς τάξεως,
> 130   γάμων, γεννήσεως, Χοῶν, ἐφηβείας,
> πολειτείας, ῥαβδοφορίας, βουλείας, ἀ
> θλοθεσίας, Πανέλληνος, γερουσίας,

θεσμοθεσίας, ἀρχῆς ἧς δή ποτε οὖν,

συνθυσίας, εἰρηναρχίας, ἱερονείκου,

135   καὶ εἴ τίς τι ἐπὶ τὸ κρεῖσσον ἰόβακχος ὢν τύχοιτο.

18. Omission of Distribution to celebrate the Panhellenia

Athens. W. Dittenberger, *I.G.*, III (1878), 1141; J. Kirchner, *I.G.*, II² (1931), 1141; P. Graindor, *Athènes sous Hadrien* p. 102, note 3; M. Mitsos, *Polemon*, IV, 1949, p. 20. This fragmentary ephebic catalogue contains the observation

καὶ ἐκ Παν[ελ]

ληνίου οὐθέν

In this year, as Graindor notes, the ephebes did not obtain their part of the distributions made on the occasion of the Panhellenia. Graindor dates the inscription between 173/4 and 178/9.

19. Agonothete of the Panhellenia

Athens. Two fragments of a circular statue base of white marble, broken all around, published by Ph. D. Stavropoullos, ᾽Αρχ. Δελτίον, XX, 1965, Χρονικά, pp. 64-66 with drawings.

A

[— — — — — — —]νεσοι ἐπὶ

[— — — — — — Π]ανελληνι

[— — — — — — — —]υτο[. . . .]

B

[— — — — — — — — — — —]νει[.]

[— — — — — — —] ἱερέα θ[ε]

[ου ῾Αδριανοῦ Παν]ελληνί ⱽ

4   [ου καὶ ἀγωνοθέτ]ην τῶν μ[ε]

[γάλων Πανελ]ληνίων · κ[αὶ]

[— — — — —]αμωνια[. .]

[— — — — — —]ιέα τὸν

Fragment B, lines 2-4 were restored by J. and L. Robert, *Bull. ép.*, 1968, No. 225.

20. Archon Casianus Antiochus called Synesius

Athens. Base in the Roman Market Place, published by Ph. D. Stavropoullos, ᾽Αρχ. Δελτ., XIII, 1930-31, Παράρτημα, p. 7; J. H. Oliver, " The Μουσεῖον in Late Attic Inscriptions," *Hesperia*, III, 1934, pp. 191-196 with photograph; [J. Kirchner, *I.G.*, II², 3712].

Ἀγαθῆι Τύχῃ
Κασιανὸν Ἀντίοχ[ον]
τὸν καὶ Συνέσιον,
τὸν ἐπὶ τοῦ Μουσίο[υ],
5   Πανελλήνων ἄρχον[τα],
[ὁ Ἄ]ριος πάγος, ἡ β[ουλὴ]
καὶ ὁ δῆμος

The second name in line 2 was originally read as Ἀντίου.

Oliver interpreted the Museum as a local corporation, but P. Graindor, " Le nom de l'Université d'Athènes sous l'Empire," *Revue belge de philosophie et d'histoire,* XVII, 1938, pp. 207-212 supported the view that Casianus was president of the Museum of Alexandria and a Greek from Egypt. Unwilling to recognize any Panhellene as a Greek from Egypt, Oliver would still see the Museum as a local corporation. The *signum* Synesius is already attested at Athens in a religious philosophical environment by *I.G.,* II², 13209, which begins Ἀντωνία ἡ καὶ Σωκρατικὴ τῷ γλυκυτάτῳ μου ἀνδρὶ Ἀντιόχῳ τῷ καὶ Συνεσίῳ, cited by Hélène Wuilleumier, " Étude historique sur l'emploi et la signification des signa," *Mém. présentés par divers savants à l'Acad. Inscr. et Belles-Lettres,* XIII, 1932, pp. 556-696. This is undoubtedly our man.

Since the man is being honored as archon of the Panhellenes, the absence of a demotic or ethnic has no significance. He could easily be an Athenian. In fact he must be an Athenian because he uses the name Casianus as a nomen like the Athenian archon Κασιανὸς Ἱεροκῆρυξ Στειριεύς attested by *I.G.,* II², 2241, which, thanks to L. Moretti, *Iscrizioni agonistiche greche,* Rome, 1953, pp. 202 f., may now be dated in 230/1. One branch of this family, to which C. Julius Casius of Steiria, Athenian archon in 125/6, and C. Julius Casianus Apollonius of Steiria, cosmete in *I.G.,* II², 2085 of 161/2, belonged, adopted this very unusual nomen in the Severan period. Since the above mentioned Athenian archon of 230/1 held the hieronymous priesthood of Sacred Herald, the Casiani were native Athenians and members of the sacred genos of the Ceryces. The nomen occurs also in *I.G.,* II², 1826 and 2203.

Many cities had Musea (Chr. Habicht, *Alt. v. Perg.,* VIII, 3, pp. 149-151, No. 152). The most important parallel at Athens would be the inscription, *Hesperia,* XV, 1946, p. 233, No. 64 (Trajanic), erected by a man who calls himself ὁ ἱερεὺς Μουσῶν Φιλοσόφων Τ. Φλάβιος Πάνταινος Φλαβίου Μενάνδρου διαδόχου υἱός. Pantaenus, who was not a *diadochos,* gave a library (of philosophy) with all its books and equipment and placed it under the protection of Athena Polias, the emperor and the Polis. This library, surrounded by arcades and serving all four Schools, may well have been the Museum or part of the Museum over which Casianus Antiochus called Synesius presided under the Severi.[8]

---

[8] The family tree may be represented as follows:

21-22. Imperial Letters Concerning Athletes who Avoided the Panhellenia

These two inscriptions are strikingly similar in subject matter, marble, thickness, original width, and lettering, but as Daniel J. Geagan notified me, they are not by the same hand. The one epistle, dated to A.D. 201, went from Septimius Severus and Caracalla to the Panhellenion. The senders and recipients of the other epistle are unknown. For instance, it could have been a letter of the same emperors to the city of Athens, or it could have been a letter of, say, Marcus Aurelius and Commodus to the Panhellenion. The same abuses often recurred.

For some reason, perhaps because too much reliance was placed on the prestige of the Panhellenia and because the prizes at Athens no longer had the real value of inflated prizes elsewhere, professional athletes were unwilling to return. After the accession of Septimius Severus, whose antipathy for Athens was well known, the tendency had to be corrected or corrected again. In 195 or soon thereafter the Athenians honored Julia Domna as " the savior of Athens." By A.D. 201 Septimius Severus was sufficiently interested and placated to intervene.

21. Athens, the Roman Market Place. N. M. Verdelis, *B.C.H.*, LXXI-LXXII, 1947-1948, pp. 34-42, with photograph of the two fragments.

καὶ Αὐτοκράτωρ]
[Καῖσαρ Λ. Σεπτιμίου] Σεουήρου Εὐσε[βοῦς]
[Περτίνακος Σεβαστοῦ Ἀραβικοῦ Ἀδια]

C. Iulius Casianus Apollonius of Steiria
anticosmete in 158/9 (*I.G.*, II², 2079)
cosmete in 161/2 (*I.G.*, II², 2085)

C. Iulius Casianus Apollonius
ephebic archon in 161/2 (*I.G.*, II², 2085)
hoplite general in 188/9 (*Hesp.* Suppl. VIII, p. 282)
archon *ca.* 200 (*I.G.*, II², 2199)

C. Iulius Casius
ephebic basileus in 161/2 (*I.G.*, II², 2085)

Casianus Antiochus called Synesius = Antonia called Socratica
director of the Museum (at Athens)   *I.G.*, II², 13209
archon of the Panhellenes

Casianus Antiochus, archon of the Panhellenes, and Casianus Hierokeryx, Athenian archon in 230/1, are closely related but probably not identical. In *Hesperia*, Suppl. VIII, p. 282 the name of the former's father should be supplied without a praenomen and Raubitschek's restoration in lines 7-8 should be resolved [στρατ]ηγοῦντ[ος ἐπὶ τὰ ὅπλα] Κασ(ιανοῦ) | [Ἀπο]λλωνίου Σ[τειριέως, but in *Hesperia*, XI, 1942, p. 60, No. 25 it reads στρατη[γοῦντος | ἐπὶ τ]ὰ ὅπλα Γ. Κασσίου Ἀπο[λλω|νίου Στ]ερι[έως, because the scribe or stonecutter resolved the abbreviation Κασ erroneously. Casianus Hierokeryx is attested as archon eponymous certainly in *I.G.*, II², 2241 and more dubiously in *I.G.*, II², 1832 and 2230 (M. Mitsos, Ἀρχ. Ἐφ., 1950-1951, p. 47, No. 29).

[βηνικοῦ Παρθικοῦ Μεγίστου υἱός, θεοῦ]
[Μάρκου Ἀντωνίνου Εὐσεβοῦς Σεβαστοῦ]
5   Γερμανικοῦ Σαρματικο[ῦ υἱωνός, θεοῦ]
Ἀντωνίνου Εὐσεβοῦς ἔκγο[νος, θεοῦ]
Ἁδριανοῦ καὶ θεοῦ Τραιανοῦ [Παρθικοῦ]
καὶ θεοῦ Νέρουα ἀπόγονος, Μᾶρκος [Αὐρήλιος]
Ἀντωνῖνος, Εὐσεβὴς Σεβαστός, δημαρχ[ικῆς]
10 ἐξουσίας τὸ δ', ὕπατος ἀποδεδιγμένο[ς],
ἀνθύπατος, τῶι Πανελληνίωι χαίρειν.
Ἐδήλωσεν ἡμεῖν Κοκκήιος Τιμάσαρχος
ὁ ἄρξας ὑμῶν, ὅτι τῶν ἀθλητῶν τινες τοῦ
ἀγῶνος καταφρονήσαντες παρέπλευσαν
15 τὰς Ἀθήνας· ἡμεῖς δὲ ἀνανεούμεθα μεν
[– – – – – – – – – – – – – – –]

The restorations are by Verdelis.

The year A.D. 201 is exactly forty-four years after the year in which the change from the archonship of Flavius Cyllus to that of Claudius Jason Magnus occurred, and since we now know that the term of the archon was four years, we may certainly infer that in A.D. 201 a change of archon occurred. Therefore Cocceius Timasarchus was probably the archon who went out of office sometime in A.D. 201.

To complain to the emperors Septimius Severus and Caracalla about the attitude of athletes toward the Panhellenia and to report the erection of statues of the emperors, the ex-archon apparently had gone on an embassy to Septimius Severus and Caracalla. Since Caracalla received the *toga virilis* and became *consul designatus* at Antioch in 201, we may infer that Cocceius Timasarchus had gone to Antioch, because Septimius Severus and Caracalla were still there on January 1, 202.[9]

22. Athens, from the Acropolis. For all practical purposes the first edition was that of W. Dittenberger, *I.G.*, III (1878), 32 from Koehler's copy. There followed that of J. Kirchner, *I.G.*, II² (1906), 1106. A photograph made in 1969 appears on Plate 7, b.

[– – – – – – – – – – – – – – – – – – –]
[– – – – – – –] τοῦτο αὐτὸ ἀπο[– – – – –]
[– – – – – – –]ς νομοθετούμενα [– – – – –]
[– – τοῖς μὲν ἀγῶ]να παρ' ὑμεῖν νενικη[κόσι],
[εὔλογον αἰτίαν ε]ἰ μὴ ἀποδείξαιέν τ[ινα]

---

[9] *Vita Severi*, 16, 8; G. Downey, *A History of Antioch in Syria from Seleucus to the Arab Conquest*, Princeton, 1961, p. 242.

5 [διότι] οὐ κατή[ρχο]ντο εἰς τὰ Πανελλ[ήνια],
[ἱερον]είκαις τὰ π[α]ρ᾽ ὑμεῖν συντάξεις [ἀφε]
[λεῖν, το]ῖς δὲ μὴ νεν[ι]κηκόσιν μὴ ἐξεῖνα[ι ἔτι]
[εἰς ἱερ]ῶν μηδένα τῶν παρ᾽ ὑμεῖν ἀγών[ων κατ]
[ελθεῖ]ν· καὶ ἡμεῖς μὲν ταῦτα τῇ συνόδ[ῳ δηλώ]
10 [σομε]ν, ὑμεῖς δέ, ὁπότε τις ἀπο[λ]ειφθεί[η χωρὶς]
[λόγο]υ, τὰ δόξαντα ἡμεῖν μην[ύ]σετε· [διηγή]
[σατο] δὲ καὶ περὶ τῶν ἀνδριάντων, οὓς [εἰς τι]
[μὴν ἡ]μῶν ἀνεστή[σα]τε· τὰς διανομὰς [ἂν πά]
[σας ἡ]δέως ἐδ[ίδο]μεν καὶ ἡμεῖ[ς – – – – – –]
15 [– – – – – – – –]ν τείμια νο[– – – – – – – –]
[– – – – – – – – – – – – – – – – – – – –]

Restorations: 3 τοῖς μὲν Oliver; ἀγῶ]να, νενικη[κότ|ας Dittenberger. 4 ε]ἰ D.; cetera Oliver. 5 Πανελλ[ήνια] D.; cetera Oliver. 6 [ἱερον]είκαις Wilamowitz (I.G., II², 1106); π[α]ρ᾽ D.; ἀφε Oliver. 7 λεῖν, ἔτι Oliver; το]ῖς, νεν[ι]κηκόσιν, ἐξεῖνα[ι αὐ|τ]ῶν D. 8 [εἰς ἱερ]ῶν, κατ] Oliver; ἀγών[ων μετ|έχει]ν D. 9 [ελθεῖ]ν Oliver; συνόδ[ῳ δηλώσ|ομεν D. 10 χωρὶς Oliver; ἀπολειφ[θείη τού|το]ν D. 11 [λόγο]υ, διηγή|σατο Oliver; μην[ύ]σετε [ἤσθη|μεν] D. 12 οὓς [εἰς τι|μὴν Oliver; οὖσ[τινα|ς D. 13 ἡ]μῶν ἀνεστή[σα]τε, [δὲ πάσ|ας D.; [ἂν πά|σας Oliver. 14 ἡ]δέως ἐδ[ίδο]μεν, ἡμεῖς D. 15 νο[μίζοντες D.

The restoration of line 4 and of lines 10-11 has been inspired by Cassius Dio, LV, 3, 2, τοῖς μὴ δι᾽ εὔλογόν τινα αἰτίαν τῆς συνεδρείας ἀπολειπομένοις.

The *synodos* mentioned in line 9 was an athletic guild,[10] the Sacred Guild of Roving Athletes Devoted to Heracles and the Emperors.

A new section begins in line 11. At the end of the line some verb indicated a speech by the ambassador. The word καί in line 12 invalidates Dittenberger's restoration ἤσθη|μεν.

23. Athenian Decree upon Geta's Accession

Athens. A. Boeckh, *C.I.G.*, I (1828), 353 from Fourmont's copy; W. Dittenberger, *I.G.*, III (1878), 10 from Koehler's copy of lines 1-20; J. Kirchner, *I.G.*, II² (1916), 1077 with the help of a squeeze.

A.D. 209/10

['Επὶ ἄρχοντος] Φλ. Διογένους Μαραθωνίου, ἐπὶ τῆς Πανδιονί
[δος – – – πρυ]τανείας, ἧς ἐγραμμάτευεν Ῥόδων Καλλίστου Μαρα
[θώνιος], ἱερε[ὺ]ς Θεόφιλος ἐπεστάτει, τῶν προέδρων ἐπεψή
[φιζεν] Ἰουλιανὸς Κασίου καὶ οἱ συμπρόεδροι, κγ̅ τῆς πρυτα
5 [νείας], μηνὸς Ποσειδεῶνος τῆς λ̕, βουλὴ συνήχθη ἐπὶ τοῖς

---

[10] Cl. A. Forbes, "Ancient Athletic Guilds," *Cl. Phil.*, L, 1955, pp. 238-252, with attention to the exemptions enjoyed by *hieronikai*. For further evidence on privileges and exemptions see the Oxyrhynchus Papyri 2475-7, published in 1962.

[εὐαγγ]ελίοις, ἀναδειχθέντος ‖[Αὐτοκράτορος Καίσαρος Ποπλίου]‖

‖[Σεπτιμίου Γέτα Εὐσεβοῦς Σεβαστοῦ]‖· ἐν ᾗ ἀνεγνώσθη

[γνώμ]η [τ]ῶν συνεδρίων διὰ τῶν ἀρχόν[τ]ων, ἀναγνόν

[τος τοῦ] στρατηγοῦ Ἀλκαμένους Λαμπτρέως γνώμην τὴν ἀναγεγραμμένη[ν]·

10 [Ἡ ἐξ Ἀρείου] πάγου βουλὴ καὶ ἡ βουλὴ τῶν Φ καὶ ὁ δημος ὁ Ἀθηναί

[ων μετὰ] τῶν ἀρχόντων, τοῦ τε ἐπωνύμου ἄρχοντος Φλ. Διογένους

[Μαραθων]ίου κα[ὶ τ]οῦ ἐπὶ τὰ ὅπλα στρατηγοῦ καὶ ἐπιμελητοῦ γυ

[μνασιαρχί]ας θε[οῦ] Ἀδρι[α]νοῦ καὶ ἀ[ντ]άρχοντος τοῦ ἱερωτάτου Ἀτ

[τικοῦ Π]ανελληνίου [Μά]ρ. Αὐρ. Ἀλκαμένους Λαμπτρέως καὶ τοῦ κήρ

15 [υκος τῆς ἐξ] Ἀρείου π[ά]γου βουλῆς καὶ ἀγωνοθέτου τῶν τῆς Σεβα

[στῆς οἰκίας ἀ]γώνω[ν Τρύ]φωνος τοῦ Θεοφίλου Ὑβάδου γνώμην ἀπο

[φαίνου]σιν κατὰ [τὰ] πάτρια· vacat Ἐπειδὴ ἡ ἱερωτάτη καὶ τε

λεω[τάτη πασ]ῶν [ἡ]μερῶν καὶ ὑπὸ πάντων ἐλπισθεῖσα διὰ τὴν ἀθάνατον ὁμόνοι

αν τῶν ὁσίων βασιλέων, Λουκίου Σεπτιμίου Σεουήρου Εὐσεβοῦς Περτίνακος

20 Σεβαστοῦ Ἀραβικοῦ Ἀδιαβηνικοῦ Παρθικοῦ Μεγίστου καὶ Μάρκου

Αὐρηλίου Ἀντωνείνου Εὐσεβοῦς Σεβαστοῦ, ὑπὸ τῶν μεγάλω

[ν βασιλέων κοινῶι κη]ρ[ύγμ]ατι πᾶσιν ἀν[θ]ρώποις δεδήλωται, ἐν [ἧι]

‖[τὸν θειότατον Αὐτοκράτορα Καίσαρα Πόπλιον Σεπτίμιον Γέταν]‖

‖[Εὐσεβῆ Σεβαστὸν]‖ τῇ οὐρανίᾳ ψήφῳ καὶ κρίσει προσει

25 [λήφασι πρ]ὸς [τὴν τῆς] αὐτοκράτορος ἀρχῆς ἰσηγορίαν ἱδρύσαντες

τοῦ κόσμου τὸ βασίλειον ἐν ὁλοκλήρῳ τῷ γένει· δεδόχθαι

[τῆι] ἐ[ξ] Ἀ[ρείου] πάγου βουλῇ καὶ τῇ βουλῇ τῶν Φ καὶ τῷ δήμῳ τῷ

Ἀθηναίων θύ[ει]ν πα[ν]γενεὶ καὶ ἑορτάζειν ἔν τε κοινῶι καὶ κα

[τ' ἰδίαν παντὶ τῶι βα]σιλείωι γένει, ἄγεσθαι δὲ καὶ τὴν τῆς κρα

30 [τίστης ἀρχῆς γενέθλ]ιον ἡμέραν ἀκολούθως ταῖς ἄλλαις αὐτῶν κρα

τίσ[ταις, καθὼς διὰ τῆ]ς ὁσίας ῥήσεως αὐτῶν μεμαθήκαμεν, καὶ δίδο

[σθαι παντὶ τῶι δή]μ[ωι δι]ανομὴν καθὰ καὶ ὁ κράτιστος πρεσβευτὴς

[αὐτῶν καὶ ἀντιστράτηγος] καὶ λογιστὴς τῆς πατρίδος ἡμῶν Γάιος Λι

[κίννιος Τηλέμαχος] δεδήλωκεν ἐν τῷ προκ[ε]ιμένῳ διατάγματι

35 σκησμ[.]ι[.....]εν εὐσέβειαν, δι' ἧς τὴν τῆς πόλεως εὐφροσύ

νην καὶ εἰωθυ[ῖ]αν εἰς τὸν Ὀλύμπιον αὐτῶν οἶκον εὐσέβει

[αν] δηλώσομεν.

The name in lines 33-34, the restorations at the beginning of lines 13, 17 and 18 are by Kirchner, that at the beginning of line 14 by Oliver, but the rest of the text is basically that published by Dittenberger. G. Klaffenbach reexamined the Berlin squeeze for me and kindly reported that syllabic division actually is violated at the end of lines 14 and 21.

The reference in line 13 is the only reference to an *antarchon* of the Panhellenion.

Koehler, who read lines 1-20, reported the final letter of line 13 as tau, which permits a new restoration 'Ἀτ|[τικοῦ on the basis of a parallel in the text from Thessalonica, No. **49**. Dittenberger and Kirchner, who did not yet know the phrase " the Attic Panhellenion," preferred to read ἀγ|ῶνος τοῦ Π]ανελληνίου, which breaks the rule of syllabic division and overfills the lacuna at the beginning of line 14. Klaffenbach writes as follows: " Zeile 13/14 bestätigt sich Ihre Vermutung τοῦ ἱερωτάτου 'Ἀτ|[τι-κοῦ Π]ανελληνίου vollkommen. Der letze Buchstabe von Zeile 13 ist ein *absolut* sicheres T."

The most important passage for our purpose is that in lines 12-14, but a translation of the whole may be of use:

" In the archonship of Flavius Diogenes of Marathon, in the – – prytany, that of Pandionis, when Rhodon son of Callistus of Marathon was secretary, priest Theophilus was epistates, and Julianus son of Casius with his fellow-proedroi put it to a vote, the twenty-third day of the prytany, the thirtieth of the month Posideon, a Council meeting was convoked upon the good tidings that ⟦Imperator Caesar P. Septimius Geta Felix Augustus⟧ had been appointed. At this session there was read a proposed resolution of the synedria drafted by the archons, the resolution here engraved. Alcamenes of Lamptrae read it.

" The Council of the Areopagus and the Council of the Five Hundred and the Demos of the Athenians [with] the archons, namely the eponymous archon Flavius Diogenes of Marathon, and the hoplite general and epimelete of divine Hadrian's gy[mnasi]archy and vice-chairman of the most sacred Attic Panhellenion M. Aurelius Alcamenes of Lamptrae, and the herald of the Council of the Areopagus and agonothete of the games for the [domus] Augusta, Tryphon son of Theophilus of Hybadae, report a resolution according to ancestral custom.

" Since the most sacred and most perfect of days and day awaited by all has through the immortal harmony of the holy emperors L. Septimius Severus Pius Pertinax Augustus Arabicus Adiabenicus Parthicus Maximus and M. Aurelius Antoninus Pius Augustus been proclaimed by our great emperors to all mankind in a joint proclamation, the day on which they have associated ⟦the most divine Imperator Caesar P. Septimius Geta Pius Augustus⟧ by their celestial vote and judgment in the equality of the imperial office, thus establishing the kingship of the world upon their whole family:

" May it be resolved by the Council of the Areopagus and the Council of the Five Hundred and the Demos of the Athenians (1) to offer sacrifices in every family and to keep holiday both publicly and privately for all the imperial family; (2) to celebrate this dies imperii in accord with their other dies imperii [as] we have learned through their holy announcement and to give a distribution [to the whole populace], just as his excellency the legatus pro praetore and logistes of our fatherland C. Li[cinnius Telemachus] has made clear in the edict he publishes – – – – piety through which we shall make clear the joy of the city and the customary loyalty to their Olympian house."

There follow catalogues of the *prytaneis* and of the *aisitoi*.

For the family of M. Aurelius Alcamenes of Lamptrae, antarchon of the Attic Panhellenion, see D. J. Geagan, *The Athenian Constitution after Sulla,* pp. 172 f.

24. Distribution of money to celebrate the Panhellenia

Athens. W. Dittenberger, *I.G.,* III (1878), 1184 from Koehler's copy; P. Graindor, *Musée Belge,* XXVI, 1922, p. 170; J. Kirchner, *I.G.,* II², 2221. This fragmentary ephebic catalogue contains the observation:

20   [Με]τ[ὰ τὰ]ς Σεβαστοφορικὰς νομὰς πάσας τὰς διὰ Πανελληνίων ἐπ᾿ ἴσης οἵ τε ἔφηβοι καὶ οἱ πε
[ρὶ τὸ Δι]ογένειον θύσαντες καὶ σπείσαντες ἐν τῷ Διογενείῳ τὰ ἐξιτήρια εὐωχήθησαν,
ο[ὐδε]νὶ δὲ ἄλλῳ συνετέλεσαν οἱ ἔφηβοι ἢ κατά τὸ ἀνανκαῖον τῷ καψαρίῳ μόνῳ.

J. A. Notopoulos, *Hesperia,* XVIII, 1949, p. 46 would date this inscription precisely in 219/20.

25. Dating by Agonothete of the Panhellenia

Athens. W. Dittenberger, *I.G.,* III (1878), 1199 from Koehler's copy; P. Graindor, *Album d'inscriptions attiques d'époque impériale* (Recueil de Travaux publiés par la Faculté de Philosophie et Lettres de l'Université de Gand, 53e et 54e fascicules), 1924, pp. 69-70, No. 103 and Planche LXXXI; J. Kirchner, *I.G.,* II², 2243. Of this ephebic catalogue the heading reads as follows:

Ὁ κοσμη[τὴς τῶν ἐφήβων]
Μέστρι[ος . . . .]
ἀνέγραψ[εν τ]οὺ[ς ὑπ᾿ αὐτῷ ἐφη]
βεύσαντα[ς] καὶ το[ὺς περὶ τὸ Διογέ]
5   νειον ἐπὶ ἀγωνοθέ[του τῶν μεγά]
λων Πανελληνίων Ἀλ[— — — — —]
ἄρχοντος Αὐρ Λανδικιανοῦ. ἀν[τικοσμήτης]
Τ Δομίτ(ιος) Προμηθεὺς Ὤαθεν. παιδο[τρίβης διὰ]
βίου Αὐρ Σεραπίων ὁ καὶ Κράτων

The *paidotribes* Kraton with several other officials of this (omitted) catalogue reappears in two securely dated inscriptions, *I.G.,* II², 2239 = III 1197 of the reign of Gordian and *I.G.,* II², 2245 = III 1202, year of the thirty-fifth Panathenaid (A.D. 255/6). For the Panathenaid Era see L. Moretti, *Iscrizioni agonistiche greche,* Rome, 1953, pp. 202 f. Our inscription belongs to a year when the Panhellenia were celebrated, 244/5 rather than 248/9 or 252/3.

26. Paramonus son of Aphrodisius

Acraephnium in Boeotia. Paul Perdrizet, " Inscriptions d'Achraephiae," *B.C.H.*, XXII, 1898, p. 246.

Ψηφίσματι βουλῆς καὶ δήμου
τὸν ἀγωνοθέτην καὶ Πανέλληνα
Παράμονον Ἀφροδεισίου · οἱ φίλοι τ[ὸν]
ἑαυτῶν εὐεργέτην ἀνέστησαν
ἐκ τῶν ἰδίων

27. Panhellene P. Cae(lius) Dionysius

Aezani in Phrygia. J. Franz, *C.I.G.*, III (1853) 3841 from de Laborde's copy (addendum on p. 1067) ; Philippe Le Bas, *Voyage archéologique en Grèce et en Asie Mineure: Inscriptions*, III, Paris, 1870, 864.

Αὐτοκράτορι Ἀδριανῷ
γενέτορι εἰσανγείλαν
τος Ποπλίου Και Διον
υσίου συνέδρου τοῦ
5 Πανέλληνος

On the pride of Aezani in its antiquity and noble origin see L. Robert, *Études anatoliennes*, Paris, 1937, pp. 301-305.

28. Epistle of the Panhellenes to Aezani about Ulpius Eurycles

Aezani (Savdere-hissar). J. Franz, *C.I.G.*, III (1853), 3832 from Keppel and Laborde; Philippe Le Bas, *Voyage archéologique en Grèce et en Asie Mineure: Inscriptions*, III, Paris, 1870, 869; W. Dittenberger, *O.G.I.* (1905), 504; [*I.G.R.*, IV (1927), 573].

A.D. 156/7

Ὁ ἄρχων τῶν Πανελλήνων καὶ ἱερεὺς θεοῦ Ἀδριανοῦ Π[ανελληνίου]
  καὶ ἀγωνοθέτης τῶν μεγάλων Πανελληνίων Τίτος [Φλάβιος Κύλλος]
  καὶ οἱ Πανέλληνες Αἰζανειτῶν τῆι βουλῆι καὶ τῶ[ι δήμωι χαίρειν]·
Καὶ αὐτοῖς ἡγούμενοι προσῆκον εἶναι τὰς πρὸς τοὺς ἀγαθοὺς ἄνδρας ἀποδείκιν
5 σθαι τειμὰς διαρκῶς καὶ ὑμεῖν συνήδεσθαι τῆς τῶν τοιούτων πολιτῶν κτή
  σεως ἀκόλουθον ὑπολαμβάνοντες, ο[ἷό]ς ἐστιν οὗτος ὁ Μ. Οὔλπιος Εὐρυκλῆς συν
  πεπολιτευμένος ἡμεῖν πάντα τὸν τῆς συνεδρείας χρόνον μετρίως καὶ ὡς
  τούς τε καθ' ἕκαστον ᾑρηκέναι φιλίαι καὶ ἐν τῶι κοινῶι ἐπὶ παιδείαι τε καὶ
  τῆι ἄλληι ἀρετῆι καὶ ἐπιεικείαι διάδηλον ἑαυτὸν πεποιηκέν[αι], εὔλογον ἤγη
10 σάμεθα μαρτυρῆσαι αὐτῶι παρ' ὑμεῖν καὶ εὐφρᾶναι ὑμᾶς ἐνδειξάμενοι

ἣν πρὸς αὐτὸν εὔνοιαν ἔχομεν πρός τε τὸ κοινὸν τοῦ Πανελληνίου καὶ ἰδίᾳ
πρὸς τὸν θαυμασιώτατον ἡμῶν ἄρχοντα Φλάβιον Κύλλον φιλοτιμίᾳ κεχρη
μένον κοσμούσῃ οὐκ αὐτὸν μόνον τὸν Εὐρυκλέα, ἀλλὰ καὶ τὴν διασημο
τάτην ὑμῶν πόλιν, ἧς ἄξια καὶ τοῦ γένους καὶ τῆς ἐκ προγόνων ἀνδραγαθίας
15   καὶ λέγων καὶ πράττων παρὰ πάντα τὸν χρόνον διατετέλεκεν. ἐ⟨π⟩εστείλα
μεν δὲ καὶ πρὸς τὸ ἔθνος ὑπὲρ αὐτοῦ καὶ πρὸς τὸν θειότατον αὐτοκράτορα, καὶ τη
λικαύτης μαρτυρίας ἄξιον αὐτὸν ὑπολαβόντες ᵛᵛᵛᵛᵛ ἔρρωσθε   vacat

" The archon of the Panhellenes and priest of the deified Hadrian Panhellenius and agonothete of the Great Panhellenia, T. Flavius Cyllus, and the Panhellenes to the council and demos of the Aezanites: Greetings.

" Considering that it becomes us constantly to confer honor ourselves upon those who are good men and judging it to be natural for you to rejoice in the possession of such citizens as is this M. Ulpius Eurycles who collaborated with us during all the time of the congress patiently and in such a way that he has captivated us individually with friendship and has in the community distinguished himself for culture and his general excellence and fairness, we decided that it was reasonable to bear witness to him among you and to gladden you by putting on record the good will which we entertain for him because he has shown toward the community of the Panhellenion and privately toward our most marvelous archon Flavius Cyllus a noble ambition which reflects credit not only upon Eurycles himself but also upon your most distinguished city. He has all the while continued to say and to do what is worthy of her and of his family and of the virtue inherited from ancestors. We wrote concerning him to the provincial assembly and to our most divine emperor, because we judged him worthy of such appreciation. Farewell."

The date, A.D. 156, was recognized by Dittenberger from the reference in the epistle of Antoninus Pius to the next synedrion of the Panhellenion, No. **29**, dated pridie Kal. Dec. of A.D. 157. But if the new synedrion took office in 157, the old synedrion may still have been in office early in 157.

This archon and his family are studied by J. A. O. Larsen, " A Thessalian Family under the Principate," *Classical Philology*, XLVIII, 1953, pp. 86-95. Compare No. **9**.

29. Letter of Antoninus Pius to the Panhellenion

Aezani. J. Franz, *C.I.G.*, III (1853), 3834 from copies by Keppel and de Laborde; Philippe Le Bas, *Voyage archéologique en Grèce et en Asie Mineure: Inscriptions*, III, Paris, 1870, 866; W. Dittenberger, *O.G.I.*, 506; [*I.G.R.*, IV, 575].
A.D. 157

[Αὐτ]οκράτωρ Καῖσαρ, θεοῦ Ἀδριανοῦ υἱό[ς],
[θεο]ῦ Τραιανοῦ Παρθικοῦ υἱωνός, θεο[ῦ]

[Νέρ]βα ἔκγονος, Τίτος Αἴλιος Ἀδριανὸς
['Αντ]ωνεῖνος Σεβαστός, ἀρχιερεὺς μέ
5 [γιστ]ος, δημαρχικῆς ἐξουσίας τὸ κ΄, αὐ
[τοκρ]άτωρ τὸ β΄, ὕπατος τὸ δ΄, πατὴρ πα
[τρίδ]ος, τῶι Πανελληνίωι χαίρειν
[Οἱ] πρὸ ὑμῶν Πανέλληνες Οὐλ
[πιο]ν Εὐρυκλέα ἀπεδέξαντο ὡς ἐπ
10 [ιει]κῆ ἔμαθον ἐκ τῶν ὑπ' αὐτῶν ἐπ
[εστ]αλμένων ^{vv} εὐτυχεῖτε · πρὸ μι[ᾶς]
[κα]λανδῶν Δεκεμβρίων ἀπὸ Ῥώμη[s]

Earliest copies seem to indicate that the letters along the left edge were still visible, but we here follow Le Bas.

Line 8, as Franz saw, refers to the Panhellenes of the last term. For lines 10-11 compare No. **28**.

30. Letter of the Panhellenes to the Greeks of Asia about Ulpius Eurycles

Aezani. J. Franz, *C.I.G.*, III (1853), 3833 from copies by Keppel and de Laborde; Philippe Le Bas, *Voyage archéologique en Grèce et en Asie Mineure: Inscriptions*, III, Paris, 1870, 867; W. Dittenberger, *O.G.I.* 507; [*I.G.R.*, IV, 576].

A.D. 157/8

Ὁ ἄρχων τῶν Πανελλήνων καὶ ἱερεὺς θεοῦ Ἀδριανοῦ Πανελληνίου
καὶ ἀγωνοθέτης τῶν μεγάλων Πανελληνίων Κλ. Ἰάσων καὶ οἱ
Πανέλληνες ^v τοῖς ἐπὶ τῆς Ἀσίας Ἕλλησι   vacat   χαίρειν ^v
Μ. Οὔλπιον Ἀπουλήιον Εὐρυκλέα τὸν Αἰζανείτην φθάνομεν ἤδη καὶ δι'
5 ἑτέρων γραμμάτων μαρτυρίας τῆς παρ' ἡμῶν ἠξιωκότες, ἐπεσταλκό
τες ὑμεῖν τε αὐτοῖς ὑπὲρ αὐτοῦ καὶ τῇ πατρίδι καὶ τῶι μεγίστωι αὐτο
κράτορι· δίκαιον δὲ ἡγησάμεθα καὶ τοῦ κρατίστου Κλ. Ἰάσονος παραλαβόν
τος τὴν ἀρχὴν μαρτυρῆσαι αὐτῶι τὰ αὐτὰ ἐπιεικείᾳ τε καὶ αἰδοῖ πάσῃ
κεχρημένωι περὶ τὴν πολιτείαν τῶν συνπανελλήνων καὶ τὸ ἀξίωμα
10 τὸ ὑπάρχον αὐτῶι ἄνωθε καὶ ἀπὸ γένους ἔτι μᾶλλον προάγοντι ἐν οἷς
λέγων καὶ πράττων διατετέλεκε παρὰ πάντα τὸν τῆς συνεδρείας
χρόνον   vacat   ἐρρῶσθαι ὑμᾶς εὔχομαι   vacat

"The archon of the Panhellenes and priest of the god Hadrian Panhellenius and agonothete of the Great Panhellenia, Claudius Jason, and the Panhellenes, to the Hellenes of Asia, greetings.

"M. Ulpius Apuleius Eurycles the Aezanite we have already commended in other letters, having deemed him worthy of a testimonial from us and having written about him both to yourselves and to his own city of origin and to his majesty the emperor. But at the moment when his excellency Claudius Jason took over the archonship we thought it right to express our appreciation of Eurycles who has shown every kind of fairness and scrupulosity in connection with the public business of his fellow-Panhellenes and to testify that he has further advanced the prestige which he enjoyed of old from family position in words and actions continuously throughout all the period of the congress."

The chief importance for us lies in the predicate of rank which Claudius Jason has and in the information that he succeeded Flavius Cyllus as archon in A.D. 157.

See No. **10**.

31. M. Ulpius Damasippus

Amphicleia, still in the old church in the cemetery on the hill, where it was examined on July 25, 1968 and found to be illegible except for a few letters along the right edge, enough to support Lolling's reading against that of Soteriades. It was first copied by W. Leake and included in *C.I.G.*, I (1828), 1738; also by Ph. Le Bas, *Voyage archéologique en Grèce et en Asie Mineure*, II, Paris, 1876, No. 831. The important edition is that of W. Dittenberger, *I.G.*, IX, 1 (1897), 218 from Lolling's copy. Other editions are by G. Soteriades, Πρακτικά, 1909, p. 129 and Ch. M. Enisledes, Ἡ Ἀμφίκλεια κατὰ τοὺς ἀρχαίους χρόνους, Διάλεξις Α´, Athens, 1938, p. 63, No. IV.

Ψ   Β   Δ
Μ. Οὔλ. Δαμάσιππον
τὸν ἀρχιερέα τοῦ με
γάλου θεοῦ Διονύσου
5   τὸν Βοιωτάρχην, πα
τρὸς Βοιωτάρχου, ἀ
γωνοθέτην, Φωκάρ-
χην, Ἀμφικτύονα, θε
ηκόλον Πανέλληνα,
10   ἄρχοντα καὶ τὰς ἄλλας
πάσας ἐν τῇ πατρίδι
τελέσαντα λιτουργί
ας Κιντυλία Πλουτάρ
χη ἡ γυνὴ τὸν ἴδιον
15   ἄνδρα εὐνοίας καὶ ἀρε
τῆς ἕνεκεν Διονύ
σου ἐν τεμένει.

M. Ulpius Damasippus, known also from an inscription at Anticyra, *I.G.*, IX, 1, 8, represents the Confederacy of the Phocians.

32. M. Ulpius Damasippus

Amphicleia, where I did not find it in 1968. G. Soteriades, Πρακτικά, 1909, p. 130.

M. Οὔλ. Δαμάσιππον
τὸν Βοιωτάρχην, πατρὸς
Βοιωτάρχου, τὸν ἀγωνο
θέτην, Φωκάρχην, ἀρχιερέ
α τῆς Βοιωτίας, Ἀμφικτύ-
ονα, θεηκόλον Πανέλλη
να καὶ ἄρχοντα καὶ τὰς ἄλ
λας δὲ πάσας ἐν τῇ πα
τρίδι τελέσαντα λιτουρ
γίας Κυντυλία Πλου
τάρχη ἡ γυνὴ τὸν ἴδι
ον ἄνδρα εὐνοίας καὶ
ἀρετῆς ἔνεκεν.

33. Primus, Panhellene from Apamea in Phrygia

W. M. Ramsey, *The Cities and Bishoprics of Phrygia*, II, Oxford, 1897, p. 475, No. 333 (apparently from Hogarth's copy); [*I.G.R.*, IV, 801]. Line division was not indicated by Ramsay.

– – – κατεσκεύα]σε ἑ[α]υτῇ καὶ τῷ ἀνδρὶ [αὐτῆς
Πρείμῳ – – – – ο]υ, ἀρχάς τε τετελεκότι πάσας καὶ
[χ]ρεοφυλακήσ[αν]τι καὶ ἀγορανομήσαντι, γρα[μματεύσαντι],
ἐργεπιστατήσαντι, καὶ Πανέλληνι γενομ[ένῳ· ζήσα]ντι
καλῶς. Π[ρ]εῖμε, ἥρως χρηστέ, χαῖρε.

κατεσκεύα]σε Oliver; *cetera* Ramsay.

34. T. Statilius Timocrates Memmianus

Argos. Francesco Scipione Maffei, *Museum Veronense*, Verona, 1749, p. XLIII; A. Boeckh, *C.I.G.*, I (1828), 1124; M. Fraenkel, *I.G.*, IV (1902), 590 from his own copy.

Ἁ πόλις ἁ τῶν Ἀργεί
ων Τ. Στατίλιον Λαμ
πρίου υἱὸν Τιμοκράτη
Μεμμιανόν, Περσέος καὶ
5   Διοσκούρων ἀπόγονον,

τὸν Ἑλλαδάρχαν καὶ ἀρχι
ερέα διὰ βίου τῶν Ἑλλάνων,
στρατηγήσαντα τῶν Ἀχαι
ῶν [γ΄], ἀγωνοθέταν Ἡραί
10 ων καὶ Νεμείων καὶ Σεβα
στείων καὶ Νεμείων καὶ Ἀν
τινοείων ἐν Ἄργει καὶ Ἀν
τινοείων ἐν Μαντινείᾳ
καὶ Ἀσκλαπείων ἐν Ἐπι
15 δαύρῳ, καὶ ἀμφικτύονα καὶ
Ἑλλαδάρχαν ἀμφικτυόνων
καὶ Πανέλληνα καὶ Ἑλληνο
ταμίαν καὶ ἀγορανομήσαντα
καὶ στρατηγήσαντα τρὶς καὶ τα
20 μιεύσαντα καὶ πρεσβεύσαν
τα ὑπέρ τε τᾶς πατρίδος
καὶ τῶν Ἑλλάνων πρός τε
τὰν σύγκλητον καὶ πρὸς βα-
σιλέας καὶ τὰ ἄλλα καὶ λό{γο}
25 γοις καὶ ἔργοις πολειτευσά
μενον ἄριστα καὶ φιλοτειμό
τατα, ἀρετᾶς ἕνεκα.

35. Archon Cn. Cornelius Pulcher

Corinth. M. Fraenkel, *I.G.*, IV (1902), 1600; B. D. Meritt, *Corinth*, VIII, i (1931), 82.

Γν Κορνήλιον Τιβ Κορνηλίου Πούλχρου υἱὸν Φαβίᾳ Πού[λ]χρον στρατηγὸν
τῆς πόλεως Κορινθίων πενταετηρικόν, ἀγωνοθέτην Καισαρείων Ἰσθμίων, ἀρχιερ[έα]
τῆς Ἑλλάδος καὶ Ἑλλαδάρχην ἀπὸ τοῦ κοινοῦ τῶν Ἀχαιῶν συ[νεδ]ρίου διὰ βίου,
Ἠπείρου
4 ἐπίτροπον, Αἰγύπτου καὶ Ἀλεξανδρείας δικαιοδότην, ἄρχον[τα τοῦ] Πανελληνίου
καὶ ἱερέα
Ἀδριανοῦ Πανελληνίου, ἄλλας τε μεγάλας δωρεὰς ἐπιδόντα καὶ τὴν ἀτέ[λειαν] τῇ
πόλει παρασχόντα
Καλπουρνία Φροντεῖνα ἡ ἀδελ[φή]

References to this man will be found in *PIR²*, C 1424. To him Plutarch dedicated his essay, *How to Profit from One's Enemies*. See also G. W. Bowersock, *Cl. Q.*, XV, 1965, pp. 269 f. and C. P. Jones, *J.R.S.*, LVI, 1966, pp. 61-63.

36. Archon Cn. Cornelius Pulcher

Corinth. J. H. Kent, *Corinth*, VIII, iii (1966), 139.

[– –]
[– – – – – – – – – – – – ἄρ]χοντα τοῦ Πανελληνί
[ου καὶ ἱερέα Ἀδριανοῦ Πανε]λληνίου, ἄλλας τε μεγά
[λας δωρεὰς ἐπιδόντα καὶ] τὴν ἀτέλειαν τῇ πόλει
4 παρασ[χόντα]   *vacat*

See the foregoing. Restorations and identification by Kent.

37. Panhellene, Maecius Faustinus the Rhetor

Corinth. J. H. Kent, *Corinth*, VIII, iii (1966), 264.

[.] Μαίκιο[ν]
[Φ]αυστεῖνο[ν],
σ[τ]ρατηγό[ν],
Παν[έ]λλ[ηνα],
5 ῥή[τορα] ἀγαθ[όν],
ἡ πα[τρ]ὶς ἐπὶ
καλο[κ]αγα[θ]
ίᾳ
ψ β

Before Maecius Faustinus was elected Panhellene, he must have held a qualifying magistracy. The duovir in Greek is called *strategos*. Is the office mentioned in line 3 the duumvirate at Corinth, a Roman praetorship, or the generalship of a league? The word πα[τρ]ίς proves that Maecius Faustinus was a Corinthian, and it suggests that he resided outside of Corinth. Therefore, he does not seem to be honored as a duovir. Nor is it proper for him to have become praetor at Rome without first being quaestor. The writer, accordingly, leans to an interpretation of the qualifying office as the generalship of the Achaean League (J. A. O. Larsen, *Greek Federal States*, Oxford, 1968, pp. 500-504). He would then have been elected Panhellene by the Achaean League.

38. Date of Foundation of the Panhellenion

P. Kabbadias, *Fouilles d'Épidaure*, I, Athens, 1891, p. 43, No. 35, and Ἀρχαιο-λογικὸν Δελτίον, 1892, p. 114; W. Dittenberger, *S.I.G.*² (1898), 391; M. Fraenkel, *I.G.*, IV (1902), 1052; F. Hiller von Gaertringen, *S.I.G.*³ (1917), 842 and *I.G.*, IV², 1 (1929), 384.

ἔτους γ̄ τῆς καθιερώσεος τοῦ Διὸ[ς]
τοῦ Ὀλυμπίου καὶ τῆς κτίσεος
τοῦ Πανελληνίου, ἔτους δὲ ῑ τῆς
Τραιανοῦ Ἁδριανοῦ Καίσαρος ἐπι
5 δημίας, ἐπὶ ἱερέος τοῦ Ἀσκληπιοῦ
Εὐτύχου) τοῦ), ὑπὲρ αὐτὸν Λε
ωνίδου τοῦ Περιγένους, Στέφανος
Εὐτύχου πυροφορήσας Ἀσκληπιοῦ καὶ
Ἠπιόνης

This inscription, one of the most important pieces of evidence for the chronology of Hadrian's reign (W. Weber, *Untersuchungen zur Geschichte des Kaisers Hadrians*, Leipzig, 1907, p. 208) shows that the dedication of the Olympieum at Athens and the foundation of the Panhellenion occurred between Sept. 130 and 132, and so the year 129, in which some scholars believed, is now usually excluded. But see Conclusions. Since the Hadrianic era began in 124, the inscription was erected in 133/4. Two years earlier was 131/2, the sixteenth year of Hadrian.

Lines 5-7 call attention to the *trigonia* of the priest Eutyches, son of Eutyches, grandson of Eutyches, and mention that Leonidas, son of Perigenes, was functioning for him.

39. Archon Q. Alleius Epictetus

Epidaurus. M. Fraenkel, *I.G.*, IV (1902), 1474; F. Hiller von Gaertringen, *I.G.*, IV², 1 (1929), 691; W. Peek, *Abh. sächs. Ak. Wiss. Leipzig*, Phil.-hist. Kl., LX, 2, 1969, pp. 130 f., No. 302 with photograph.

[Κύι]ντον Ἀλλήιον Ἐπίκτητον [.........]τος υἱόν, ἱε[ρέα]
τοῦ σωτῆρος Ἀσκληπιοῦ α[ὐ]θ[αίρε]το[ν], στρατηγόν, ἀγω
νοθέτην τῶν μεγάλων Ἀσκληπείων, ἐπώνυμον ἄρχον
τα τῆς λαμπροτάτης Ἀθηναίων πόλεως, ἐπὶ τὰ ὅπλα στρα
5 τηγὸν καὶ ἐπιμελητὴν γυμνασιαρχία[ς] θεοῦ Ἁδριανοῦ, κή
ρυκα τῆς ἐξ Ἀρίου πάγου βουλῆς, ἄρχον[τα τῶν] σ[εμν]οτάτων
Πανελλήνων καὶ ἀγωνοθέτην τῶν [μ]εγ[άλ]ων [Παν]ελληνί
ων, [ἱερέα Διὸς Ὀ]λυμπίου, ἐπι[μελητ]ὴν [τῆ]ς λαμπρο[τάτ]ης [Ἀρ]γεί
ων πό[λε]ω[ς ἔτ]η ιε ʹ τῶν Ἐπιδαυρίων [ἡ πόλ]ις τὸν [ἑαυτῆς]
10 [πάτρωνα καὶ] εὐεργέτην [– – – – – – – – – – – – – ἐπιδόν]
[των τὸ ἀργ]ύριον τὸ λοιπὸν τῶν [– – – – – – – – – – – – –]

Peek's reading is so superior to those of his predecessors that no apparatus need be presented. In line 8 Fraenkel restored ἱ]|ε[ρέα Διὸς Ὀ]λυμπίου ἐπι[στάτην τῆ]ς λαμπρο[τάτης and in line 11 ἐπι|δόντα τὸ ἀργύ]ριον. In line 2, where Peek reads α[ὐτ]οκράτο[ρα with dots under most letters, I have risked α[ὐ]θ[αίρε]το[ν. In line 9, where Peek has υ]ῆιε (to me incomprehensible), I have substituted ἔτ]η ιε.

The inscription (from the second century) has a special interest because it attests the name, wealth and career of an archon of the Panhellenion. The order of the *cursus honorum* is as follows: first the Epidaurian honors, of uncertain date, namely volunteer priest of Asclepius, *strategos*, agonothete; then the Athenian honors in chronological order, namely archon, hoplite general and herald of the Areopagus; then the Panhellenic honors of archon and agonothete and perhaps priest of Zeus Olympius (at Athens), if ἱερέα rather than τοῦ or τῶν is the correct restoration in line 8; and finally an undated term of fifteen years as epimelete of Argos.

Honored at Athens in *I.G.*, II², 3625, he may have been an Epidaurian originally, Members of his family seem to appear later in *I.G.*, II², 1794 and 2125.

40. Sebon of Gortyn

Gortyn. A. Taramelli, *A.J.A.*, VI, 1902, p. 148, No. 3; M. Guarducci, *Inscriptiones Creticae*, IV (1950), 326.

[– – – – – – –] οὔνεκα Κεκροπίδαι με
[– – – – – – –] Πανέλληνές τε Σέβωνα
[– – – – – – – –]ει σὺν κλεινο[– – –]
[– – – – – – –] στῆσαν ἄγαλμα πάτρῃ

41. Panhellene, Pardalas

Lyttos. M. Guarducci, *Inscriptiones Creticae*, I (1935), p. 205, No. 56 from Spratt's copy; G. Klaffenbach, *Klio*, XXX, 1937, p. 255.

Ψηφισαμ[έν]ου [τοῦ]
κο[ι]νοῦ τῶν Κρητῶν
καὶ τῆς Λυττίων πό[λ]
εος Παρδαλᾶ[ν τ]
5 ὸν πρωτόκοσμον
καὶ Πανέλληνα ἀπο[δ]
ειχθέντα τοῦ συν[ε]
[δ]ρίου Μᾶρκος Ἰούν
ιος Σωτήριος τὸν
10 [ἑαυ]τοῦ φίλον

The lettering, says the editor, dates from the second century. The office in lines 6-8 was deciphered by Klaffenbach.

42. Panhellene, C. Curtius Proclus

Megara. A. Boeckh, *C.I.G.*, I (1828), 1058 from copies by Fourmont and Pococke; Ph. Le Bas and P. Foucart, *Inscriptions grecques et latines*, II, Paris, 1848 and 1873, No. 43; W. Dittenberger, *I.G.*, VII (1892), 106.

[Γάιον Κούρτιο]ν Πρόκλον
[Γαίου Κ]ουρτίου Πρόκλου
[υἱ]όν · ἡ βουλὴ καὶ ὁ δῆ
μος ἀγωνοθέτην Πυ
5   θαήων καὶ [σ]υστράτηγον
καὶ ἀγορανόμον, φιλο
τειμησάμενον μονο
μάχων ζεύγη κ΄ καὶ βοι
ωταρχήσαντα ἀπὸ τῆς
10   πατρίδος τὸ β΄ καὶ ἀμφι
κτυονεύσαντα τὸ γ΄ καὶ
πρῶτον Πανέλληνα, ῥή
τορα, προστάτην διὰ βίου,
υἱὸν τῆς πόλεως καὶ πατέ
15   ρα βουλῆς, ἀρετῆς ἕνεκεν
καὶ τῆς πρὸς τὴν πατρίδα
εὐνοίας

The restorations are assured by comparison with *I.G.*, VII, 107, in honor of Flavia Lais, daughter of C. Curtius Proclus.

L. Robert, *Les gladiateurs dans l'orient grec*, Paris, 1940, p. 262, rightly says (against Foucart and Dittenberger) that C. Curtius Proclus was the first Megarian in the Panhellenion. The Panhellene, however, represented the Boeotian Confederacy rather than the city, I think. He was also a rhetor who thrice had served in the Delphic Amphictyony. His wealth and generosity in giving a gladiatorial show brought him the highest honors at home.

For the phrase υἱὸν τῆς πόλεως see L. Robert, *R.É.A.*, LXII, 1960, p. 311 and *R.É.G.*, LXXIX, 1966, p. 369.

43. Panhellene, Dionysius the Rhetor

Methana. E. Dodwell, *A Classical and Topographical Tour through Greece . . .*, II, London, 1819, p. 283; A. Boeckh, *C.I.G.*, I (1828), 1192; M. Fraenkel, *I.G.*, IV (1902), 858 from his own copy; A. Wilhelm, *Glotta*, XIV, 1925, p. 79.

Διονύσιον πᾶσαν πολιτείαν πολε[ι]
τευσάμενον, γενόμενον δὲ Πανέλληνα,

Ἑρμογένης τὸν θεῖον κατὰ τὴν βούλησιν
τοῦ πατρὸς τὸν ῥήτορα

44. Panhellenes, Coranus and Heraclius

Pagae. Ph. LeBas, *Voyage archéologique en Grèce et en Asie Mineure pendant 1843 et 1844*, II, Paris, 1870, No. 16 (transcription and commentary by P. Foucart); K. Keil, " Zur Sylloge inscriptionum Boeoticarum," *Jahrbücher für classische Philologie,* Supplementband IV, 1863, p. 507, No. IV from R. Schillbach's copy compared with LeBas; W. Dittenberger, *I.G.,* VII (1892), 192.

Πανέλλη[νες]
Κόρανος [– – –]
δος καὶ Ἡρ[άκλει]
ος Ἡρακλεί[ου]
5 τ[ῇ] ἱερᾷ συν[όδῳ]
τῶν Ἡρακλ[εισ]
τῶν προῖκ[α]
[τ]ὸν Ἡρακλέα
[ἀνέ]στησαν

Restorations: 1, 3-4 Keil. 5 Dittenberger. 6-9 Foucart.

See Cl. A. Forbes, " Ancient Athletic Guilds," *Cl. Phil.,* L, 1955, p. 245.

45. Panhellene, A. Cornelius Postumus, and affairs of Sardis

Athens, on the Acropolis. One fragment (b) was published by W. Dittenberger, *I.G.,* III (1878), 14 and by J. Kirchner, *I.G.,* II² (1916) 1089 from Koehler's copy; a second fragment, found in a modern house wall, was identified by J. H. Oliver, who published a photograph of both pieces, *Hesperia*, X, 1941, pp. 82 f., No. 35.

Shortly after A.D. 132.

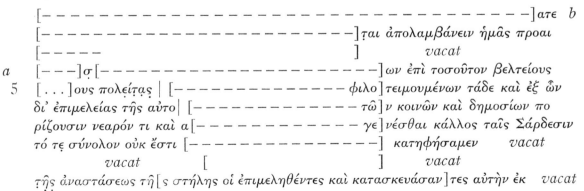

10 τῶν ἰδίων σύνεδροι Γ [– –]χος καὶ   vacat
Α. Κορνήλιος Πόστομ[ος –]

In his notes on fragment *b* Koehler correctly pointed out that it was very similar to, but not a part of, the stele engraved with a record of Hadrian's benefactions to Thyatira. The latter was set up in Athens as the seat of the Panhellenion and center of the Greek world. From lines 7, 9, and 10 it appears that this inscription was erected at Athens for the same reasons by the delegates of Sardis to the Panhellenion, the foundation of which in A.D. 132 constitutes a *terminus post quem*.

46. Panhellenes from Sparta

Sparta. Lost stone known only from Fourmont's copy, edited by W. Kolbe, *I.G.*, V, 1 (1913), 164 and A. M. Woodward, *B.S.A.*, XLIII, 1948, pp. 244 f.

[– – – – – –]
Ἀπολλωνίο[υ καὶ]
Σ. Ἰούλ Ἀρέτω[ν] Φ[ι]
λαθηναίου ἐπ[ι]
στάται τῆς ἀν[αθέ]
5   σεως·
[Π]ανέλληνες·
[Ξ]εναγόρ[ας]
[Π]ασικρ]ατ–]
[. .]σσ[– – –]
10   [. .]ι[– – – –]
[– – – – – –]

Kolbe and Woodward make the stone begin with the first line preserved in Fourmont's time. Woodward reads the first name as Ἀπολλώνιο[ς Ἐρά]|στου, because a man so named appears in *I.G.*, V (1), 71. In line 2 Kolbe reads [Γάιο]ς Ἰούλ Ἀρέτω[ν], but the praenomen is less likely to have been written out when the nomen was abbreviated. In fact, Woodward thinks that nothing is lost before the sigma in line 2, but his own reconstruction (Λ. Ἀρέτω[ν]) of what follows arouses distrust. I have restored a genitive in line 1 and the word καί at the end of line 1. Moreover, I adopt Woodward's reconstruction of Fourmont's line 4 as a garble of two lines, 4 and 5.

The importance of the inscription lies in the plural Panhellenes, which, accompanied by two names, suggests that Sparta like Cyrene and Sardis had just two Panhellenes. The inscription unfortunately fails to prove this because lines 9-10 might have contained something other than the restorations suggested by Kolbe, [πρ]έσ[βυς φει|δι]τ[ίου.

47. Panhellene, Neon son of Neon

Sparta. A. M. Woodward, *B.S.A.*, XXVII, 1925-1926, p. 239.

Νέων⟨, παρά
δοξος, σύν
δικος, γραμ
ματοφύλαξ,
5   νομοφύλαξ,
Πανέλλην,
συναγορανό
μος Αἰλίῳ
Ἀλκανδρίδα,

10   συνπατρονό
μος Λάμπιδος
τοῦ⟨,
γερουσίας,
ἱεροθύτης
15   σεβαστός,
συνπ[ατ]ρο
νόμ[ος — —]
.ου [— — —]

The date could be Hadrianic.

Panhellene, C. Julius Arion

Sparta. The text is given above on p. 78 as No. **2.**

48. Panhellene Spendon of Sparta

Mistra. W. Kolbe, *I.G.*, V(1), 47 from Prott's copy.

Σπένδων (Σπένδοντος) συνέ
φηβος Ἀριστέος,
σύνδικος καὶ δαμο
σιομάστας, συνθύτ[ας]
5   ἰς Ῥόδον, Πανέλλην,
γερουσίας ἐπ[ὶ] Ἰου
[λίου — — — — — —]

Compare this monument for a Panhellene from Sparta with No. **2.**

49. Archon T. Aelius Geminius Macedo

Thessalonica. M. N. Tod, *J.H.S.*, XLII, 1922, pp. 167-180 from a copy made by Captain A. E. W. Salt in 1918. J. H. Oliver personally reexamined the inscription in 1934. Many of the letters in lines 5-15 were then missing, but others, including some overlooked or miscopied by Capt. Salt, were still visible. See Plate 8, a and b.

Ἡ πόλις
Τ. Αἴλιον Γεμείνιον Μακεδόνα,
τὸν ἄρξαντα τοῦ Ἀττικοῦ Πανελληνίου
καὶ ἱερατεύσαντα θεοῦ Ἀδριανοῦ καὶ ἀγο
5   νοθετήσαντα τῶν μεγάλων Πανελλη

νίων ἐν τῇ ηι΄ Πανελληνιάδι, ῥάψαντα
διὰ βίου τοῖς αὐτοκράτορσιν, πρῶτον γε
νόμενον ἄρχοντα Πανελλήνων ἀπὸ τῆς
λαμπροτάτης Θεσσαλονεικέων πόλεως,
10   γυμνασιαρχήσαντα καὶ πρωταρχήσαν
τα ἐν τῇ λαμπρᾷ ταύτῃ πόλει, δόντα ἐξ ὑπο
σχέσεως εἰς τὴν βασιλικὴν ταύτην ξύλων
πήχ(εις) μυρίους, λογιστεύσαντα ἐκ θείας
προστάξεως τῆς Ἀπολλωνιατῶν πόλε
15   ως τῆς πρὸς τῷ Ἰονίῳ κόλπῳ, Γεμεινία
Ὀλυμπιὰ[ς] ἡ θυγάτηρ τὸν πατέρα
εὐτυχῶς.

The reader is referred to Tod's masterly commentary on most of this inscription. The word ῥάψαντα in line 6 is certain. On p. 180 Tod asks if it is possible that Macedo was a kind of poet laureate to the Imperial house. But διὰ βίου in line 7 is a mere error for διάλογον, " ceremonial speech," as in *I.G.*, II², 2086, lines 34-38.

The inscription contributes the information that the Great Panhellenia occurred at regular numbered intervals. The eighteenth Panhelleniad, if the first occurred in 131/2, would fall in 199/200, but this date seems to belong to the archonship of Cocceius Timasarchus (No. **21**). However, the first Panhelleniad may have belonged to the first regular term, A.D. 133-137, and then the archonship of Geminius Macedo could be placed in A.D. 201-205.

50. Decree of Thyatira

Athens, on the Acropolis. Eight fragments published by W. Dittenberger as *I.G.*, III (1878), 12 (a, b, c, d, e) and 13 (f) and 15 (g) and 3985 (h); J. Kirchner, *I.G.*, II² (1916), 1088 (a, b, c, d, e, f) and 1090 (g). All eight fragments as part of the same inscription are republished with photographs, measurements and previous history, by J. H. Oliver, *Hesperia*, X, 1941, pp. 363-368.

A.D. 132-138   c, f, d, a
        Ἀγαθῇ   [Τύχῃ]
[τοῦ θειοτάτο]υ Αὐτοκράτορ[ος Καίσαρος Τραιανοῦ Ἀδριανοῦ Σεβαστοῦ Ὀλυμπίου]
[ἔδοξεν τῇ Θυα]τειρηνῶν πόλ[ει, – – – – – – – – – – – – – – – ἐπειδὴ παρὰ τοῦ]
μ[εγίστου Αὐτο]κράτορος Καίσα[ρος Τραιανοῦ Ἀδριανοῦ Σεβαστοῦ Ὀλυμπίου σωτῆρος]
5   καὶ [εὐεργέτο]υ πατρὸς τῆς πα[τρίδος ἔτυχεν ἡ ἡμετέρα πόλις μεγάλων δωρεῶν, δι']
ὧν [πάντα τὰ ἔθ]νη τῆς ἁπάσης Ἑ[λλάδος εὐεργετεῖται, καὶ τὸ συνέδριον τὸ Πανελ]
λήνι[ον ἐψηφίσα]το πάντα ἃ Μέττ[ιος – – – ὁ] τοῦ σ[υνεδρίου – – – – – εἶπε, ἀνα]
γράψα[ι Ἀθήνησι] ἐν Ἀκροπόλει ἐ[ν στήλῃ πάσ]ας δωρεὰς ὡς [ἔκασται ἐδόθησαν ὑπὸ τοῦ]

μεγίσ[του τῶν π]οτε βασιλέων Αὐ[τοκράτορ]ος Καίσαρος Τραια[νοῦ Ἀδριανοῦ Σεβαστοῦ]
10 Ὀλυμπί[ου Πανελλ]ηνίου Διός, ἐφ' [ὅτου τὸ τοι]οῦτο ἔδοσεν· ἀγα[θῇ τύχῃ δεδόχθαι τῷ Θυα]
τε[ι]ρην[ῶν ......]τῷ δήμῳ τό[δε μὲν τὸ ψήφι]σμα ἐνχαράξαι λίθ[ῳ καὶ προσαναθεῖναι, ὅπω]
ς [ἂν] ἐν [........] ἔκδηλον [ὑπάρχῃ τοῖς Ἑλ]λησι ἅπασιν ὅσων [εὐεργεσιῶν τ]έτ[ευχ]ε
α[ὐτὸ παρὰ τοῦ βασι]λέως ὅτ[ι ἰδίᾳ καὶ κοι]νῇ πᾶν τὸ τῶν Ἑλλή[νων ἔθνος ε]ὐεργέ[τ]ησ[εν]
ὁ βα[σιλεὺς − − − −]ν ἐξ αὐ[− − − − − τ]ὸ συνέδριον ὡς [− − − − − −]ιμι[.]ν κοινῇ
15 ε[− − − − − − − −]θηι[− − − − − − − −]ν Εὐεργέτιν Καρπ[οφόρον διὰ τῶ]ν Μυστηρίω[ν]
ο Λ[− − − − − − − − − − − − − Πανε]λλήνιον δι' ὧν ἐψη[φισ − − − − ὁ]μολογουν[− −]
[− − − − − − − − − − − − − − − − ἰ]δίᾳ τά τε ἔθνη κ[αὶ − − − − − το]ύτου τοῦ τ[−]
[− − − − − − − − − − − − − − − −]ν καὶ τὴν ἡμ[ετέραν πόλιν − − ἐκδ]ήλως καὶ πολλ[α]
[− − − − − − − − − − − − − − − − − − − −]πων ἔτι τὴν
20 [− λα]μβάνων ὑπε[ρ]
[− − − − − − − − − − − − − − − − − − −] τῶν ὑδάτων α[−]
[− − − − − − − − − − − − − − − − − −] α τὰς ἁπάντων
[− − − − − − − − − − − − − − − − − − − −]ε ΔꓥΥ[−]

b

[− − − − − − − − − − − − −]ειν προσ[− − − − −]
25 [− − − − − − − − − − − − − −]ı * μυριάδας εἴκοσιν χάριν
[− − − − − − − − − − − − −]ην τὴν περὶ τὸν πυρὸν ἄφθο ᵛ
[νίαν − − − − − − − − − − τῆς τοῦ βασ]ιλέως φιλοδωρίας, ἀλλὰ καὶ τὴν
[− − − − − − − − − − −]ως αὐτὸς σχὼν πολλάκις, ἡνίκα
[− − − − − − − − − − ἔχουσ]ιν εἰσαεὶ τὴν τῶν ὅρων ἀμε ᵛ
30 [τακίνητον ἀσφάλειαν − − − − − − − − − διὰ τ]ῆς τοῦ βασιλέως προνοίας, ἔτι δὲ
[− − − − − − − − − − − − − − − − −]ι ἐπιτρέψας αἰτήσασιν παρ' αὐτοῦ
[− − − − − − − − − − − τὰ χρήμα]τα εἰς ἕτερον ἔργον καταλεί ᵛ
[πειν − − − − − − − − − − − − −] τῆς γῆς φόρους ἴσους γενέσ ᵛ
[θαι −]

e

35 μ[− −]
φαν[− −]
ψηφ[ισ −]
μεν[− −]
Σακε[ρδω − − − − − − − − − − − − − − − − − − −]
40 καὶ Ἰου[λι − − − − − − − − − − − − − − − − − − −]
τῆς ἀ[ναγραφῆς καὶ ἀναστάσεως τῆς στήλης Ἀθήνησι ἐπιμελείσθω ὁ ἀρχιερεὺς τῶν]
Σεβα[στῶν −]
Τι · Κλ · Μ[− − − − − − − − − − − − − − − − − − −]
vacat

g

] πόλιν [

τὸ σεμνότα]τον Πανε[λλην–

]συ[νκ]λήτου κα[

]ον δῆλος δὲ ἐσ[τι

κ]αὶ εὐεργετῶν τ[

] εὐεργέτησε[

]εν παρὰ τοῦ[

]χι παρὰ[

h

]ε[

]ιν μει[

]τροφω[

]του μ[

] ‾νε[

]ωσ[

] ‾ωγ[

Restorations are my own except for the following, which I have adopted from my predecessors, or which, proposed by my predecessors, have suggested my own:

(1) Pittakys. (2) τοῦ θειοτάτο]υ Αὐτοκράτορ[ος, Dittenberger. (3) Θυα]τειρηνῶν, Dittenberger. (4) Αὐτο]κράτορος Καίσα[ρος, Pittakys; Τραιανοῦ Ἁδριανοῦ Σεβαστοῦ Ὀλυμπίου, Dittenberger. (5) πα[τρίδος, Pittakys. (6) Πανελ, Dittenberger. (7) Μέττ[ιος and ἀνα, Dittenberger. (8-12) Αὐτοκρά-τορ]ος Καίσαρος Τραια[νοῦ (9) and Πανελλ]ηνίου (10), Pittakys; ἀνα]|γράψα[ι ἐν στήλῃ λιθίνῃ τ]ὰς δωρεὰς ὡ[ς ἕκασται ἐδόθησαν ὑπὸ τοῦ] μεγίσ[του Αὐτοκράτορ]ος Καίσαρος Τραια[νοῦ Ἁδριανοῦ Σεβαστοῦ] | Ὀλυμπί[ου Πανελληνίου· τ]οῦτο ἔδο⟨ξ⟩εν· ἀγα[θῇ τύχῃ, δεδόχθαι καὶ τὸ τῆς | Θυα]τε[ι]ρην[ῶν πόλεως ψήφι]σμα ἐνχαράξαι λίθ[ωι καὶ στῆσαι - - - ὅπω]|ς [ἂν φα]ν[ερὸν γένηται τοῖς Ἕλ]λησι ἅπασιν, Ditten-berger. (13) Ἑλλή[νων, Pittakys; βασι]λέως and ἔθνος, Dittenberger. (14) βα[σιλεὺς and φιλοτε]ιμί-[α]ν, Dittenberger. (15) θεὰ]ν Εὐεργέτιν Καρπ[οφόρον, Dittenberger. (16) Pittakys. (17) καὶ κοινῇ καὶ ἰ]δίᾳ, Dittenberger. (18) ἡμ[ετέραν, Dittenberger. (20) Dittenberger. (27) ἀφθο|[νίαν οὐ μόνον τῆς τοῦ βασι]λέως φιλοδωρίας, Pittakys. (29-30) ἔχουσ]ιν εἰς ἀεὶ τὴν τῶν ὅρων ἀμε|[τακίνητον ἀσφάλειαν διὰ τ]ῆς, Dittenberger. (32-34) Dittenberger. (35-36) στε|[φάν[ω, Pittakys. (37) ψήφ[ισμα, Pittakys. (41-43) τῆς ἀ[ναγραφῆς καὶ ἀναστάσεως τῶν στηλῶν ἐπιμελείσθω ὁ ἀρχιερεὺς τῶν] | Σεβα[στῶν καὶ ἄρχων τοῦ σεμνοτάτου συνεδρίου τῶν Πανελλήνων] | Τι : Κλ. Ἡ[ρώδης Ἀττικὸς Μαραθώνιος], Dittenberger. (Fragment g) ἐσ[τι Rangabé; τὸ σεμνότατ]ον Πανε[λλήνων συνέδριον, Dittenberger.

The inscription is particularly interesting because it shows a city of the Panhellenion publishing its honorary decree for the emperor at Athens, not because the decree concerned Athens particularly but because the benefactions of Hadrian concerned all the Hellenes and Athens was now the capital of the Hellenic world. In the *Bulletin épigraphique,* 1951, 2, p. 122 (cf. 1956, 144) it is indicated that in *I.G.,* II², 1075 Louis Robert has discovered a decree of Synnada similarly erected at Athens in connection with the Panhellenion.

The decree reflects the *Philippus* of Isocrates in its attitude toward benefactions. Compare G. Dobesch, *Untersuchungen zum Korinthischen Bund,* I, Vienna, 1968, pp. 160-212.

In line 10 Hadrian receives the epithets *Olympios Panhellenios.* So also at Chios (*Bull. ép.* 1956, No. 215).

In lines 39-43 three men of Thyatira are mentioned, perhaps Claudius Socrates Sacerdotianus and his son the high priest Tib. Claudius Menogenes Caecilianus, and an unknown Julius.

51-58. Agonistic Inscriptions

No. **51**, at Chios, is best consulted in the edition of Werner Peek, " Aurelius Heras," *Wiss. Zeitschr. Halle-Wittenberg*, IX, 1960, pp. 191-204; [*S.E.G.*, XIX, 589]. It dates apparently from the time of Marcus Aurelius.

On the front an epigram cataloguing the victories reads in line 5:

$$[\kappa\alpha\acute{\iota} \ \mu\epsilon] \ \Pi\alpha\nu\epsilon\lambda\lambda\acute{\eta}\nu\omega\nu \ \kappa\rho\iota\tau\grave{o}\varsigma \ \grave{\alpha}\nu\delta[\rho\hat{\omega}\nu \ \overset{\text{´}}{\epsilon}]\sigma\tau\epsilon\phi\epsilon \ \lambda[\alpha\acute{o}\varsigma]$$

On the right side there is a list of victories which include one at the Πανελ[λήνια.

In addition we have some agonistic inscriptions collected by Luigi Moretti, *Iscrizioni agonistiche greche* (Rome, 1953).

52. At Olympia monument for P. Aelius Artemas, herald, *ca*. 140, Moretti No. 70, which ends: καὶ τὰ πρώτως Πανελλήνια ἀχθέντα ἐν Ἀθήναις πρῶτος κηρύκων.

53. At Adada in Pisidia, monument for M. Aurelius Abas, runner in the *dolichos,* second half of second century, Moretti No. 76, which ends Πανελλήνεα ἐν Ἀθήναις.

54. At Naples tablet for M. Aurelius Hermagoras, wrestler, second half of second century, *I.G.*, XIV, 1102 = Moretti No. 77, with a record of victories including Πανελλήνια β΄.

55. At Rome marble base for M. Aurelius Asclepiades called Hermodorus, pancratiast, *ca*. 200, Moretti No. 79, who won among many victories five at Athens, including one at the Panhellenia.

56. At Sardis monument for M. Aurelius Demostratus Damas, pancratiast and pugilist, A.D. 212-217, Moretti No. 84, which lists among others ten victories at Athens including three at the Panhellenia.

57. At Megara monument for an unknown athlete, middle of third century, *I.G.*, VII, 49 = Moretti No. 88 with list of victories including Πανελλήνια ἐν Ἀθήναις.

58. At Athens monument for Valerius Eclectus, herald, *ca*. 253-257, *I.G.*, III, 129 = *I.G.*, II², 3169/70 = Moretti No. 90 with a list of victories including one at the Panhellenia.

To the epigraphical evidence cited above we should add
Three references from Philostratus, *Lives of the Sophists:*

P. 44 Kayser, p. 110 Wright: The famous sophist Polemo delivered the address when the Olympieum at Athens was finished and dedicated. He was there on the emperor's invitation rather than as a representative of Smyrna to the newly established Attic Panhellenion.

P. 58 Kayser, p. 146 Wright: The millionaire Herodes Atticus is said to have performed as liturgies the eponymous archonship at Athens, also the *agonothesiai* of the Panhellenia and Panathenaea. One might ask if he was serving as archon of the Panhellenes when he undertook the *agonothesia*; P. Graindor, *Athènes sous Hadrien*, p. 53, n. 1 denies it.

P. 100 Kayser, p. 248 Wright (discussed above in connection with No. **14**): The sophist Aurelius Rufus of Perinthus presided over the Panhellenia with great distinction (in the Severan Period). He too had vast wealth and was related to consulars.

One reference from Cassius Dio, LXIX, 16, 1-2:

Hadrian completed the Olympieum at Athens, in which his own statue also stands, and dedicated there a serpent, which had been brought from India. He also presided at the Dionysia, first assuming the highest office among the Athenians, and arrayed in the local costume, carried it through brilliantly. He allowed the Greeks to build in his honor the shrine which was named the Panhellenium, and instituted a series of games in connection with it; and he granted to the Athenians large sums of money, an annual dole of grain, and the whole of Cephallenia. (Loeb translation of E. Cary)

One reference in Pausanias, I, 18, 9:

Hadrian built also other things for the Athenians, a temple of Hera, one of Zeus Panhellenius and a Pantheon.

CONCLUSIONS

The three grounds on which Magnesia on the Maeander was admitted to the Panhellenion according to No. **5** were (1) Hellenic origin, (2) cooperation with Ionians, Dorians and Aeolians, (3) good relations with Rome. In the dossier at Cyrene, No. **7**, the representation of the Cyrenaeans was justified on the basis of Achaean and especially Dorian descent.

Constituencies were both city states and federal states. Of the former we have Athens and Sparta certainly. Of the latter we have the Thessalian League (No. **9**) and the Cretan League (No. **41**) certainly. Also the Achaeans (Nos. **34**, **37**, **38** and **39**), the Boeotians (Nos. **26**, **42** and **44**), the Phocians (Nos. **31** and **32**) and others probably belonged as federal states rather than as cities, though the federal states consisted of cities.

Cornelius Pulcher of Argos, whom the Panhellenion probably owed to the Achaean League (Nos. **35** and **36**), and Maecius Faustinus of Corinth (No. **37**) look like men of Italian descent. Thessalonica, though a Roman colony, contributed an archon of the Panhellenion (No. **49**). Sardis, long a non-Hellenic town, had received Hellenic elements into its population, so that it could call itself in *Sardis,* VII, i, 63 and 68 a first city of Hellas, but one of its delegates, A. Cornelius Postumus, looks again like a man of Italian descent (No. **45**). A delegate, presenting his credentials, was expected to have three generations of good birth (No. **1**, E 78-79).

While some of the Panhellenes are recognizable chiefly as men of inherited wealth, others like Flavius Sulpicianus Dorion of Hierapytna (No. **11**), Aurelius Rufus of Perinthus (No. **14**), the Athenian Casianus Antiochus called Synesius (No. **20**), Maecius Faustinus of Corinth (No. **37**), Curtius Proclus of Megara (No. **42**), Dionysius of Methana (No. **43**) strike one particularly as men of culture.

Of course a barbarian city like Emesa had no place in this organization, but even Alexandria and Antioch seem to have had no connection. The Old Hellas of Europe and what Aelius Aristides (Panathenaic, 57) calls "the Asian counterpart facing the Old Hellas" constituted the core. It would not be exact to identify the area from which the Panhellenes came as the Greek-speaking world, nor to call the Panhellenes of Italian descent men of supposedly pure Greek blood.

Still the Panhellenion, as the name declares, was a congress representing the Hellenes, but the word Hellene has been reinterpreted as if the founders had the famous passage of Isocrates, IV, 50 in mind, that the Hellenes were those not of a race but of a culture, less those of a common Hellenic origin than of a common education stemming from Athens. Hellenic education binds all the Panhellenes together, men who have had civilized fathers and grandfathers and been themselves trained in the disciplines and arts of discourse. When Aelius Aristides at the beginning of his Panathenaic calls the Athenians foster-parents of all those who belong in any way to the Hellenes, he too interprets the word Hellenes in this broader sense.

Two inscriptions connect the Panhellenion with (annual)? contributions to the sanctuary at Eleusis (Nos. **15** and **16**), and several inscriptions attest a close connection with the Eleusinian sanctuary in some unspecified way. Above all, Athens itself was the seat of the Panhellenion and the place where the Panhellenes published their own decrees and those of their constituent cities (Nos. **5**, **45** and **50**). The Athenian cult of the Olympian Zeus served as a focal point of their religious interest (No. **38**), and his temple may have been a gathering place for their meetings.

As Nörr[11] rightly points out, Plutarch, who had excellent relations with the Romans, considered the Romans foreigners, and it was the contrast with barbarians which led to the development of an empire patriotism. A decree of Messene from A.D. 2[12] concerning P. Cornelius Scipio quaestor pro praetore, who, " having made a vow, completed the Caesarea and then learned that the son of Augustus, Gaius Caesar, who was fighting the barbarians for the security of all mankind (τὸν ὑπὲρ τᾶς ἀνθρώπων πάντων σωτηρίας τοῖς βαρβάροις μαχόμενον), was in good health and, after escaping perils, had taken vengeance on the enemy," reveals the way a Roman official represented the war in Armenia to the people of Achaia, as early as the time

---

[11] Dieter Nörr, *Imperium und Polis in der hohen Prinzipatszeit* (Münchener Beiträge zur Papyrusforschung und antiken Rechtsgeschichte, L), 1966, p. 97.

[12] A. K. Orlandos, "Ἀνασκαφὴ Μεσσήνης," Πρακτικά, 1960 (published 1964), pp. 216-217.

of Augustus. All the wars of Domitian and Trajan renewed in Roman leaders an appreciation of Hellenism not only for its own sake but as an ally in an unending struggle against barbarism. But it was the foreign wars of Trajan, particularly the Parthian War, which stirred the Hellenes.

The establishment of the Panhellenion attests a recognition of the value of Hellenic civilization as an ally in the right order of the habitable world. Its establishment at Athens, " the oldest city within memory," as Aristides, Panathenaic, section 6 called it, attests a recognition of the primacy of Athens in the world of city states, at least in the East. The success of the idea owes much to the support and perhaps inspiration of Plutarch,[13] but it is due above all to the policy of Hadrian, who consistently fostered Hellenism and who turned away from the military activity and expansionism of Trajan to a concern for the domestic problems of the empire. It received encouragement from Antoninus Pius and special attention from Marcus Aurelius, so that its best days coincide with the humanistic empire of Hadrian and the Antonines. Freedmen and the enemies of the Roman order would have had no use for it, and there is no apparent reason why it should have appealed to *viri militares*.

The date at which the Panhellenion was founded seems to have been A.D. 131/2 as Weber recognized on the basis of No. **38** from Epidaurus. The term of an archon and presumably of a Panhellene may be defined as four years, because the new inscription from the Roman Market Place at Athens in lines 23-24 refers to a term of four years for the archon and in lines 14-20 shows that Panhellenes were elected for some term, which could be four years. The Panhellenion, though founded in 131/2, may have begun operating somewhat later. The Panhellenes had to be elected first, and this may well have dragged on for two years, since the institution was new and some cities were far away and had at first to establish their credentials. No. **29** from Aezani shows that by the end of November, A.D. 157, the emperor at Rome addressed the Panhellenion as a group of *synedroi* who had just taken office. Accordingly the first year of this group would be 157/8, and if we roll the terms back to the foundation, we arrive at 133/4 or 129/30 for the beginning of the first term. If the year 133/4 was the third year after the dedication of the temple of the Olympian Zeus and the third year after the foundation of the Panhellenion (No. **38**), the first regular term would seem to have been that between 133/4 and 137/8. Whether enrolled or invited by Hadrian himself, or elected, some group represented Greece in 131/2, when the temple was completed and the Panhellenion was officially " founded." The question, however, remains: Can one speak of a term antedating by two years the official ceremony with which the temple was dedicated and the Panhellenion was founded? The answer must be that in 131/2 the Panhellenion was officially inaugurated, but actually it began either in A.D. 133 or 129. Since the letter of Hadrian to the Cyrenaeans in 134 shows the archon of the Panhellenes consulting the emperor on

[13] Plutarch, *Pericles*, 17, and *Demetrius*, 8.

basic questions of organization, the date 133 seems far more likely than 129 for the beginning of operations.

We assume then that the Panhellenion was founded in 131/2 ceremoniously. Cities and federal states were invited to elect representatives, and their elected representatives gathered for the first time perhaps in 133. A list of known archonships of the Panhellenion can be arranged as follows.

Cn. Cornelius Pulcher	Hadrianic	Nos. **35** and **36**
Q. Alleius Epictetus	under Hadrian or	No. **39**
	Antoninus Pius	
T. Flavius Cyllus	A.D. 153-157	Nos. **9** and **28**
Tib. Claudius Jason Magnus	A.D. 157-161	Nos. **10** and **30**
Flavius Sulpicianus Dorion	A.D. 161-165	No. **11**
Flavius Xenion	A.D. 165-169	No. **12**
Papius Rufus	A.D. 169-173	No. **1**
Julius Damostratus	A.D. 173-177	No. **1**
Flavius Amphicles	A.D. 177-181 or 181-185	No. **15**
Cocceius Timasarchus	A.D. 197-201	No. **21**
T. Aelius Geminius Macedo	A.D. 201-205	No. **49**
Casianus Antiochus called Synesius	third century	No. **20**

Aristaeus (No. **16**) remains undated.

It is not known how the archon was chosen, but Julius Damostratus presided at the very beginning of his own term at the trials concerning the credentials of newly elected members. The emperor may have appointed the archon. Every known archon and the one known antarchon (No. **23**) were also Roman citizens.

One meeting must have occurred in Athens at the time of the Panhellenia. How many other meetings occurred we do not know. Cyrene and Sardis (Nos. **7** and **45**) sent two Panhellenes each; how many the others sent we do not know.

The Panhellenion can be traced as late as 244/5 (No. **25**) and even 255 (No. **57**). It withered with the decline of the cities in the third century and its place was eventually taken by the Senate of Constantinople.[14]

The Greek aim, as it seems to me, was to put an end to ancient Hellenic rivalries

---

[14] As the seat of the Panhellenion Athens was the second capital of the empire. Its place was eventually taken by Constantinople, whose early senators were recruited from all over the Greek East. They were not as well chosen (see P. Petit, " Les sénateurs de Constantinople dans l'oeuvre de Libanius," *L'Antiquité Classique,* XXVI, 1957, pp. 347-382) as the Panhellenes of the " humanistic empire," but they were more or less representative geographically, even socially. They were not ex-magistrates, but the Greeks no longer thought of the empire as a league of cities. The aims were different in a different empire (see A. Alföldi, *The Conversion of Constantine and Pagan Rome,* Oxford, 1948, Ch. IX) ; nevertheless, Flavius Dorion of Hierapytna, Flavius Xenion of Gortyn, and Aelius Geminius Macedo of Thessalonica were institutional precursors of those senators at Constantinople.

and to unite all Hellenes and men of Hellenic education in support of the traditional Hellenic culture, to unify the world of city states against the encroachment of barbarism within the empire, and to promote the loyalty of the cities to the old Hellenic cults and to the vicar of Zeus on earth, the Roman emperor. The Hellenes cherished their ancient freedom and never quite trusted the city state of Rome, but they saw in the emperor, as Nörr [15] rightly says, the champion of their freedom against foreign domination. In a league like the Panhellenion they retained something of the polis character which they inevitably lost as they were absorbed in the empire, and they acquired a better means of resisting arbitrary abuses and of approaching their champion, the emperor. The provincial leagues [16] were more provincial and old-fashioned, less panhellenic, more representative of wealth than of culture, by no means outdated but insufficient to represent all of a renewed world of city states. Secondly, since the Senate at Rome was of old patronizing and indifferent, a new kind of partnership may have called for an institution on which a new relationship could be built or through which some irritations of the past could be relieved.

While the senators individually were the most important officials of the empire, the Senate as an organ of government had become far less important in the administration. Certain Hellenes at least were less likely to turn to the Senate at Rome for redress or even a sympathetic airing of their aspirations or complaints, and it may well have appeared advisible to relieve the Senate of what to them seemed trivialities. A synedrion of a different kind replaced the Senate for Hellenic affairs, a synedrion that was not another senate for imperial affairs but was like the Senate an assembly of notables. The case of Athenodorus son of Agrippa against the administrators of the estates of Herodes Atticus (No. **1**, E 23-27) would have come, if not before a Roman magistrate, then before the Senate, except that the Panhellenion now existed and was able to relieve the Roman government. The Panhellenion partially corrected the vice which Plutarch, *Political Precepts*, 814e-815a denounced in his countrymen, the servility which made them ask for a Roman decision on any and every matter.

If the Panhellenes were to have a prestige comparable with that enjoyed by members of the *amplissimus ordo,* the Panhellenion had to have social standards of recognized validity and similar standards of political experience, too. That is why the Panhellenes were elected and were elected from ex-magistrates. The magistracy could of course be one in the man's paternal city or league; perhaps one at Rome was a recognized alternative. The insistence on the three-generation rule comes from the policy of Augustus just as the refusal of divine honors became a fixed policy for " good " emperors through the reign of Marcus Aurelius.[17]

[15] D. Nörr, *op. cit.*, ch. V.

[16] J. Deininger, *Die Provinziallandtage der römischen Kaiserzeit von Augustus bis zum Ende des dritten Jahrhunderts n. Chr. (Vestigia,* 6), 1965.

[17] M. P. Charlesworth. " The Refusal of Divine Honors. an Augustan Formula." *Papers of the*

In regard to the Senate Julius Caesar had a policy which could have been justified, whether or not he did so justify it to anyone, as philosophically more truly aristocratic, whereas the senate the opposition favored suffered all too obviously from the well known defects of oligarchy. A true aristocracy reflects, one might argue, contemporary excellence, not wealth or fame inherited from ancestors. Julius Caesar chose his senators without much regard to their birth. Octavian, on the other hand, compromised with traditional standards. He too was glad to introduce new men into the Senate, but he respected tradition more, and so he preferred wherever possible, collaborators from the famous old families in whom, after centuries of hereditary patronage, the many had confidence, and he refrained from outraging conservative sentiment by advancing the sons of freedmen to the highest classification, the Senatorial Order. Above all, he recognized the Equestrian Order as an élite from whom new senators might be recruited, a conservative élite chosen not just on the basis of wealth, yet chosen from men who had an interest in protecting property rights. Augustus helped to establish somewhat similar standards in Greek cities for the highest posts.

Tiberius particularly continued the policy of Augustus, and in the East the Panhellenion was created by Hadrian with standards similar to those which Augustus prescribed for the Roman Senate. In the first place the Panhellenes had to come from families in which three generations of free birth were demonstrable. There may well have been a minimum census, though this cannot be proved. Secondly, however, they were selected from an élite comparable to the cream of the Equestrian Order. That is, they were chosen in each participating community from ex-magistrates.

One may now object that the Panhellenion was much more representative of Greek cities than the Senate of other Roman cities, though both the Senate and the Panhellenion were based on elections. This is true but not necessarily a departure from the intention of Augustus. The proper parallel to the genuinely Hellenic cities which participated in the Panhellenion would be the kind of Roman city called a *colonia*. Suetonius, *Divus Augustus*, 46, after mentioning colonies, says, *etiam iure ac dignatione urbi quodam modo pro parte aliqua adaequavit, excogitato genere suffragiorum, quae de magistratibus urbicis decuriones colonici in sua quisque colonia ferrent et sub die comitiorum obsignata Romam mitterent.* Augustus had wanted to bring the colonies into a closer relation with the recruitment of the Senate at Rome, which was now to be recruited from Italians who lived all over the Mediterranean, and by Italians we mean men of Italic stock and culture or natives who had completely assimilated themselves.

The plan of Augustus in respect to colonies failed to arouse much interest. The

British School at Rome, XV, 1939, pp. 1-10. New examples occur in a letter of Claudius (*Études Thasiennes*, V, No. 179) and in the letter of Marcus Aurelius and Commodus cited above as No. 4, Epistle IV.

intention deserved praise but the method was ill conceived. But when Hadrian re-organized the empire with a more genuine partnership of Italians and Hellenes, he improved on one aspect of the plan of Augustus for the participation of colonies. Hadrian established a synedrion which united elected representatives of old Greek cities, Greek federal states, and Greek colonies. Just as the Italians of the colonies which Augustus sought to attach more closely were, on the one hand, men who lived in cities organized on a peculiarly Roman pattern, and, on the other hand, men of Italic stock and culture or natives who had completely assimilated themselves, so the cities which joined in forming the Panhellenion were cities of a peculiarly Hellenic type, the polis, the cities which could claim colonists of old Hellenic stock. If the majority of the population were Hellenes or completely assimilated to Hellenes, the Eastern *colonia* (Corinth or Thessalonica) might be treated either as a colony or a mother city of Hellenes. Roman Corinth, for instance, appears as a mother city in *I.G.*, VII, 24 and *Corinth*, VIII, iii, 269. Certainly their interests had to be weighed with those of neighboring cities.

The status of a colony may have been of no practical advantage but it was clearly a source of pride. The pride may be explained as a consciousness of the superiority of Mediterranean civilization. From the Hadrianic Period every center of Graeco-Roman civilization wished to be regarded as one of the great mother cities or daughter cities of the Mediterranean " Receptacle." The mother cities were Athens, Rome and ancient cities of Greece, and in a secondary sense the mother cities of Asia. The daughter cities were the colonies with the *eugeneia* of noble ancestry. Pausanias, I, 18, 6 reports that in front of the columns of the Temple of the Olympian Zeus at Athens stood bronze statues of colonies (ἄποικοι πόλεις), and if the Temple of the Olympian Zeus was the meeting place of the Attic Panhellenion, the statues recalled the religious bond of inherited institutions.

The difference between Rome and a Greek city was often effaced.[18] In the Pan-hellenion, which brought the daughter cities together, the colonies of Rome in the East seem to be treated like the colonies of Athens in the East. Naples, Tarentum, Marseilles, Syracuse, were they members? No colonies, either Roman or Greek, in the West are so far attested as sending *synedroi* to the Attic Panhellenion.

We must not leave the impression that the emperor and his advisers were con-cerned merely with feeding human vanity.

One purpose of the Panhellenion may have been to bring to the emperor's atten-tion and to that of the Roman Senate the men in the East who were most suitable for the imperial service and for enrollment in the Senatorial Order. They were all men of free birth with freeborn fathers and freeborn paternal grandfathers and were all men elected to office and chosen by their fellow-citizens into a synedrion of ex-

---

[18] E. Gabba, " Il Latino come dialetto greco," *Miscellanea di studi alessandrini in memoria di Augusto Rostagni*, Turin, 1963, pp. 188-194.

magistrates. Some were already members of the Equestrian or Senatorial Order.

Another purpose may have been to provide an incentive to work for the good of the city and of all the cities and so for the empire. By advancing the community of cities the Panhellenion contributed to empire patriotism in men who visualized the empire as a league of old cities and their colonies, a league of cities and federal states in the Hellenic tradition.

Still another purpose may have been religious. Christianity and even Judaism had been expanding, and Christianity at least was developing a unified organization. The old pagan world of the Greek cities had no real religious unity because the older Panhellenic festivals now were spiritually less important and no longer attracted such influential spectators. So the Panhellenion, apart from all its other advantages, served as a rallying point for the leaders of the old pagan world of the urban upper class and provided a festival of its own. The Jews had combined in Crete and other provinces to inflict much injury on Hellenes; the Christians in many cities came under suspicion. It is altogether possible that the establishment of the Panhellenion should be understood as partly a reaction to the Jewish Disturbances and to the rise of Christianity.

Above all, the aim of the Panhellenion was to make possible a crystallization of public opinion among *homines politici* in Greek cities and to acquaint the emperor therewith.

To appreciate the unity behind the Panhellenion one should remember the Panathenaic Discourse of Aelius Aristides with its emphasis on the spread of city state humanism by the sending out of colonies of civilized men and with its repudiation of barbarism visualized as the East encroaching upon the world of Hellenic civilization.

When a man was identified as archon or ex-archon of the Panhellenes, perhaps even as Panhellene, it was normal to omit the ethnic. The interests which he championed were not narrowly those of the city or federal state that sent him but those of the wider fatherland. He was supposed to be no longer ἐνδεδεμένος in local ties but ἄφετος.

One must not be misled by the silence of historians. The Panhellenion did not accomplish all that Hadrian, Antoninus Pius, Marcus Aurelius and the Hellenes of the cities and federal states during the second century expected of it, but the successful appeals to the emperor and the attempts of new men to break into it show that it offered a great hope and did enough to keep that hope very much alive for at least three generations. The Hellenic public, including the descendants of Italian settlers, took it seriously, and so did Marcus Aurelius and his Eastern advisers, and so also presumably the senatorial officials of the Greek provinces. In the crisis of A.D. 193 disastrous dissensions arose among the Hellenes, as Herodian, *Ab excessu divi Marci*, III, 2, 7-8 reports; the Panhellenion will have failed conspicuously to perform its function. But not until then.

The Hellenes still had a great spokesman in the widely read Isocrates, who for Philip of Macedon had outlined with intentional vagueness a glorious role as *hegemon*, *prostates* and reconciler for one who as a Heraclid and king stood outside all the cities. He was not to be their ruler but their *hegemon* against the barbarians, the protector of their freedom, and a reconciler whom they needed in order to transcend the recurrent enmities and jealousies which afflicted the Greek world. When we think of Hadrian and Marcus Aurelius occasionally adapting themselves to the inherited role of an ideal reconciler, we must never forget that the ideal *diallaktes* of Isocrates was not one who reconciled Hellenes with non-Hellenes but one who reconciled true Hellenes among themselves.

Thus the *Philippus* of Isocrates had an effect upon the attitude of the Roman emperor toward his own responsibility, but also the educational role which Isocrates in his *Areopagiticus*, 37-38 claimed for the Areopagus in the life of mature Athenians influenced the position of the Areopagus in Roman Athens and affected the Roman emperor in what he expected of the Areopagus and of the Panhellenion. For it carried over to the latter. What the idealized Areopagus had been to Athens in an idealized past the Panhellenion was to be to the whole genuinely Greek world, not only a court but an educational institution.

INDEX

GREEK INDEX OF WORDS AND NAMES IN "EDICT" OF MARCUS AURELIUS

LIST OF PASSAGES CITED

(References are to pages)

145

GENERAL INDEX

AALDERS, G. J. D.: 54

Abas. *See* M. Aurelius A.

Achaean League: 119, 130

Achaia, Roman: Plutarch represents Hadrian in 70-71; proconsul's court 16, 17, 66; Quintilii in 1, 67

Acraephnium in Boeotia: 113

Adada in Pisidia: 129

Adoption: 13

Adrian, sophist at Athens: 81, 82

Aelius Ameinias: 18, 31

Aelius Aristides: delivers a Panathenaic address at Athens 83. *See also* List of Passages cited

P. Aelius Artemas: 129

Aelius Dionysius: 11, 28, 38, 39

T. Aelius Geminius Macedo: 125, 133

Aelius Praxagoras: 11, 13, 17, 18, 26, 28, 30, 31, 40, 66

Aelius Themison: 11, 18, 28, 31

Aezani in Phrygia: 113-115, 132

Agathocles, son of Agathocles: 18, 30, 41

Agonothesia, agonothete: 15, 105, 111, 112, 114, 115, 121, 130

Agoranomoi: 55-56

Agriculture: 72-73; later importance of slave labor in 73

Agrippa, son of Asmenus: 14-15

Ahrens, F. H. L.: 80

Akribeia: 97-98

Albini, Umberto: 26

Alcamenes. *See* M. Aurelius A.

Alexander the Great: 93

Alexandria, Alexandrians: 16, 22, 131

Alföldi, A.: 133

Alföldi, G.: 102

Q. Alleius Epictetus: 120-121, 133

de Almeida, F.: 101

Aly, W.: 14

Ameinias. *See* Aelius A.

Amelotti, Mario: 16

Amphicleia: 116, 117

Amphicles: of Chalcis, student of Herodes Atticus 104. *See also* Flavius A.

Annius Libo, widow of: 77

Anticyra: 116

Antigonus and Demetrius: 93

Antioch: 108, 131

Antiochus. *See* Casianus A.

Antoninus Pius: xv, 14, 18, 42, 76; letter to the Panhellenion 114-115; Panhellenic policy of 132, 137

Apamea: 11, 117

Apollonia near Cyrene: 99-100

Apollonius, Athenian sophist: 84. *See also* C. Julius Casianus A.

Appeals: 1, 12-18, 37-42, 64, 69, 92, 137

Areopagus, Areopagites: 13, 15, 16, 19, 20, 23, 28, 30, 33, 44, 56, 58, 59, 62, 76, 77, 91, 92, 111, 138; as aristocratic body 53; as citizenship court 40, 64; as dicasts 64-65; eligibility for 23-24, 31, 32, 44, 45, 47-48, 55, 61, 62; Herald of 59, 111, 121; and Panhellenion 92, 138; posting of bond on appeals 38, 41; *summa honoraria* for admission to 56

Argos: 117, 121, 130

Arion. *See* C. Julius A.

Aristaeus: 104, 133

Aristocracy: at Athens 44, 45, 57, 73, 76, distinction under emperors 46, imitated by new families 60, 61, under Marcus Aurelius xv, 20, 91, preservation in constitution 56; character of 90, 135

Armenia: 131

Artemas. *See* P. Aelius A.

Asclepiades. *See* M. Aurelius A.

Asmenus called Agrippa: 15

Asmenus of Eitea: 15

Astoi: 62, 91

Astynomoi: 55-56

Athena: as patron of education 84; Polias 106

Athenaeum at Rome: 84

Athenodorus, son of Agrippa: 14-15, 19, 29, 31, 39, 134

Athens, Athenians: 124; *aisitoi* 112; archons, archonship 11-13, 15-16, 23-24, 29, 34, 43-47, 53, 55-56, 59-60, 62-63, 77, 92, 106, 111,

151

Cyllus. *See* T. Flavius C. of Hypata
Cyrene: 12, 16, 25, 96-101, 124, 130, 132, 133

DADOUCHOS. *See* Priest
Damas. *See* M. Aurelius Demostratus D.
Damasippus. *See* M. Ulpius D.
Dascalakis, Ap.: 26
Date of No. **1**: 34-35
Day, James: 20, 56
Day, John: 73
Deininger, J.: 134
Delos: 49
Delphic Amphictyony: 93, 122
Delz, J.: 64
De Martino, Fr.: 25
Democratic element: 57-63; in Greek political development 72; strengthened by Cleisthenes 47, 56, 63
Demophanes: 99
Demostratus. *See* Claudius D.
De Robertis, Francesco M.: 73
Dicasteries: 12, 13, 64-65
Diehl, Ch. and Cousin, G.: 66
Diller, A.: 45
Dioecesis in Late Empire: 70
Diogenes. *See* Flavius D.
Diogmitae: 101
Dionysius. *See* Aelius D.
Dionysius. *See* P. Cae(lius) D.
Dionysius the rhetor: 122, 131
Discrimination in Greek cities: 46, 60-61, 72, 75
Dobesch, G.: 128
Dobiáš, Josef: 69, 82
Dodwell, E.: 122
Dorians, at Thera: 97-98
Dorion. *See* Fl. Sulpicianus D.
Dow, S.: 59
Downey, G.: 108
Duff, A. M.: 21
Duncan-Jones, R.: 10
Duovir: 119

ECDEMUS: 99
Eclectus. *See* Valerius E.
Edictum: 35-37

Egypt: governor of 17; *ingenui* in 22
Eleusis: as base for a Panhellenic League 94; connection with Panhellenion 131; festival at 13; Ingenuus' court at 32; invaded by Costoboci 69-70, 83; Lucius Verus initiated 83; Marcus Aurelius initiated 83; priesthooods 43
Emesa: 131
Emperor, Roman: balance preserved in Athenian polity 54; Greek view of 134; Hellenic culture as ally against barbarians 131-132; Isocrates' influence on 138; Panhellenic role of 93-94, 133, 137; as *prostates* 92, 93, 94, 134; refusal of divine honors 134
Embassy, expenses of: 18, 30, 41
Enisledes, Ch. M.: 116
Enktesis: 50
Ephebate in Hellenic world: 49. *See also* Athens
Ephesus, Ephesians: 93; membership in Council 28
Ephialtes, Reforms of: 24, 63
Epictetus: 91. *See also* Q. Alleius E.
Epicurean Schoool at Athens: 16
Epidaurus: 120-121, 132
Epigamia: 50-53
Epigonus, son of Epictetus: 14, 18-19, 31, 40
Epimelete: 15, 111, 121
Epistula: 1-37, 85-90, 96-99, 107-109, 113-116. *See also Edictum*
Equestrian Order: 10, 21, 24, 28, 48, 62, 64, 135, 136; Claudius Jason Magnus 101; free birth as requirement for 58; promotion of Greeks to 75
Era: Hadrianic 120, 125, 136; Panathenaid 112; Panhelleniad 126
Eudemus, son of Aphrodisius: 14, 19, 29
Eugeneia: 53, 57, 58, 91, 136
Eumolpidae: 13, 29, 39
Euodus, son of Onesimus: 10, 18, 31
Euphras, son of Nicon: 30
Eupraxides. *See* Claudius E.
Eutyches, son of Eutyches: 120
Exetasis: 28, 58, 59

FABIUS RULLIANUS: 21, 54

Faustinus. *See* Maecius F.
Favorinus, the sophist: 93
Ferrara, G.: 63
Fitz, Jenö: 82
Flaccus. *See* T. Flavius Sulpicianus F.
Flavia Habroea, wife of Ulpius Leurus: 100
Flavia Lais: 122
Flavius Amphicles, archon of Panhellenes: 103-104, 133
Cn. Flavius Cn. f.: 54
T. Flavius Cyllus of Hypata: 100-101, 108, 114-115, 133
Flavius Diogenes of Marathon: 111
T. Flavius Pantaenus: 106
T. Flavius Straton of Paeania: 13
Flavius Sulpicianus Dorion, of Hierapytna (father and son): 101-102, 131, 133
Flavius Sulpicianus Dorion Polymnis: 102
T. Flavius Sulpicianus Flaccus: 102
Flavius Xenion: 74, 75, 102, 133
Forbes, C. A.: 109, 123
Forgery, testamentary: 40-41
Foucart, P.: 43, 122, 123
Fraenkel, M.: 117-120, 122
Franz, J.: 95, 113, 115
Fraser, P. M.: 60, 96-99
Free birth: in Aristotle 22; at Athens 21, 23, 24, 31-33, 61; in Greek cities 54; Marcus Aurelius' definition of 20, 22; as requirement for eligibility to Council 58; in Roman type of *trigonia* 56; at Rome 22
Freedmen: 20, 22, 57, 73; admission to citizenship 59, 75; antipathy to Hellenism 132; of Claudius Atticus 19, 75; descendants of 28, 33, 54, 57-61, 76, 77; Hadrian's attitude toward 54; of Herodes Atticus 15, 19, 75, in alliance against Herodes 61; influence with Lucius Verus 77; political status, in Athens 59, in Greek cities 58, 59, 61, 77; preeminence 60, 75, 77; receive Roman citizenship, 58, 59; as scapegoats 75
Frend, W. H. C.: 75
von Fritz, K.: 24
Froehner, W.: 94

Gabba, E.: 136

Galba: 94
Galerius: 70
Garnsey, Peter: **16, 37, 42**
Garzetti, A.: 22
Gavinius Saturninus: 16, 17, 30, 40, 41
Gavius Maximus: 78
Geagan, Daniel J.: 2, 25, 44, 56, 58, 107, 112
Gennetai: 44
German Invasions: 75, 83
Gerusia: of Ephesus 18. *See also* Athens
Geta: 109-112
Gilliam, J. F.: 75
Gordon, Mary L.: 58
Gortyn: 102, 121
Graindor, Paul: 25, 33, 34, 53, 66, 67, 80, 104-106, 112, 130
Greece. *See* Hellas
Groag, Edmund: 66, 67, 69, 102
Guarducci, M.: 121
Gythium: 10

Habicht, Chr.: 106
Hadrian: attitude toward freedmen 54, 73, 76; benefactions, to Athens 130, to Thyatira 124, 128; and Epicurean School 16; influenced by Aristotle 54; interest in domestic problems of the Empire 132; Jewish Disturbances under 93; letter to the Cyreneans 96-99, 132; Panhellenic policy of 93-94, 98, 132, 137; and Panhellenion 13, 33, 40, 54, 92, 94, 99, 100, 132, 135, 136; Panhellenius 114, 115, 128; Peace during reign of 76; Plutarch represents 70-71; Polemo, invitation to 129; presides at Dionysia 130; as *prostates* 94; recodification of laws at Athens 48, 54; Spanish influence on 94; statue at Olympieum 99-100, 130
Halicarnassus, Hellenistic Law at: 19
Hampl, F.: 82
Hanslik, R.: 67, 69
Harmon, A. M.: 80
Harsh, P. W.: 75
Hatzfeld, J.: 66
Hegemonia (a court): 66-67
Hellas, Hellenes: 69-71, 115, 131, 134; Athens as capital of 128, 131, 133; dissensions of A. D. 193, 137; encroachment of barbarism

PLATE 1

a. Marcus Aurelius Inscription, No. 1, Fragment A (Agora Museum)

b. Marcus Aurelius Inscription, No. 1, Fragment B (Agora Museum)

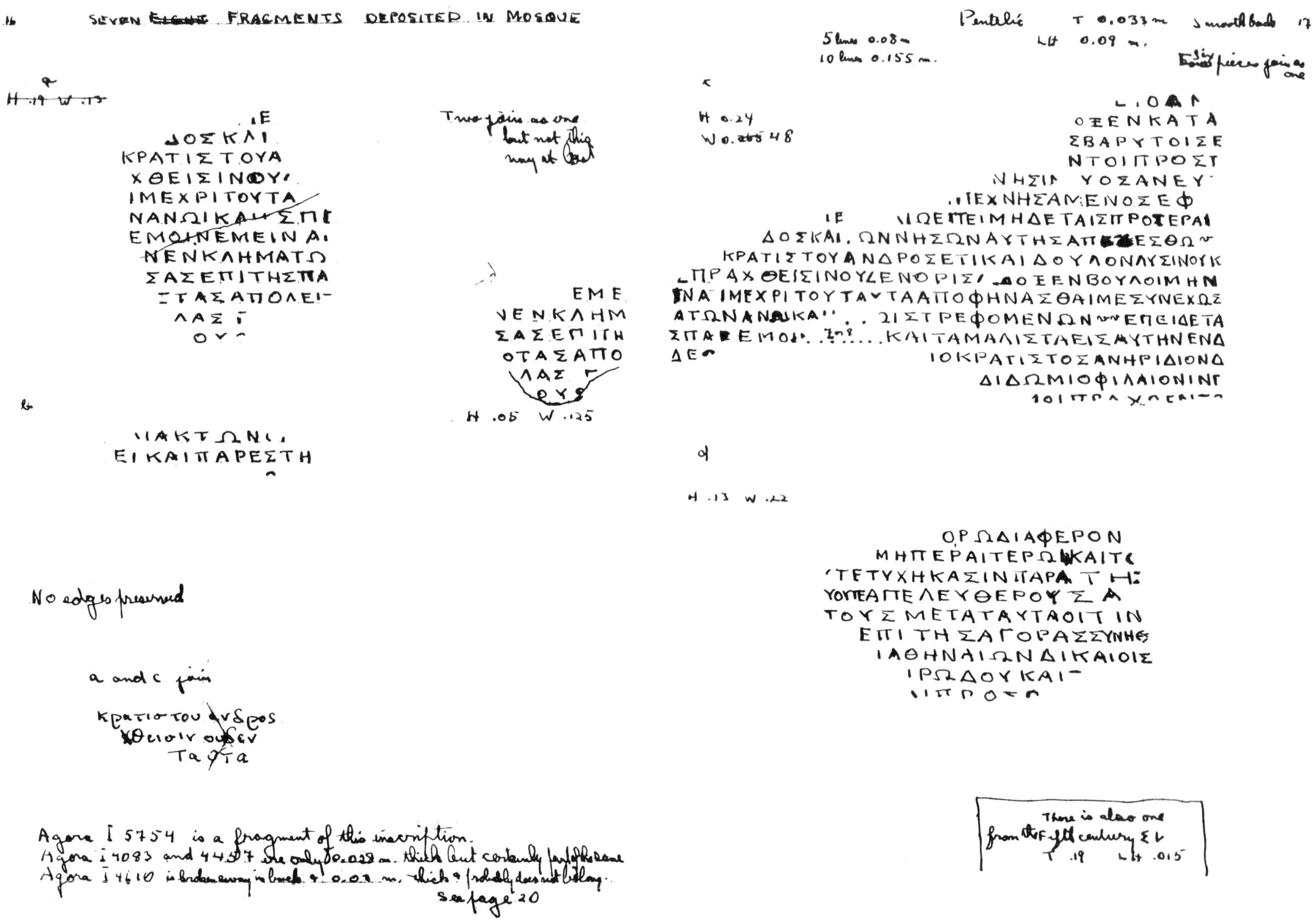

PLATE 2

SEVEN FRAGMENTS DEPOSITED IN MOSQUE

Pentelic

Marcus Aurelius Inscription, No. 1, Rough Copy of Fragments C and D in May 1940

Agora I 5754 is a fragment of this inscription.
Agora I 4083 and 4434 ...
Agora I 4610 ...

PLATE 3

Marcus Aurelius Inscription, No. 1, Fragment E (=EM 13366)
(Courtesy of the Epigraphical Museum)

Marcus Aurelius Inscription, No. 1, Fragment E, upper half (Courtesy of the Epigraphical Museum)

PLATE 5

Marcus Aurelius Inscription, No. 1, Fragment E, lower half
(Courtesy of the Epigraphical Museum)

PLATE 6

Marcus Aurelius Inscription, No. 1, Fragments F, D and C (Courtesy of the Greek Archaeological Service)

PLATE 7

a. No. 5, Decree of the Panhellenes about Magnesia ad Maeandrum
(Courtesy of the Musée du Louvre)

b. No. 22, Imperial Letter at Athens concerning Athletes
who avoided the Panhellenia
(Courtesy of the Epigraphical Museum)

PLATE 8

Η ΠΟΛΙΣ

(a. Copy by A. E. W. Salt in 1918)

ΗΠΟΛΙΣ
ΤΑΛΩΝΓΕΜΕΙΝΙΟΝΜΑΚΕΔΟΝΑ
ΤΟΝΑΡΞΑΝΤΑΤΟΥΑΤΤΙΚΟΥΠΑΝΕΛΛΗΝΙΟΥ
ΚΑΠΕΡΑΤΥΣΑΝΤΑΘΕΟΥΑΔΡΙΑΝΟΥΚΑΙΑΓΟ
ΝΟΘΕΤΗΣΑΝΤΩΝΜΕΓΑΛΩΝΠΑΝΕΛΛΗ
ΝΙΩΝΕΝΗΙΤΤΑΝΕΛΛΗΝΙΑΔΙΡΑΨΑΝΤΑ
ΛΙΑΒΙΟΤΟΙΣΑΥΤΟΚΡΑΤΟΡΕΙΝΤΙΠΡΩΤΟΝΕ
ΝΟΜΕΝΟΝΑΡΧΟΝΤΑΤΤΑΝΕΛΛΗΝΩΝΑΠΟΗΣ
ΛΑΙΡΝΡΟΠΑΤ...ΣΟΣΣΣΑΛΟΝΕΙΚΕΩΝΠΟΛΕΩ
ΓΥΜΝΑΕΙΑΡΧΗΣΑΝΤΑΚΑΠΙΡΩΤΑΡΧΗΣΑ
ΤΑΕΝΗΛΛΑΜΠΡΑΤΑΥΤΗΤΟΛΕΙΔΩΝΑΕΞΥΠ
ΕΧΕΧΩΕΕΙΣΤΗΝΒΑΣΙΛΙΚΗΝΤΑΥΤΗΝΞΥΝΤΝ
ΠΗΧΜΥΡΙΟΣΛΟΓΙΣΕΥΣΑΝΤΑΕΚΘΕΙΑΣ
ΠΡΟΣΤΑΞΕΩΣΤΗΣΑΠΟΛΛΩΝΙΑΤΩΝΠΥΛΕ
ΩΣΗΣΠΡΟΣΤΩΙΟΝΙΩΚΟΛΠΩΤΕΜΕΙΝΙΑ
ΔΑΥΜΤΑΘΟΥΓΑΤΗΡΤΩΝΠΑΤΕΡΑ
ΕΥΤΥΧΩΣ

a. Copy by A. E. W. Salt in 1918

b. Copy by J. H. Oliver in 1934

No. 49. Geminius Macedo Inscription at Thessalonica